Chi's Sweet Home

チーズ スイートホーム

4

Konami Kanata

contents
homemade 57~74

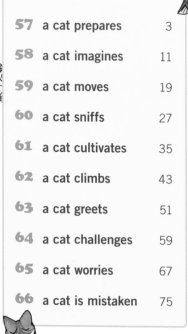

homemade 57: a cat prepares

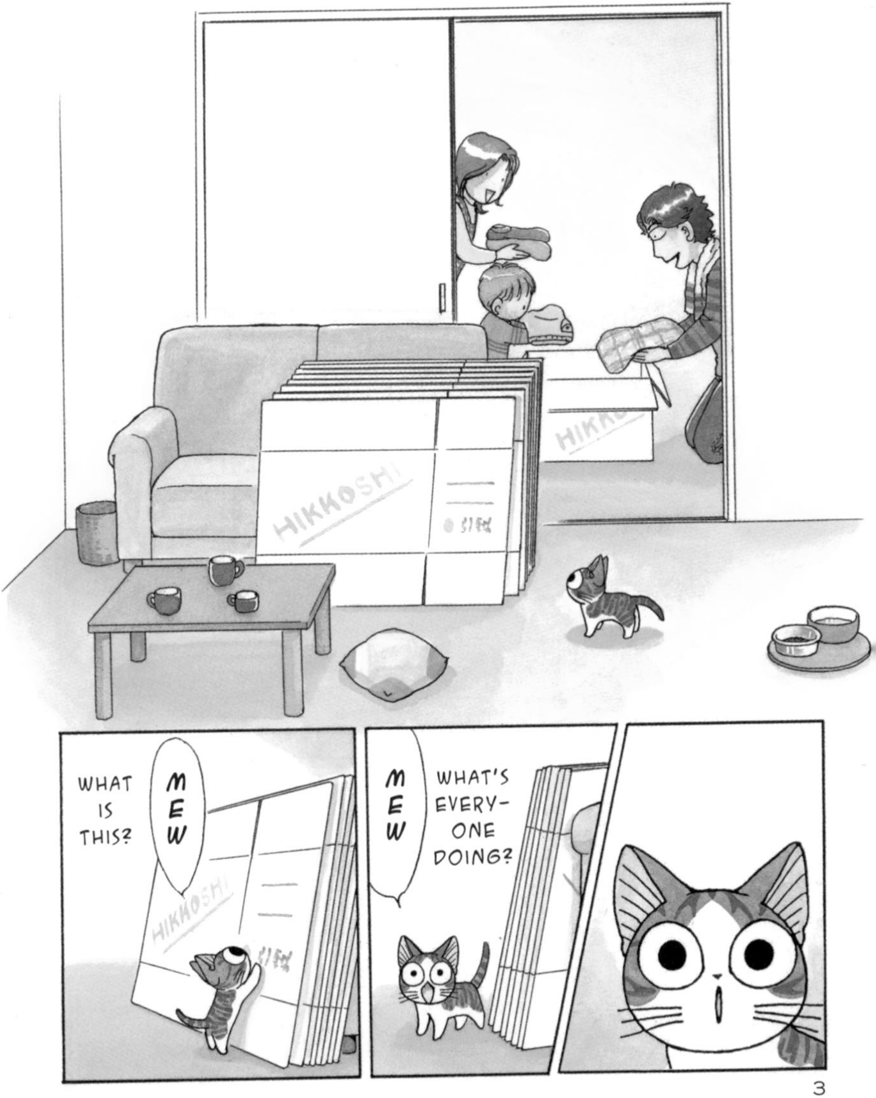
HIKKOSHI
HIKKOSHI
WHAT IS THIS?
MEW
HIKKOSHI
MEW
WHAT'S EVERYONE DOING?

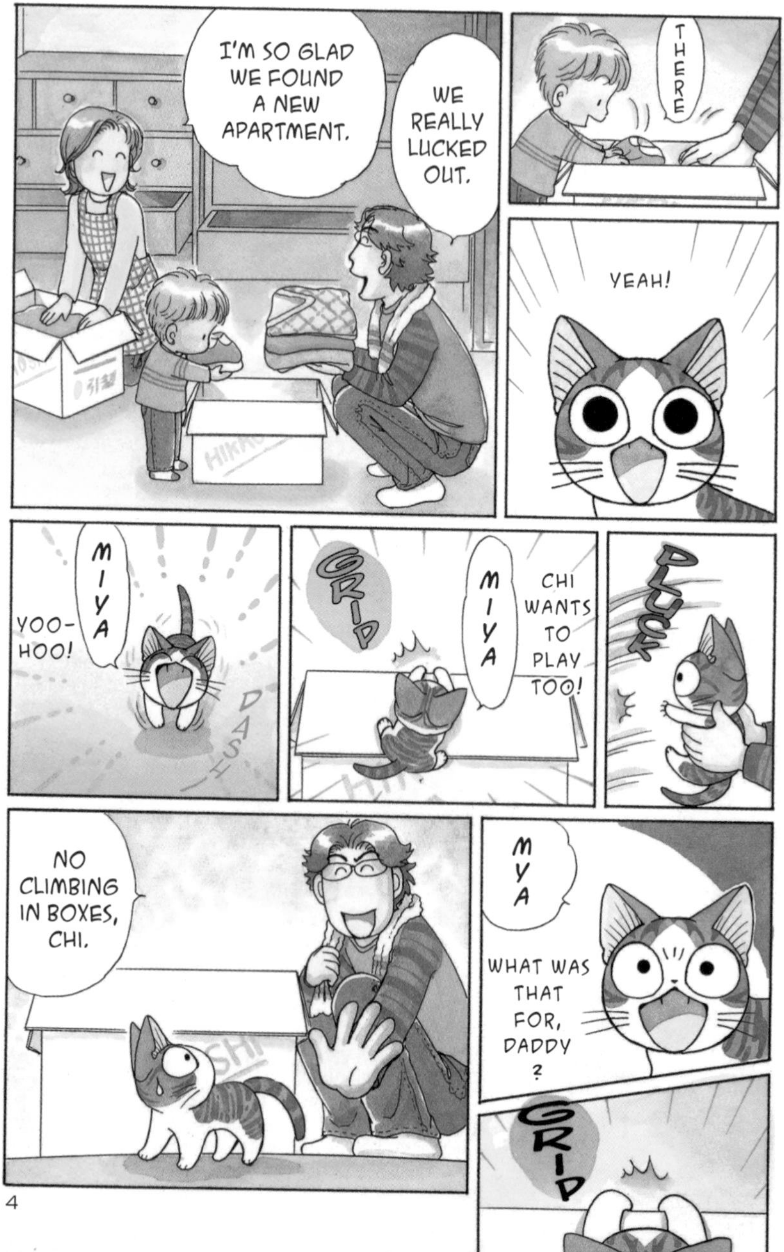
I'M SO GLAD WE FOUND A NEW APARTMENT.
WE REALLY LUCKED OUT.
THERE
YEAH!
MIYA
YOO-HOO!
DASH
GRIP
MIYA
CHI WANTS TO PLAY TOO!
PLUCK
NO CLIMBING IN BOXES, CHI.
MYA
WHAT WAS THAT FOR, DADDY?
GRIP

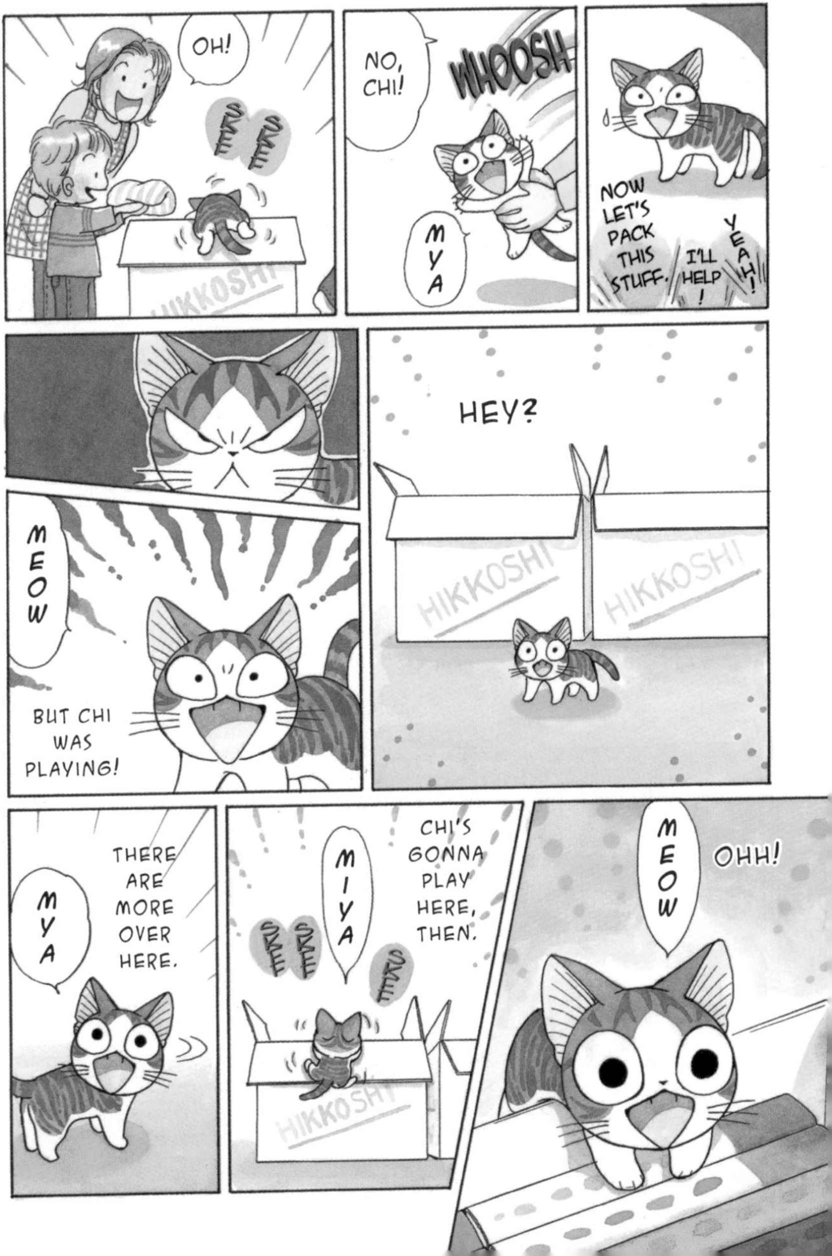
OH!
SKEE SKEE
NO, CHI!
WHOOSH
MYA
NOW LET'S PACK THIS STUFF.
I'LL HELP!
YEAH!
HIKKOSHI
MEOW
BUT CHI WAS PLAYING!
HEY?
HIKKOSHI
HIKKOSHI
MYA
THERE ARE MORE OVER HERE.
SKEE SKEE
MIYA
CHI'S GONNA PLAY HERE, THEN.
SKEE
HIKKOSHI
MEOW
OHH!

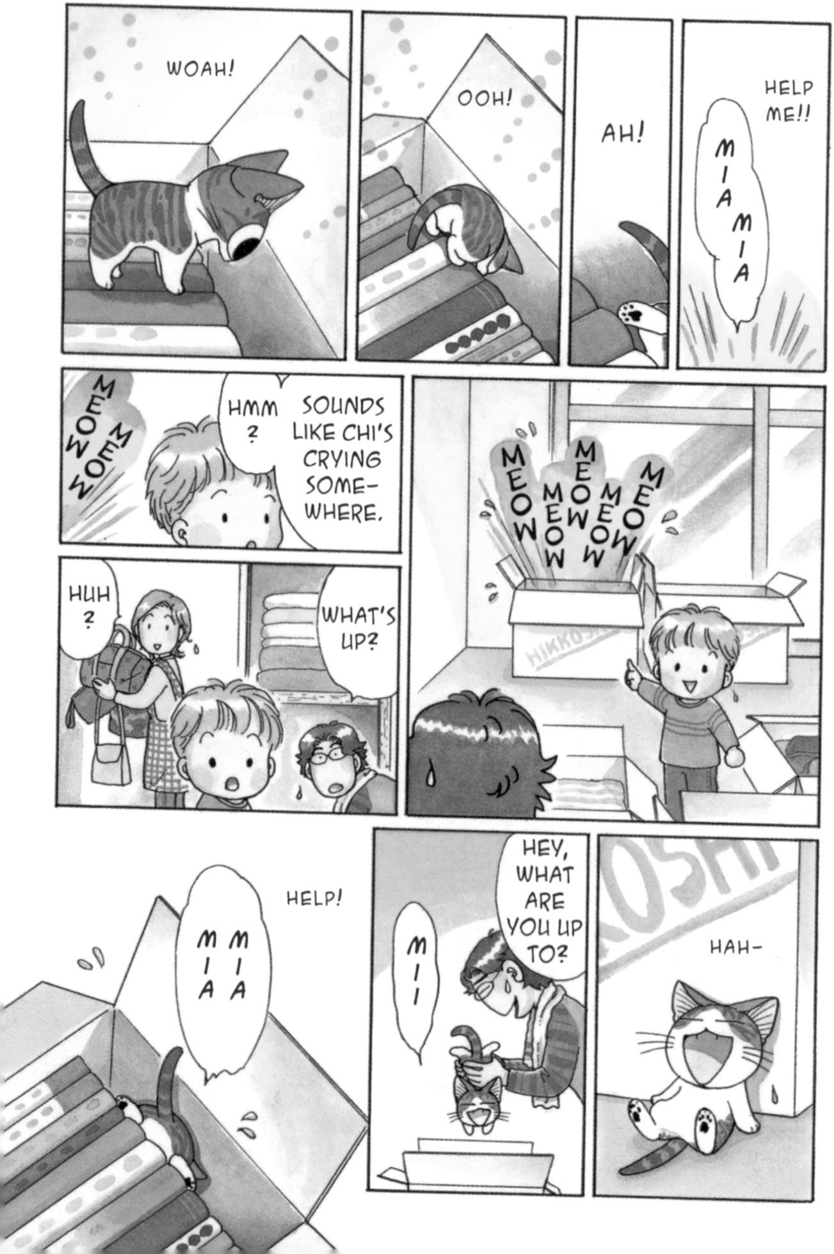
WOAH!
OOH!
AH!
HELP ME!!
MIA MIA
MEOW MEOW
HMM?
SOUNDS LIKE CHI'S CRYING SOME- WHERE.
HUH?
WHAT'S UP?
MEOW MEOW MEOW MEOW MEOW MEOW
HIKKOSHI
HELP!
MIA MIA
MII
HEY, WHAT ARE YOU UP TO?
HAH-

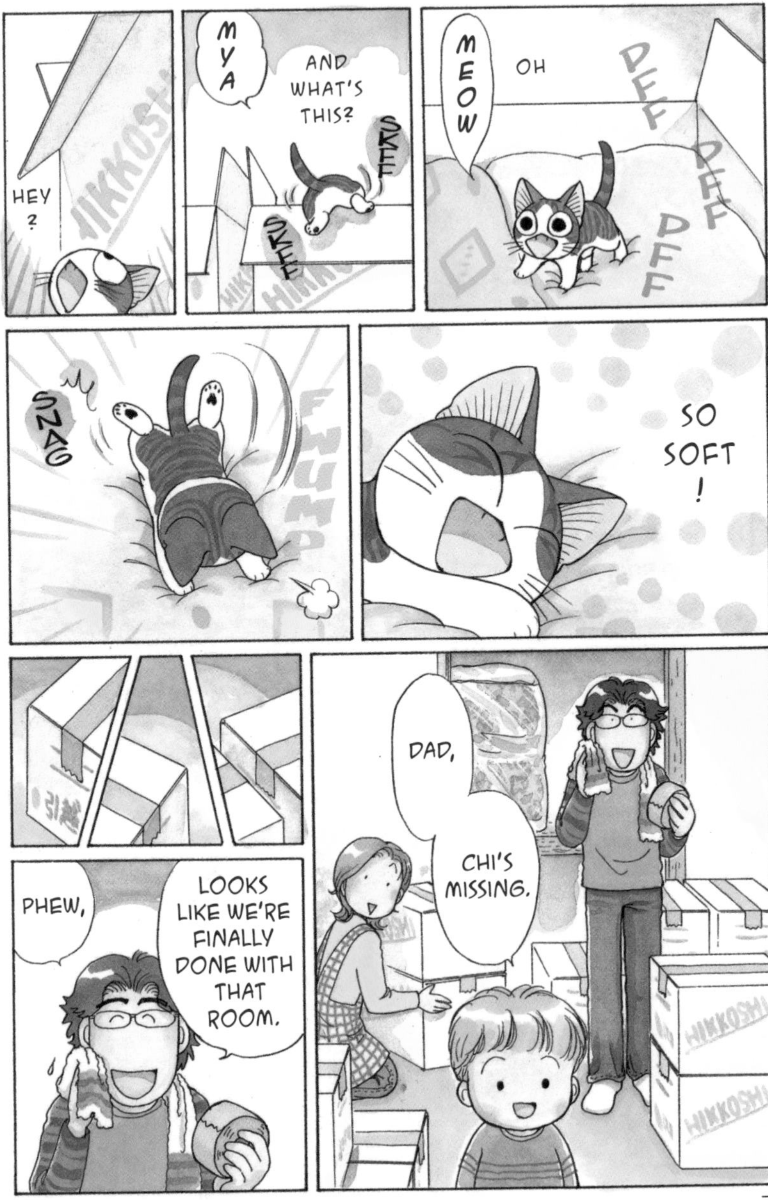
HIKKOSHI
HEY ?
MYA
AND WHAT'S THIS?
SKFF
SKFF
MEOW
OH
DFF
DFF
DFF
DFF
SNAG
FWUMP
SO SOFT !
PHEW,
LOOKS LIKE WE'RE FINALLY DONE WITH THAT ROOM.
DAD,
CHI'S MISSING.
HIKKOSHI
HIKKOSHI

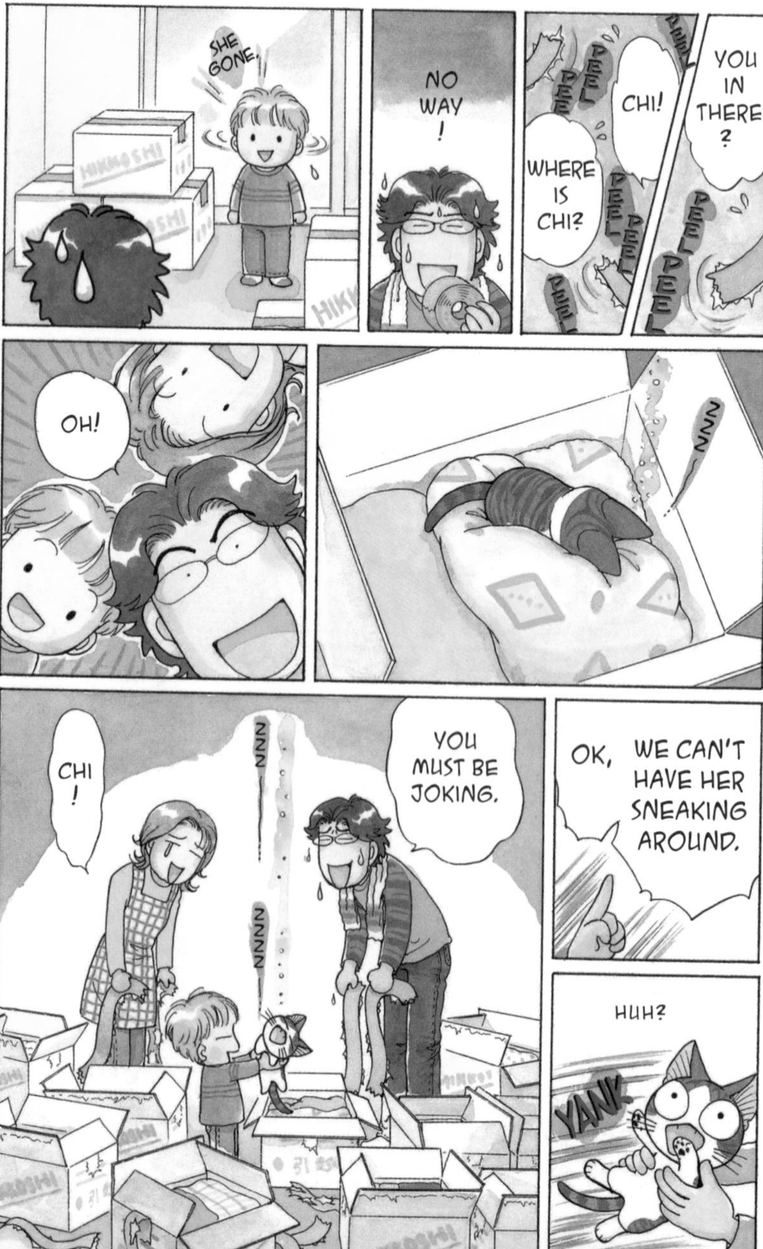
SHE GONE.
HIKKOSHI
NO WAY!
PEEL PEEL
CHI!
WHERE IS CHI?
PEEL PEEL PEEL
YOU IN THERE?
PEEL PEEL
OH!
ZZZ
CHI!
ZZZZ
ZZZZ
YOU MUST BE JOKING.
OK, WE CAN'T HAVE HER SNEAKING AROUND.
HUH?
YANK

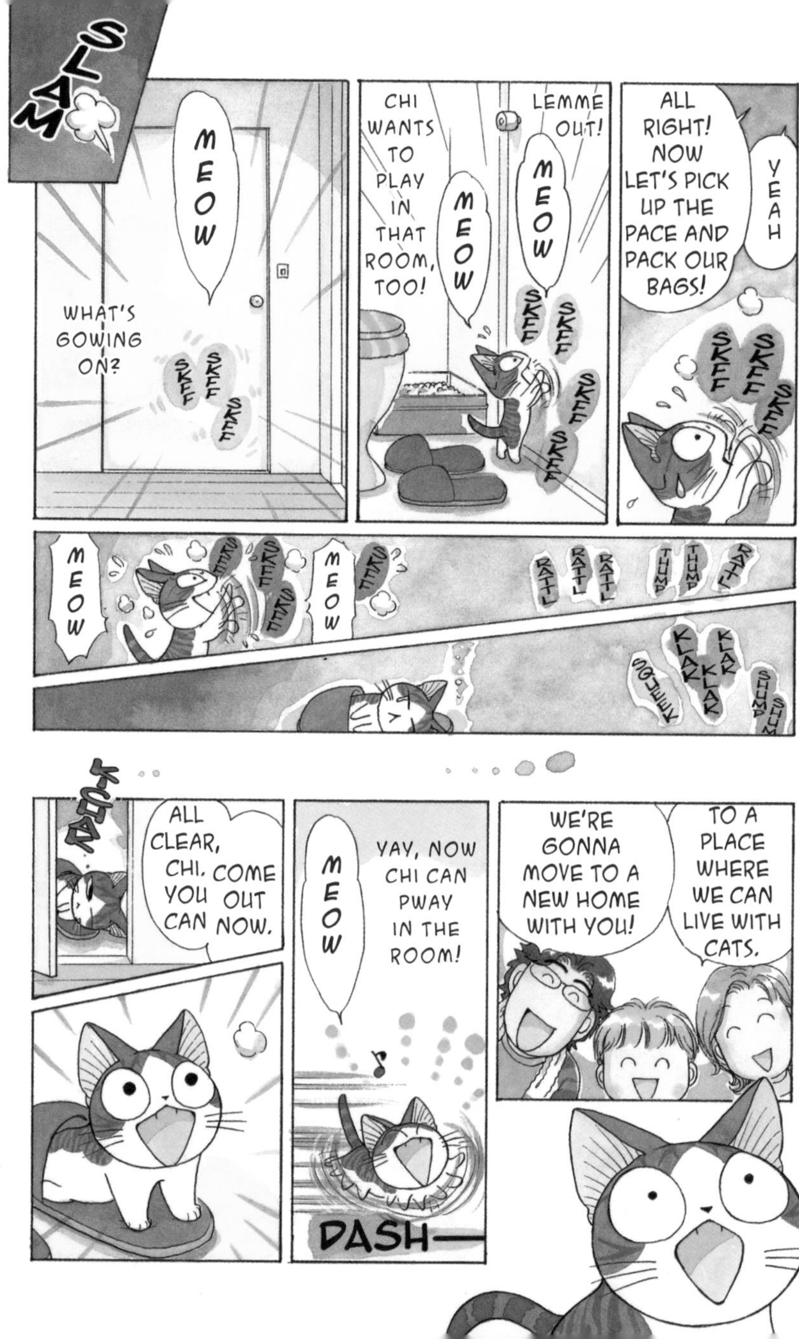
SLAM
MEOW
WHAT'S GOWING ON?
SKFF SKFF SKFF
CHI WANTS TO PLAY IN THAT ROOM, TOO!
MEOW
LEMME OUT!
MEOW
SKFF SKFF SKFF SKFF
ALL RIGHT! NOW LET'S PICK UP THE PACE AND PACK OUR BAGS!
YEAH
SKFF SKFF SKFF
MEOW
SKFF SKFF SKFF
MEOW
SKFF
RATTL RATTL RATTL
THUMP THUMP RATTL
SQUEEK
KLAK KLAK KLAK
SHUMP SHUMP
KICHA
ALL CLEAR, CHI.
YOU CAN COME OUT NOW.
MEOW
YAY, NOW CHI CAN PWAY IN THE ROOM!
DASH—
WE'RE GONNA MOVE TO A NEW HOME WITH YOU!
TO A PLACE WHERE WE CAN LIVE WITH CATS.

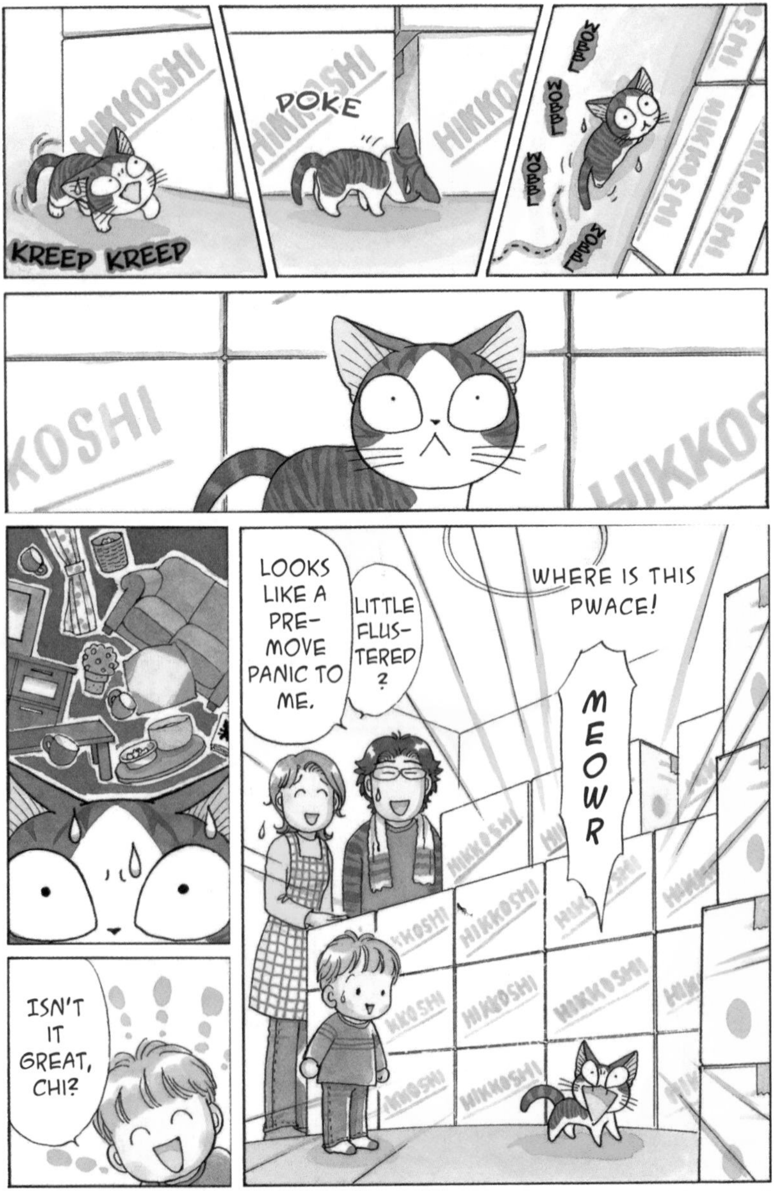
KREEP KREEP
POKE
WOBBL
WOBBL
WOBBL
WOBBL
ISN'T IT GREAT, CHI?
LOOKS LIKE A PRE-MOVE PANIC TO ME.
LITTLE FLUSTERED?
WHERE IS THIS PWACE!
MEOWR

the end

homemade 58: a cat imagines

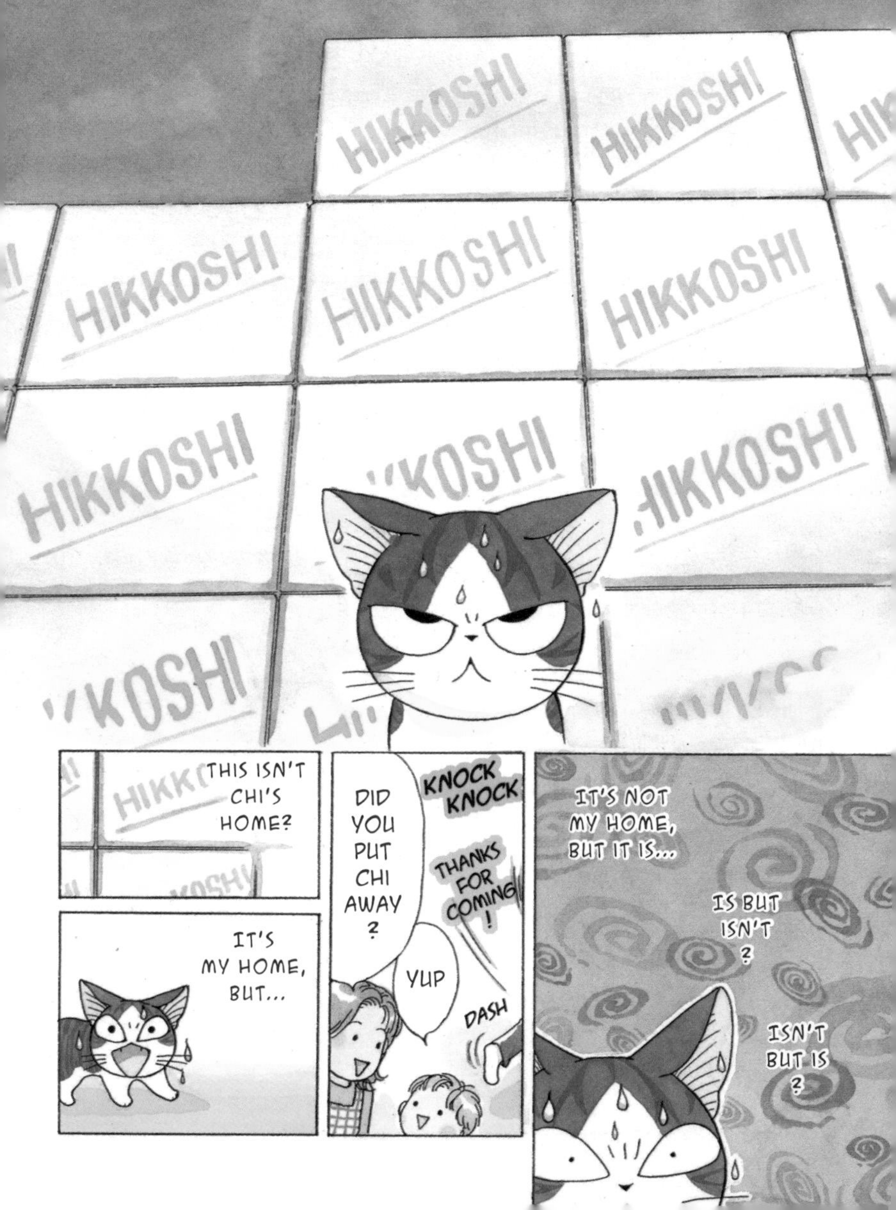
HIKKOSHI
THIS ISN'T CHI'S HOME?
IT'S MY HOME, BUT...
DID YOU PUT CHI AWAY?
KNOCK KNOCK
THANKS FOR COMING!
YUP
DASH
IT'S NOT MY HOME, BUT IT IS...
IS BUT ISN'T?
ISN'T BUT IS?

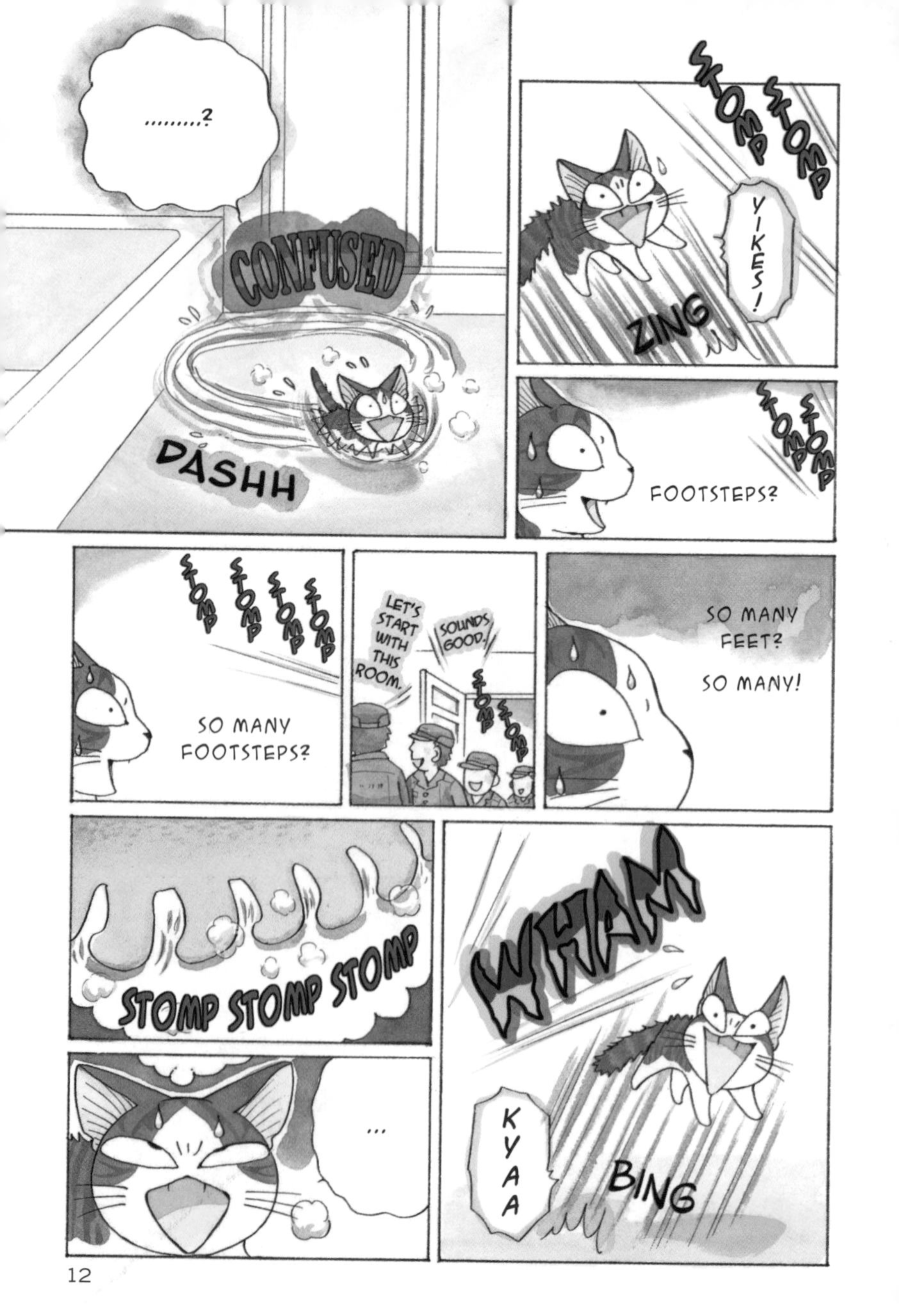

.........?
CONFUSED
DASHH
STOMP STOMP
YIKES!
ZING
STOMP STOMP
FOOTSTEPS?
STOMP STOMP STOMP STOMP
SO MANY FOOTSTEPS?
LET'S START WITH THIS ROOM.
SOUNDS GOOD.
STOMP STOMP
SO MANY FEET?
SO MANY!
STOMP STOMP STOMP
...
WHAM
KYAA
BING

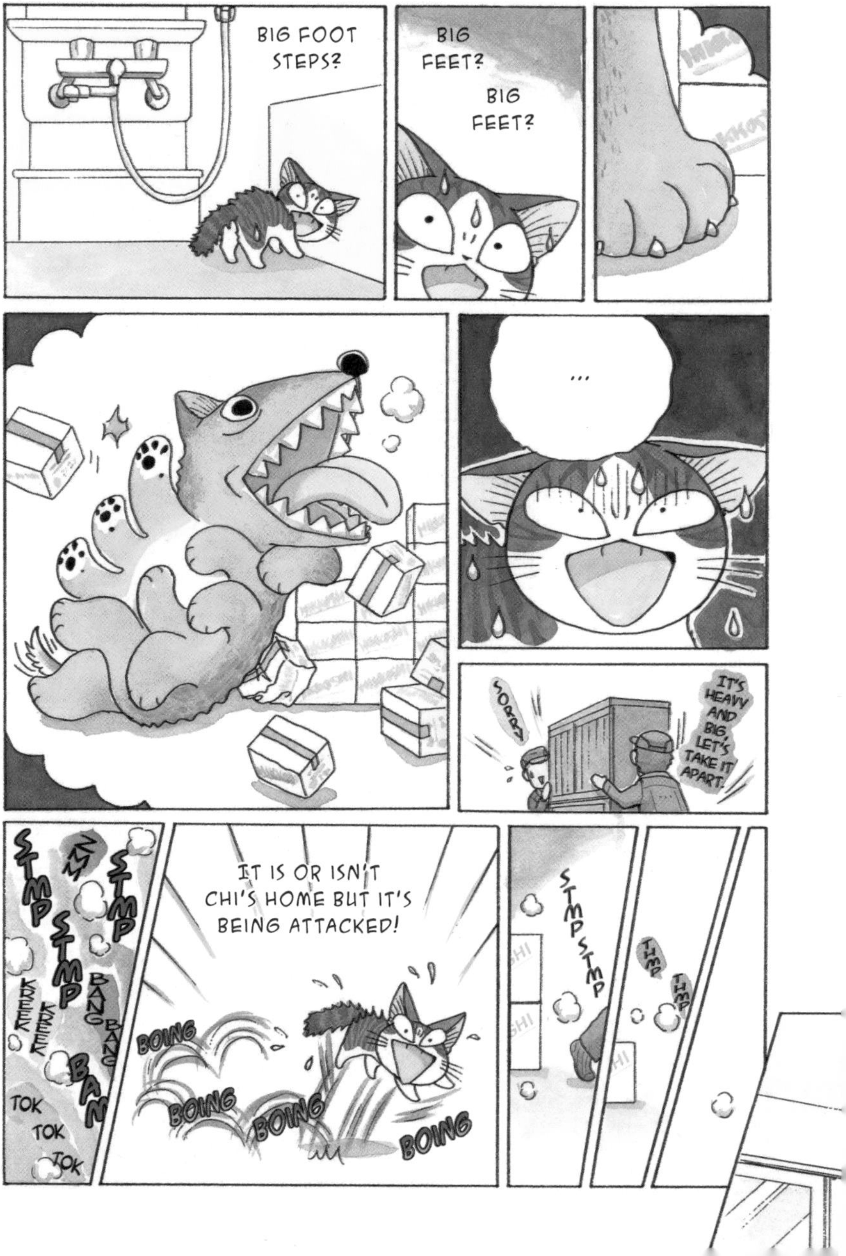
BIG FOOT STEPS?
BIG FEET?
BIG FEET?
...
SORRY
IT'S HEAVY AND BIG, LET'S TAKE IT APART.
STMP
STMP
STMP
STMP
BANG BANG
BAN
KREEK KREEK
TOK TOK TOK
IT IS OR ISN'T CHI'S HOME BUT IT'S BEING ATTACKED!
BOING
BOING
BOING
BOING
STMP STMP
THMP
THMP

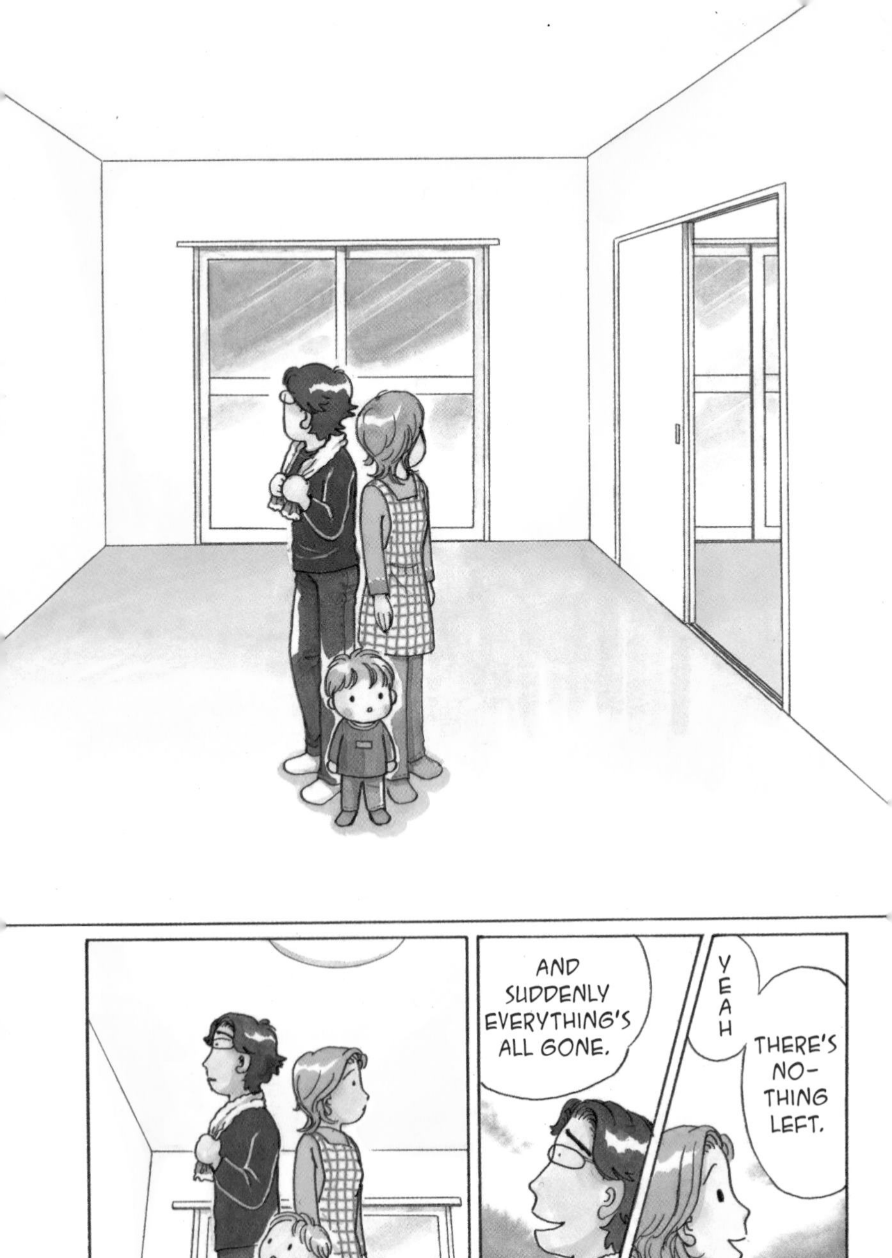
AND SUDDENLY EVERYTHING'S ALL GONE.
YEAH
THERE'S NO-THING LEFT.

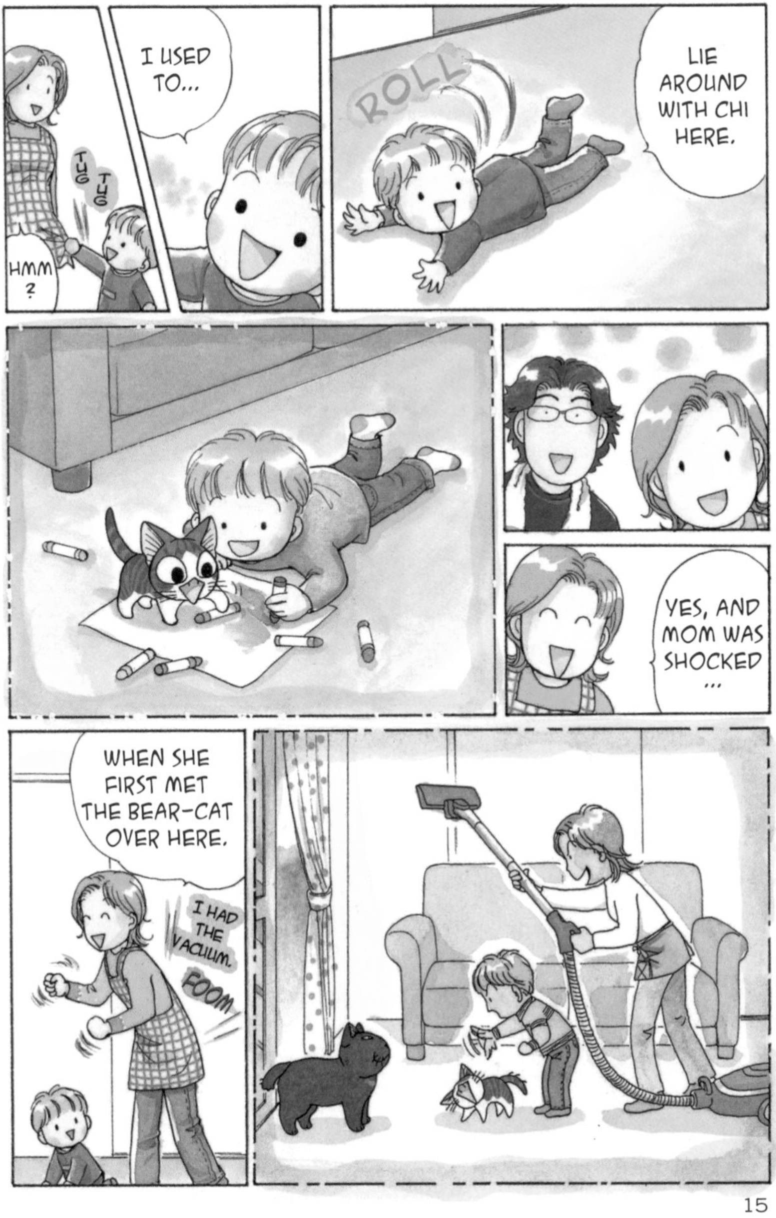
TUG TUG
HMM?
I USED TO...
ROLL
LIE AROUND WITH CHI HERE.
YES, AND MOM WAS SHOCKED...
WHEN SHE FIRST MET THE BEAR-CAT OVER HERE.
I HAD THE VACUUM.
FOOM

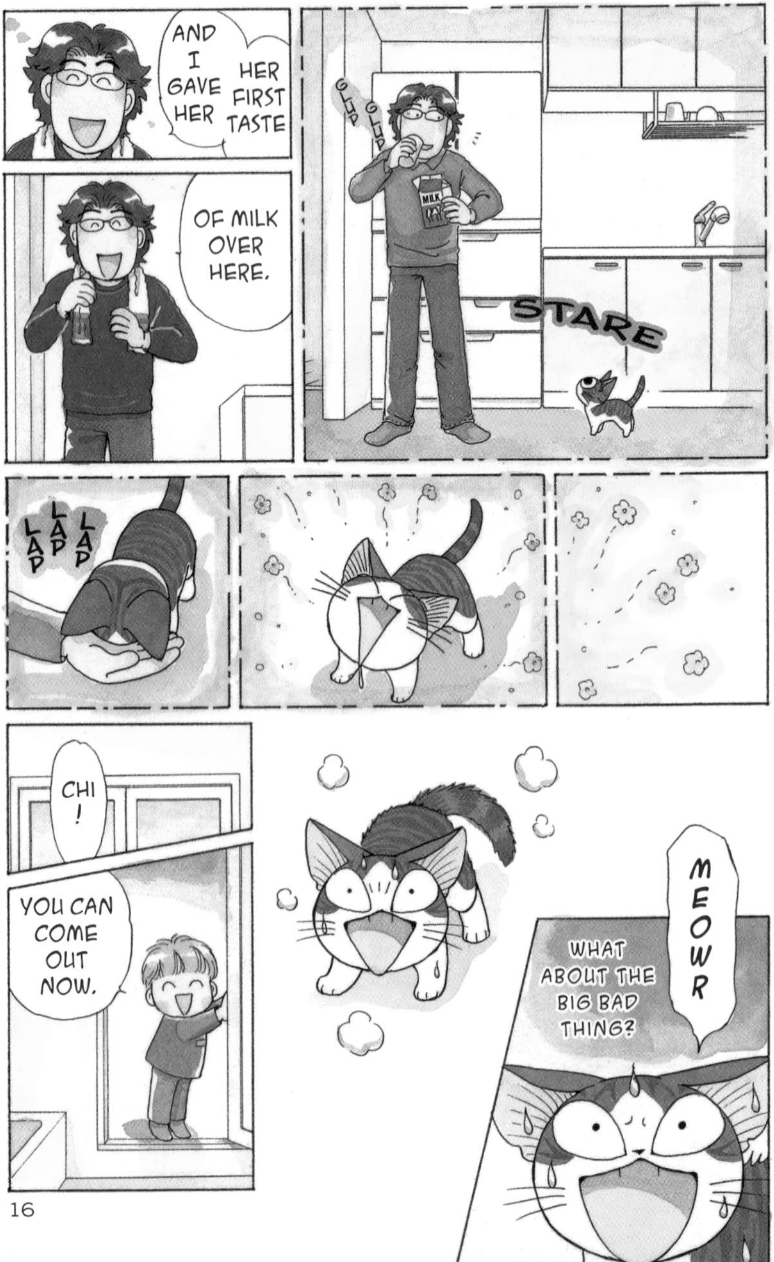
AND I GAVE HER HER FIRST TASTE
OF MILK OVER HERE.
GLUP GLUP
MILK
STARE
LAP LAP LAP
CHI!
YOU CAN COME OUT NOW.
MEOWR
WHAT ABOUT THE BIG BAD THING?

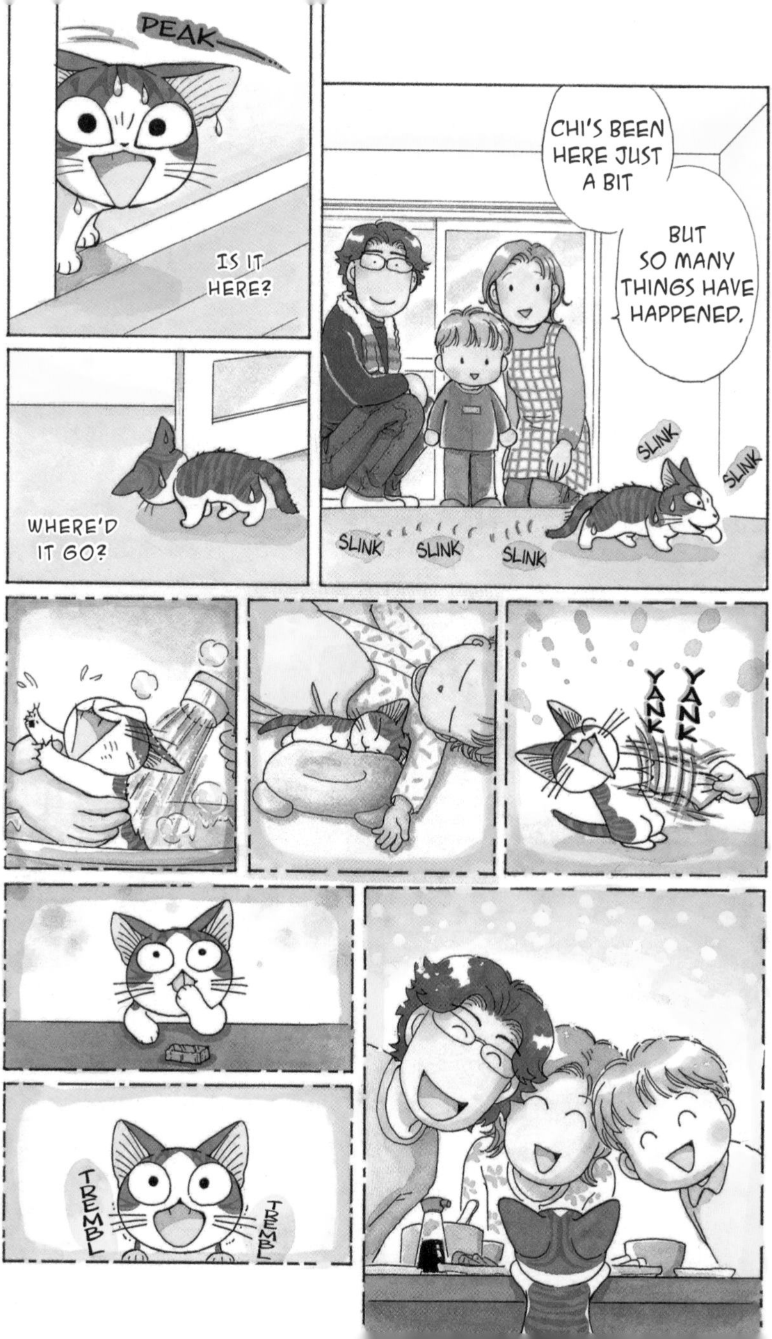

PEAK
IS IT HERE?
WHERE'D IT GO?
CHI'S BEEN HERE JUST A BIT
BUT SO MANY THINGS HAVE HAPPENED.
SLINK
SLINK
SLINK
SLINK
SLINK
YANK YANK
TREMBL
TREMBL

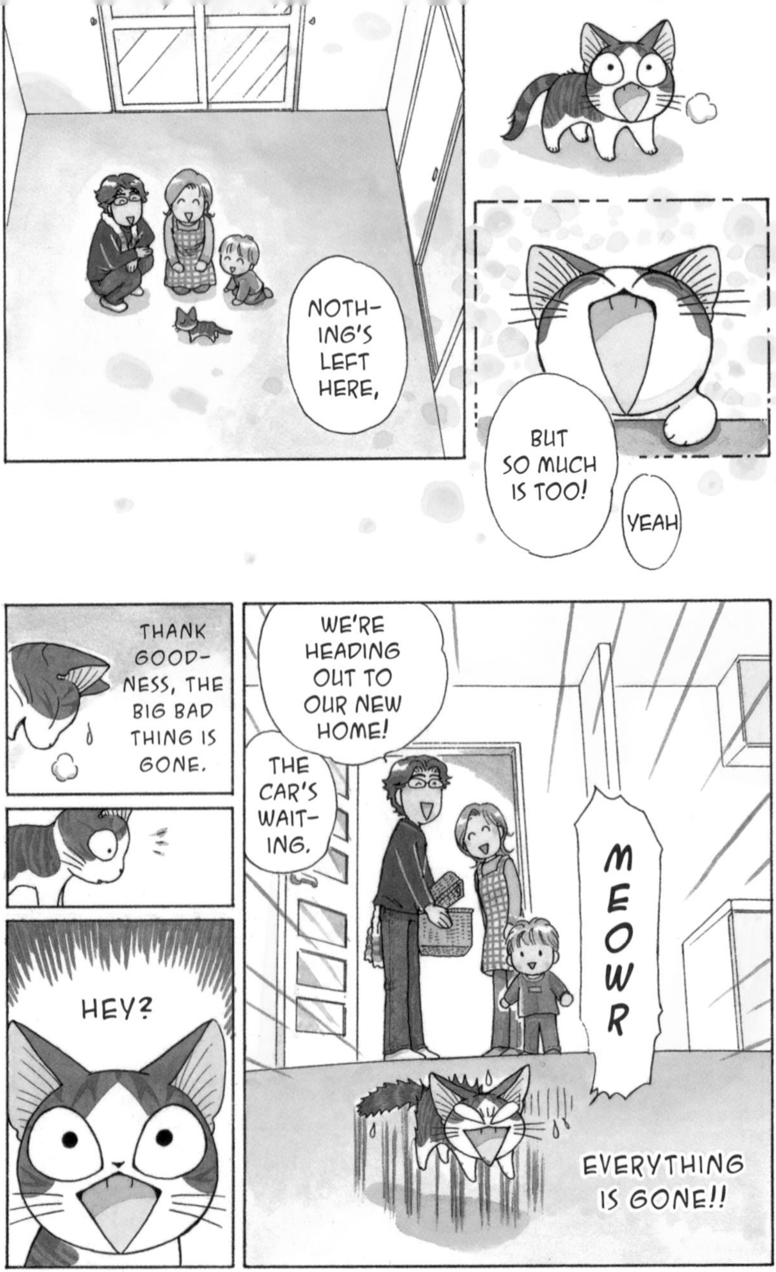
NOTHING'S LEFT HERE,
BUT SO MUCH IS TOO!
YEAH
THANK GOODNESS, THE BIG BAD THING IS GONE.
HEY?
WE'RE HEADING OUT TO OUR NEW HOME!
THE CAR'S WAITING.
MEOWR
EVERYTHING IS GONE!!

the end

homemade 59: a cat moves

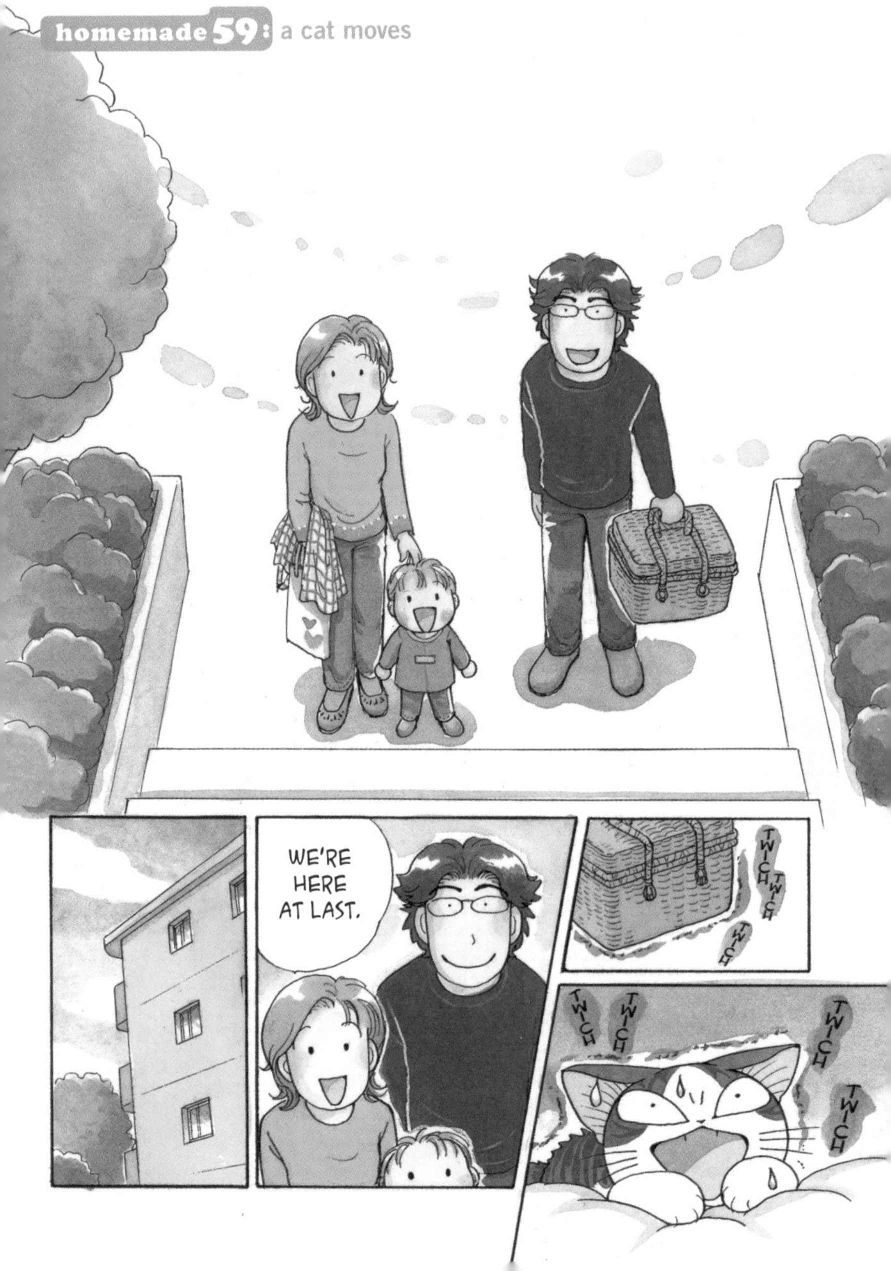
WE'RE HERE AT LAST.
TWICH TWICH
TWICH
TWICH TWICH
TWICH
TWICH

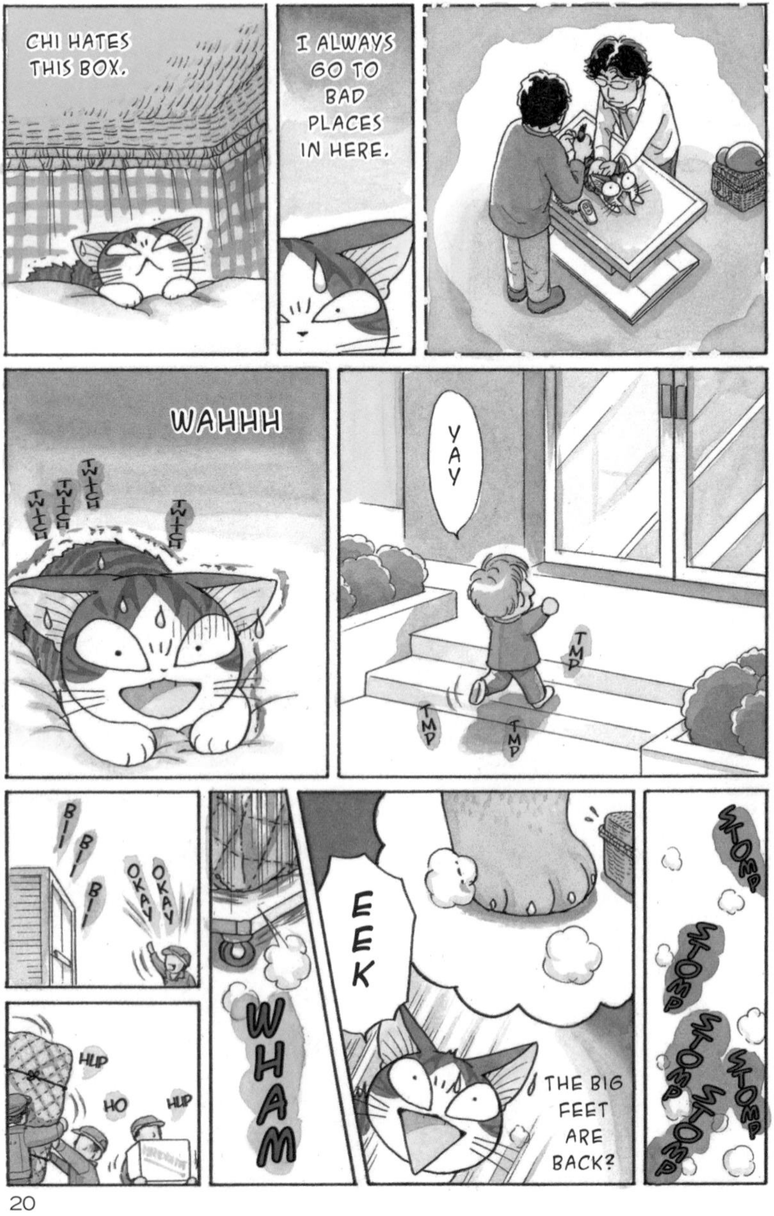
CHI HATES THIS BOX.
I ALWAYS GO TO BAD PLACES IN HERE.
WAHHH
TWITCH
TWITCH
TWITCH
TWITCH
YAY
TMP
TMP
TMP
BI
BI
BI
OKAY
OKAY
HUP
HO
HUP
WHAM
EEK
THE BIG FEET ARE BACK?
STOMP
STOMP
STOMP
STOMP
STOMP

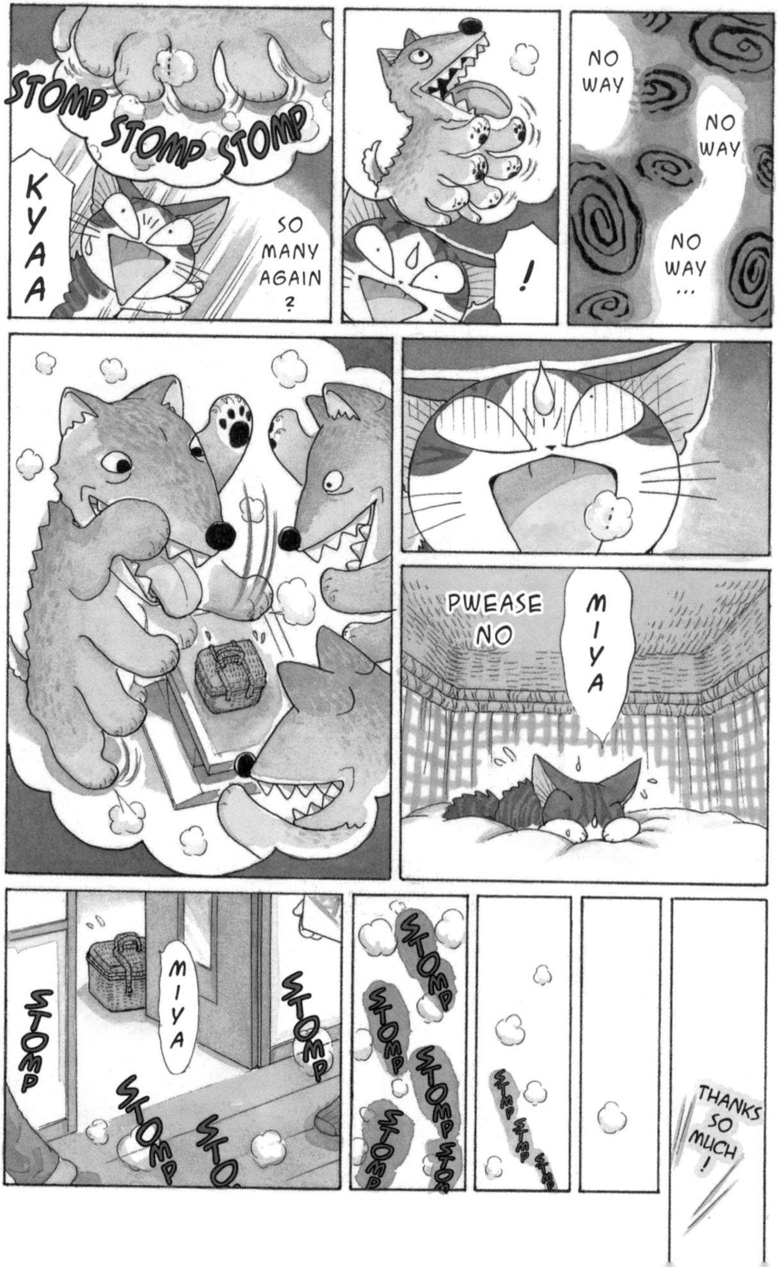
STOMP STOMP STOMP STOMP
KYAA
SO MANY AGAIN?
!
NO WAY
NO WAY
NO WAY...
PWEASE NO
MIYA
STOMP
MIYA
STOMP
STOMP
STO
STOMP
STOMP
STOMP
STOMP
STOMP
STOMP STOMP STOMP
THANKS SO MUCH!

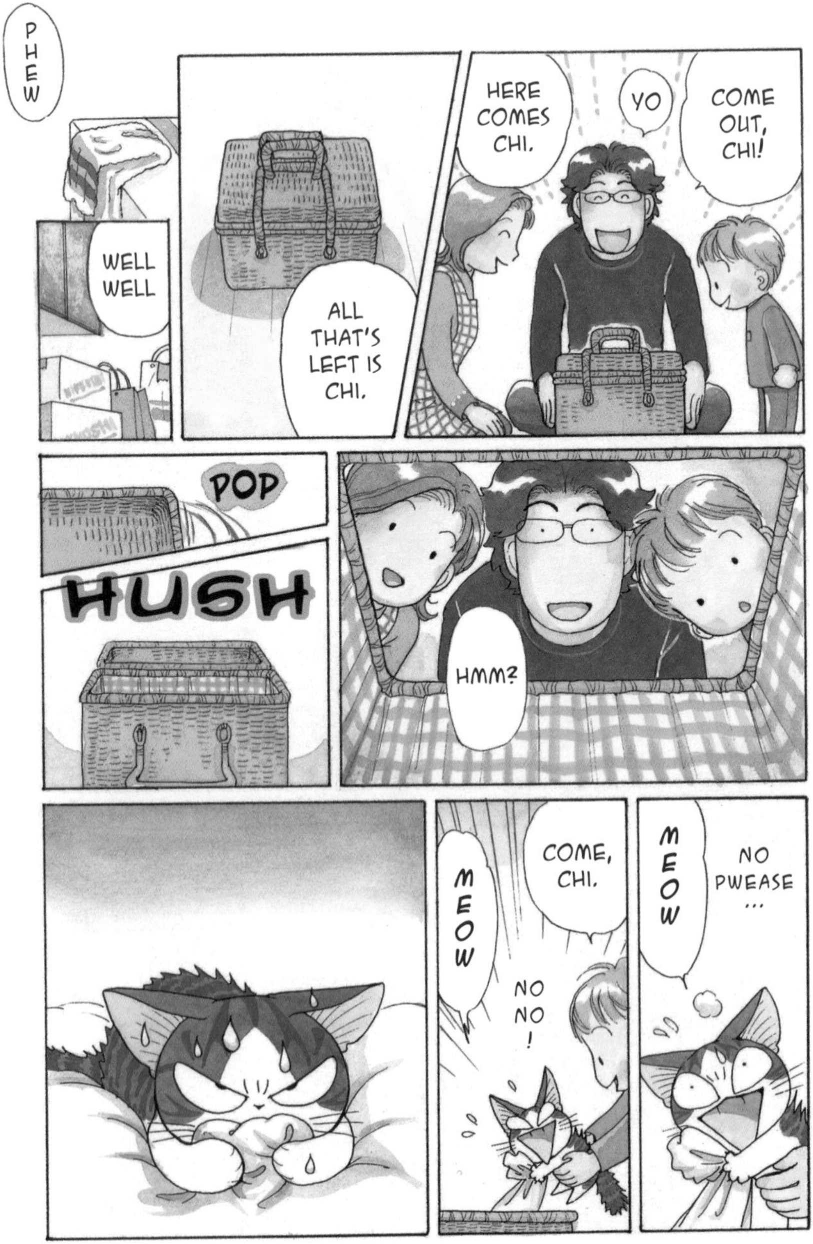
PHEW
WELL WELL
ALL THAT'S LEFT IS CHI.
HERE COMES CHI.
YO
COME OUT, CHI!
POP
HUSH
HMM?
MEOW
COME, CHI.
NO NO!
MEOW
NO PWEASE ...

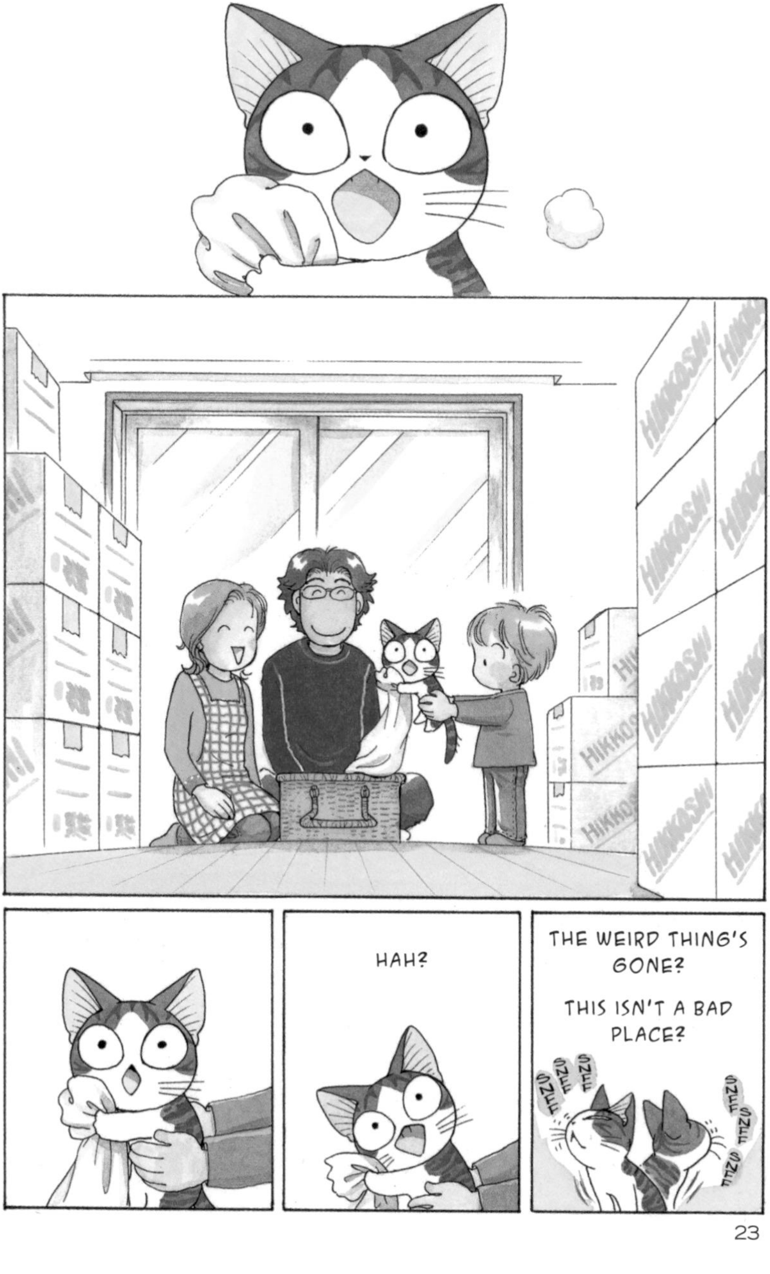
HIKKOSHI
HAH?
THE WEIRD THING'S GONE?
THIS ISN'T A BAD PLACE?
SNFF SNFF
SNFF SNFF

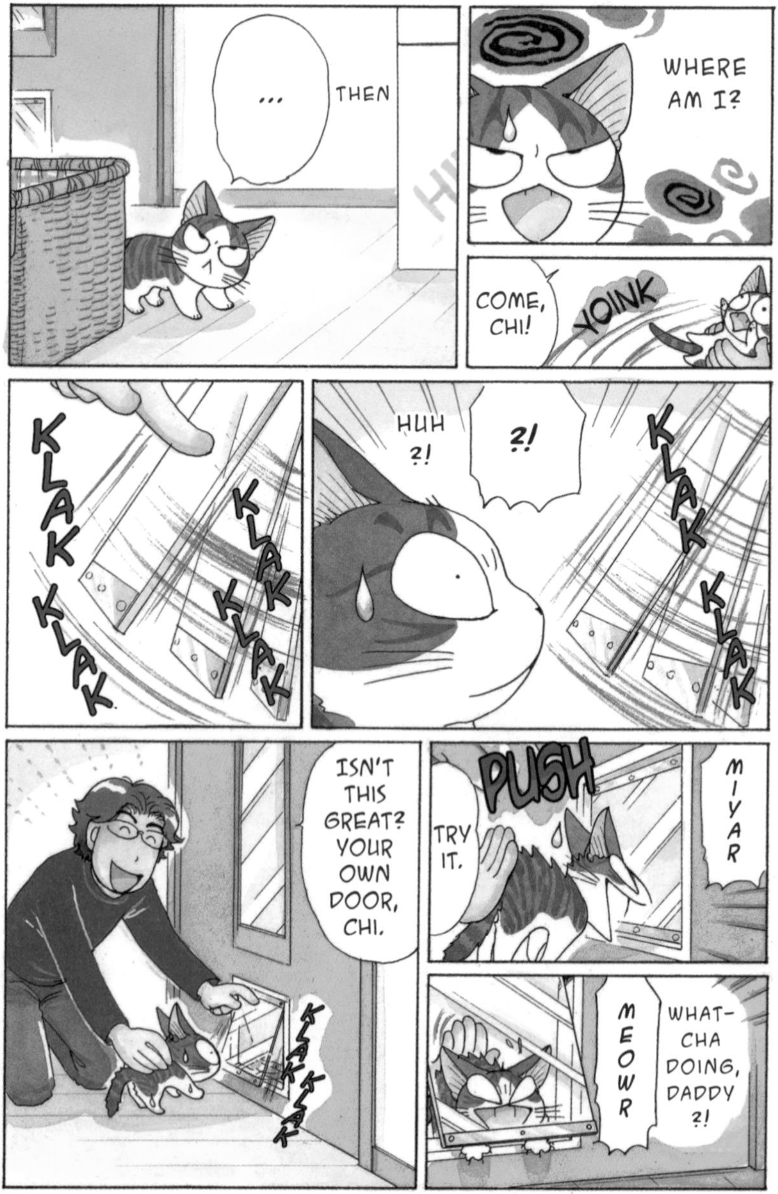
...
THEN
WHERE AM I?
COME, CHI!
YOINK
KLAK
KLAK
KLAK
KLAK
HUH ?!
?!
KLAK
KLAK
ISN'T THIS GREAT? YOUR OWN DOOR, CHI.
KLAK KLAK
PUSH
TRY IT.
MIYAR
MEOWR
WHAT-CHA DOING, DADDY ?!

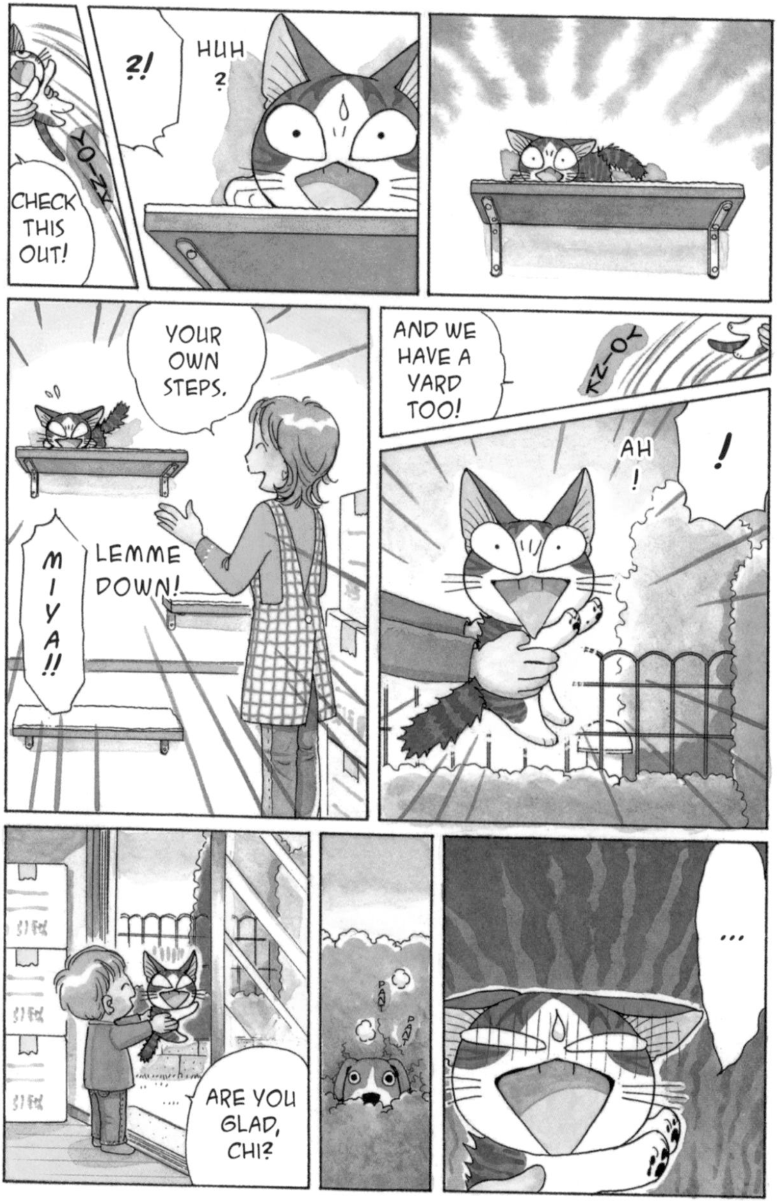
CHECK THIS OUT!
YO-INK
?!
HUH ?
YOUR OWN STEPS.
MIYA!!
LEMME DOWN!
AND WE HAVE A YARD TOO!
YO-INK
AH !
!
....
ARE YOU GLAD, CHI?
PANT
PANT
...

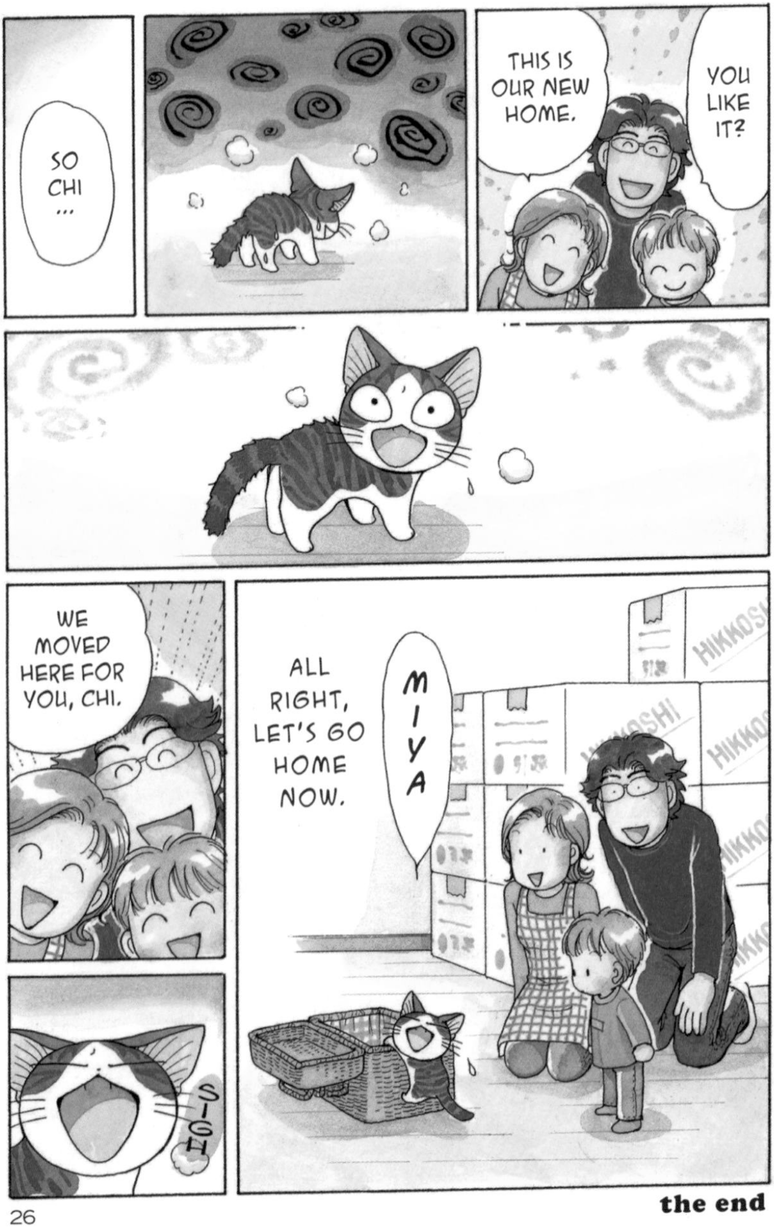
SO CHI ...
THIS IS OUR NEW HOME.
YOU LIKE IT?
WE MOVED HERE FOR YOU, CHI.
SIGH
ALL RIGHT, LET'S GO HOME NOW.
MIYA
HIKKOSHI

the end

homemade 60 : a cat sniffs

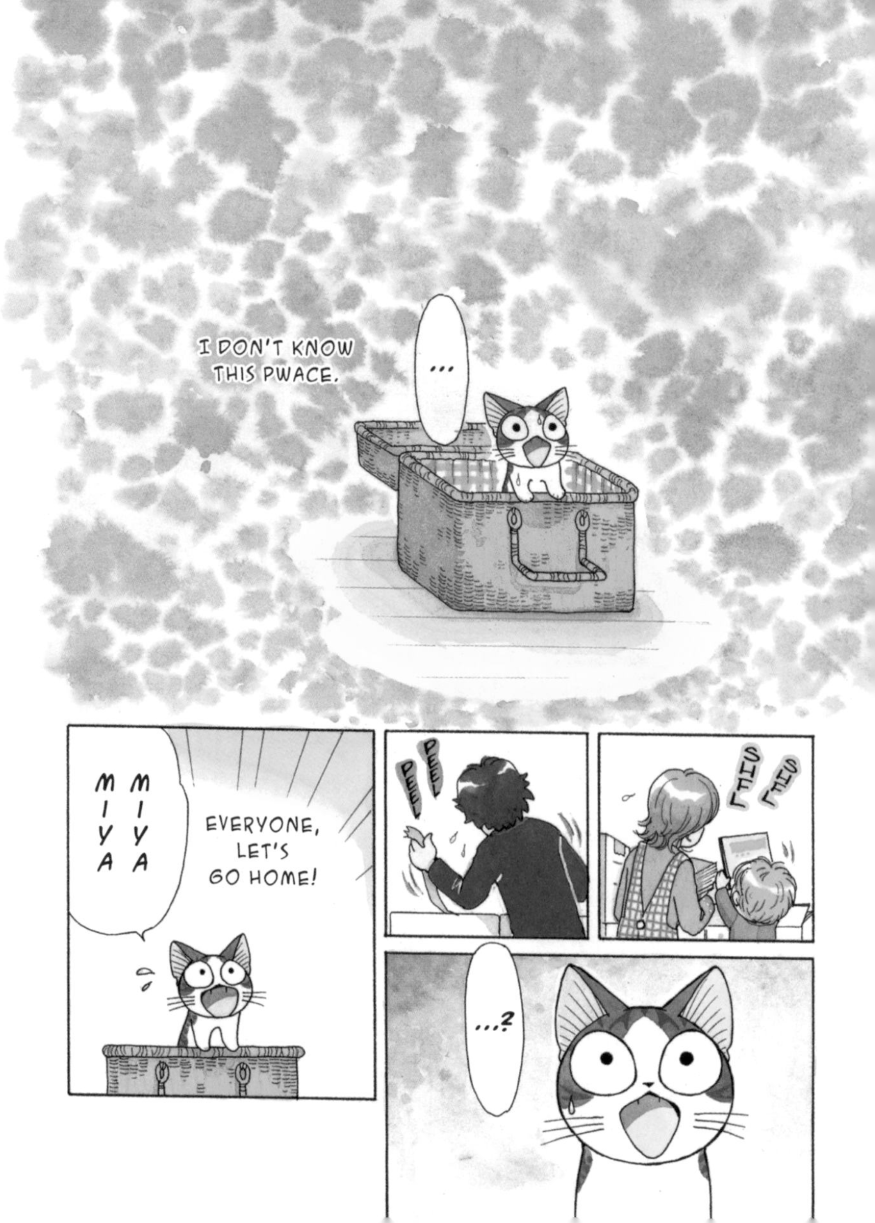
I DON'T KNOW THIS PWACE.
...
EVERYONE, LET'S GO HOME!
MIYA MIYA
PEEL PEEL
SHFF SHFF
...?

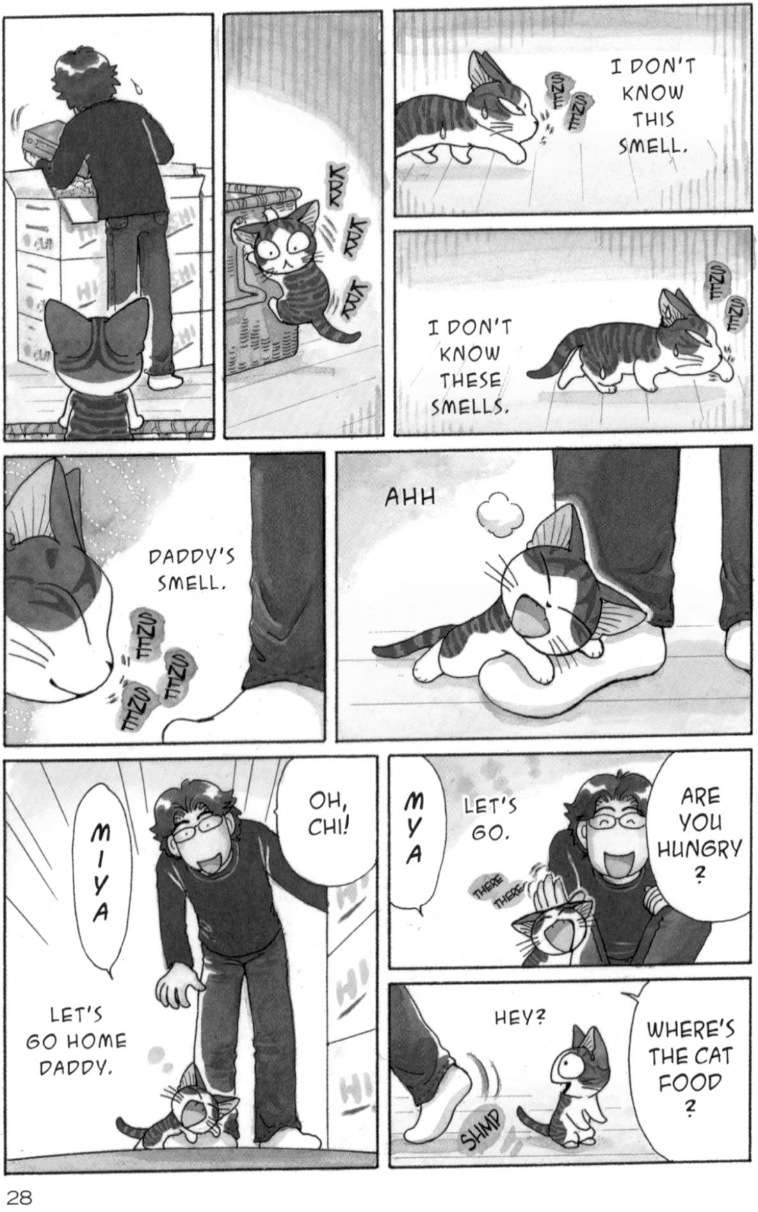
KRK
KRK
KRK
SNFF
SNFF
I DON'T KNOW THIS SMELL.
I DON'T KNOW THESE SMELLS.
SNFF
SNFF
DADDY'S SMELL.
SNFF
SNFF
SNFF
AHH
MIYA
OH, CHI!
LET'S GO HOME DADDY.
MYA
LET'S GO.
ARE YOU HUNGRY?
THERE THERE
HEY?
WHERE'S THE CAT FOOD?
SHMP

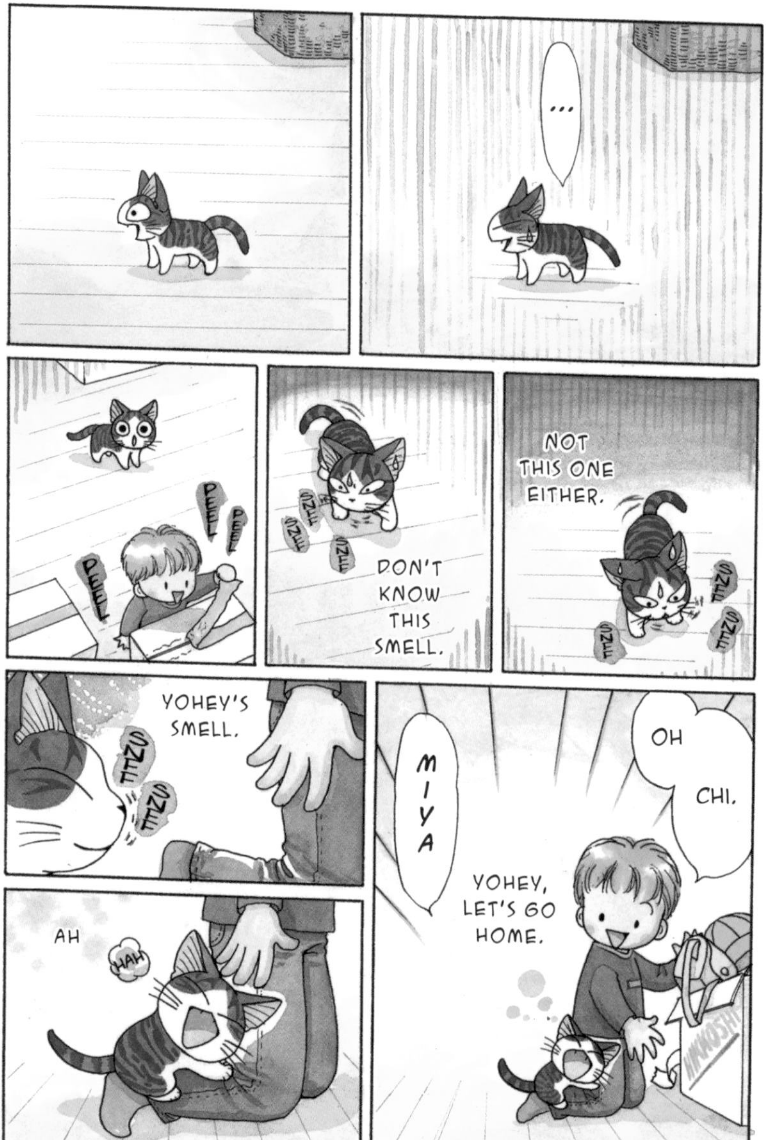
...
PEEL
PEEL
PEEL
SNFF
SNFF
SNFF
DON'T KNOW THIS SMELL.
NOT THIS ONE EITHER.
SNFF
SNFF
SNFF
YOHEY'S SMELL.
SNFF
SNFF
AH
HAH
MIYA
OH CHI.
YOHEY, LET'S GO HOME.

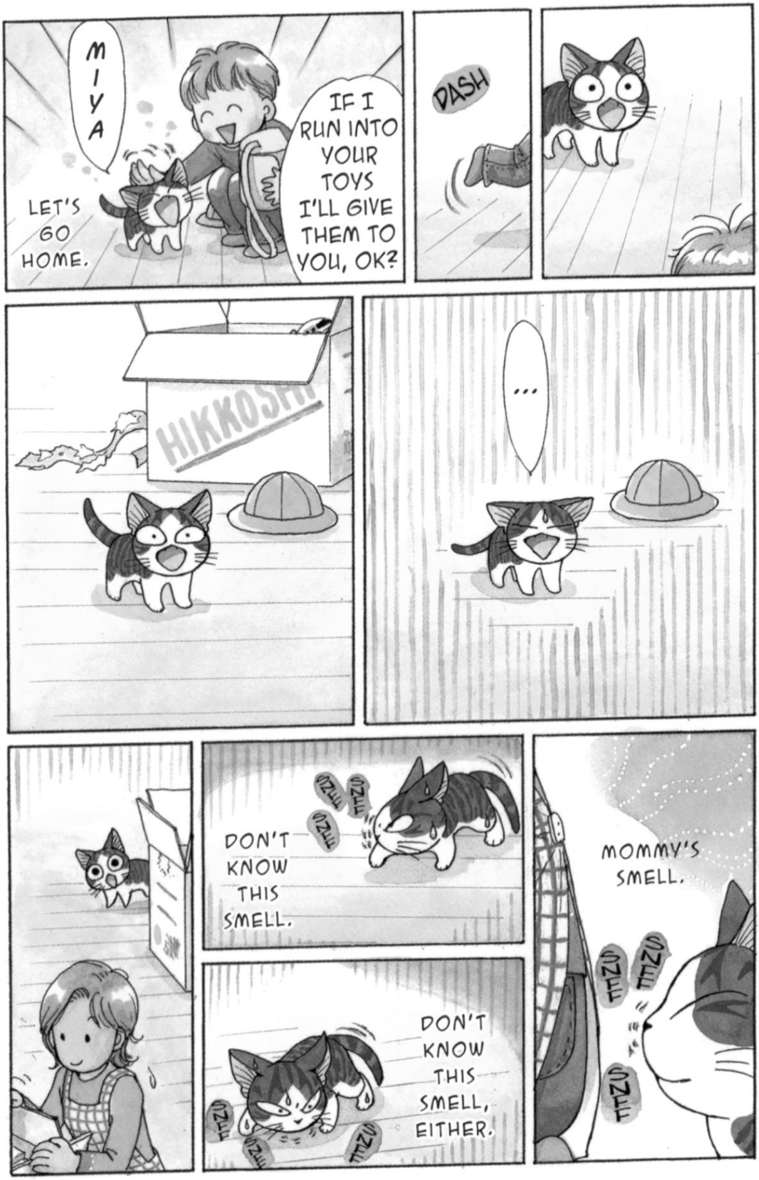
MIYA
IF I RUN INTO YOUR TOYS I'LL GIVE THEM TO YOU, OK?
LET'S GO HOME.
DASH
HIKKOSHI
...
SNFF
SNFF
SNFF
DON'T KNOW THIS SMELL.
DON'T KNOW THIS SMELL, EITHER.
SNFF
SNFF
SNFF
MOMMY'S SMELL.
SNFF
SNFF
SNFF

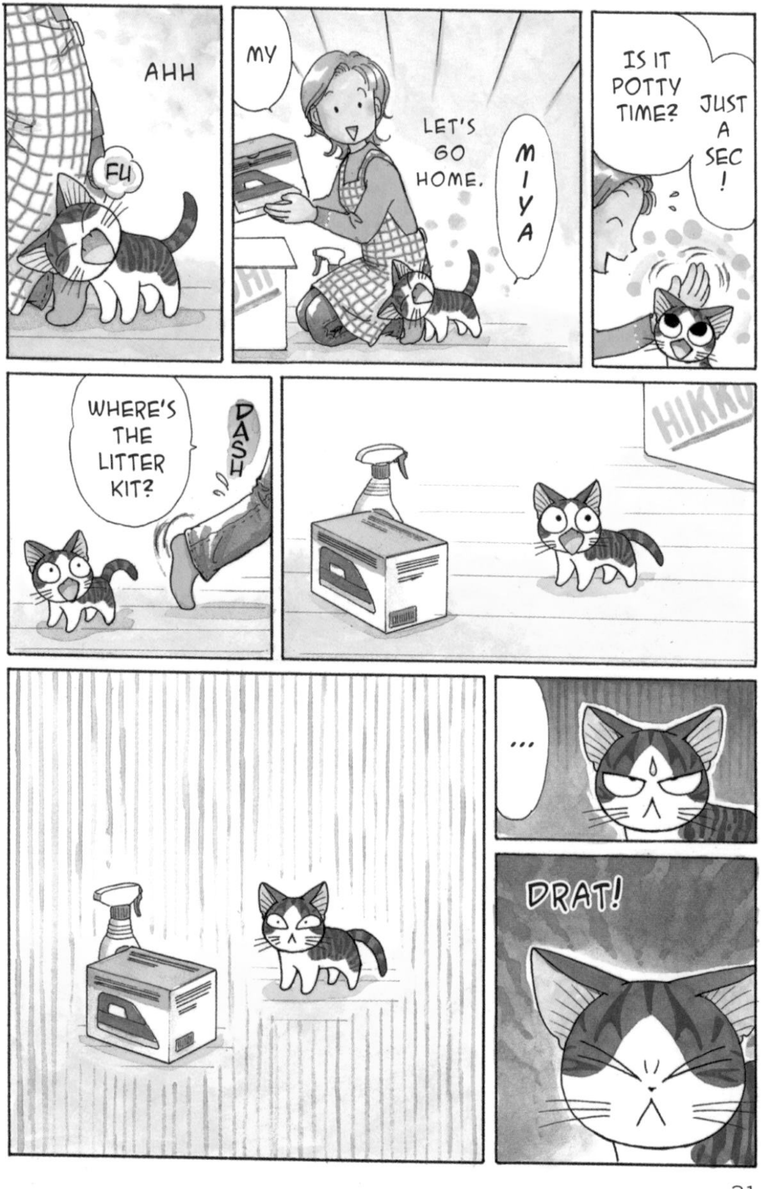
AHH
FU
MY
LET'S GO HOME.
MIYA
IS IT POTTY TIME?
JUST A SEC!
WHERE'S THE LITTER KIT?
DASH
HIKKO
...
DRAT!

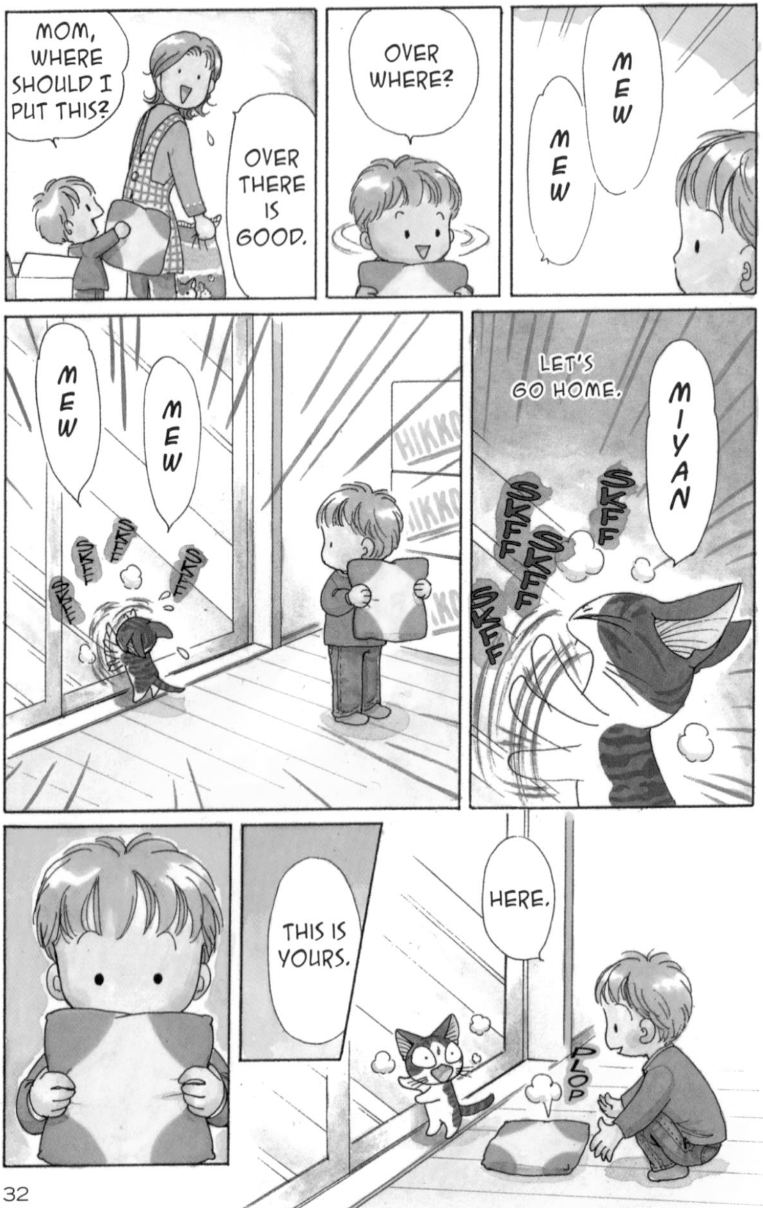
MOM, WHERE SHOULD I PUT THIS?
OVER THERE IS GOOD.
OVER WHERE?
MEW
MEW
MEW
MEW
SKFF SKFF SKFF SKFF
HIKKO
LET'S GO HOME.
MIYAN
SKFF SKFF SKFF SKFF
HERE.
THIS IS YOURS.
PLOP

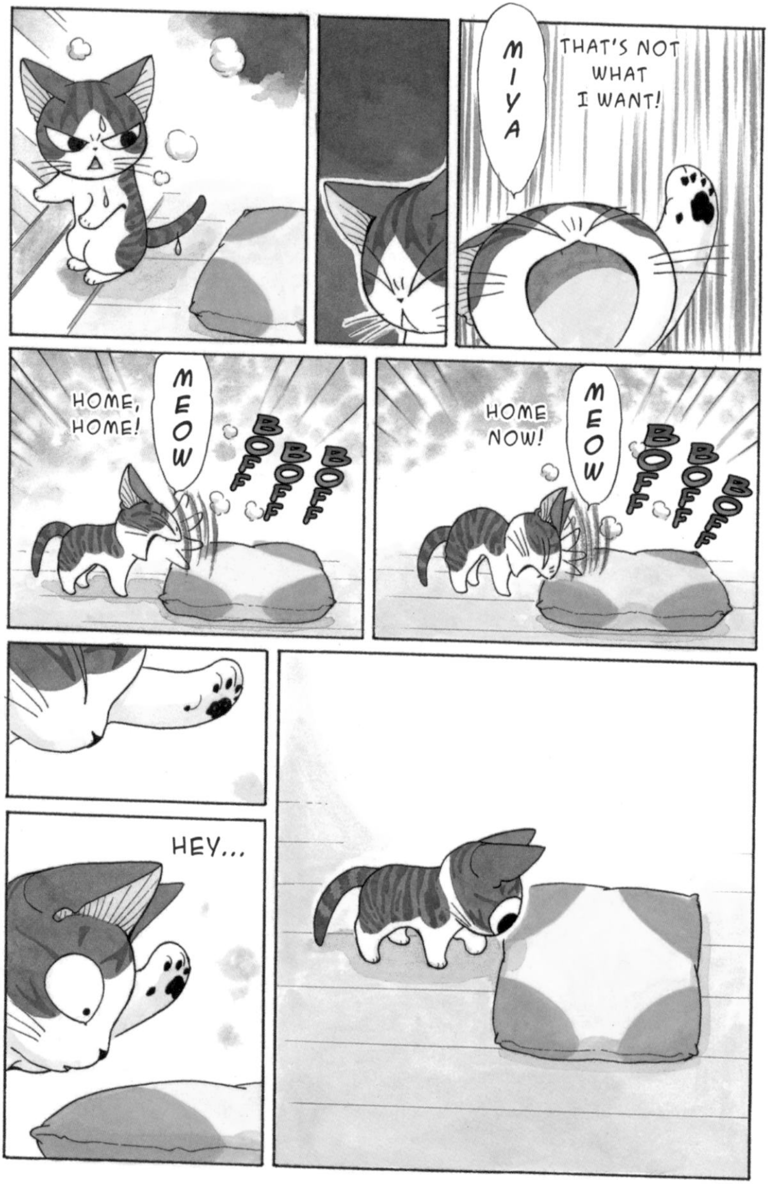
MIYA
THAT'S NOT WHAT I WANT!
HOME, HOME!
MEOW
BOFF BOFF BOFF
HOME NOW!
MEOW
BOFF BOFF BOFF
HEY...

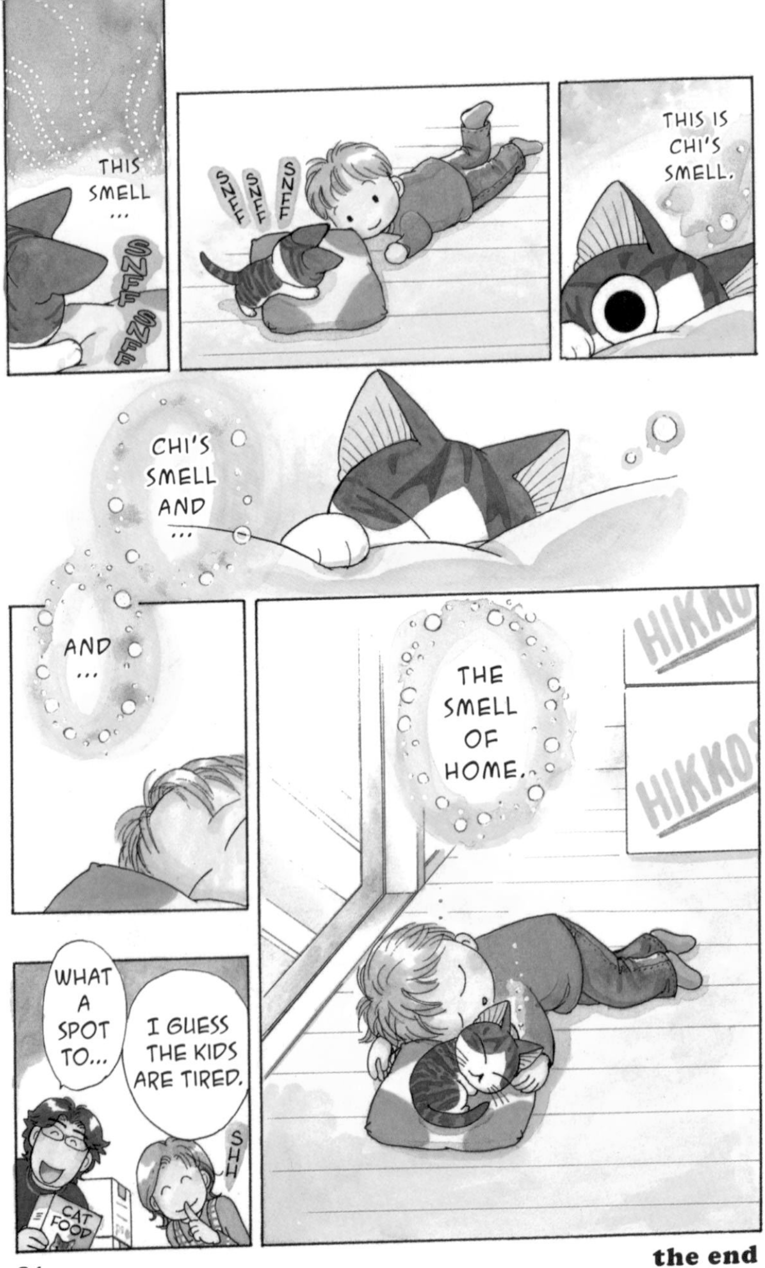
THIS SMELL ...
SNFF SNFF
SNFF SNFF SNFF
THIS IS CHI'S SMELL.
CHI'S SMELL AND ...
AND ...
THE SMELL OF HOME.
WHAT A SPOT TO...
I GUESS THE KIDS ARE TIRED.
SHH
CAT FOOD

the end

homemade 61: a cat cultivates

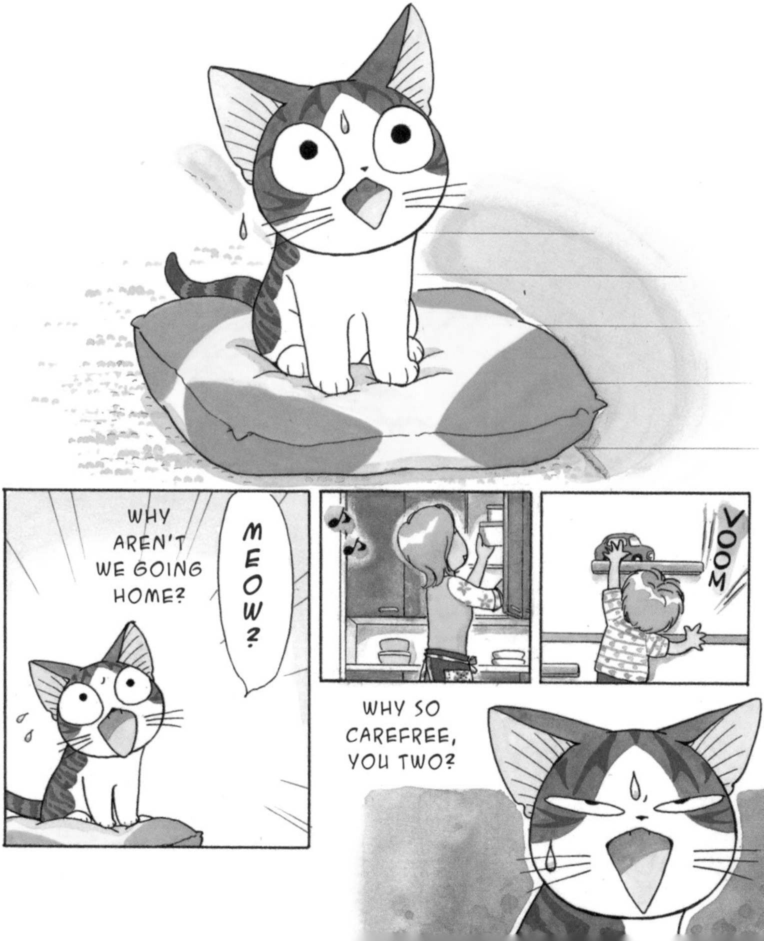
WHY AREN'T WE GOING HOME?
MEOW?
VOOM
WHY SO CAREFREE, YOU TWO?

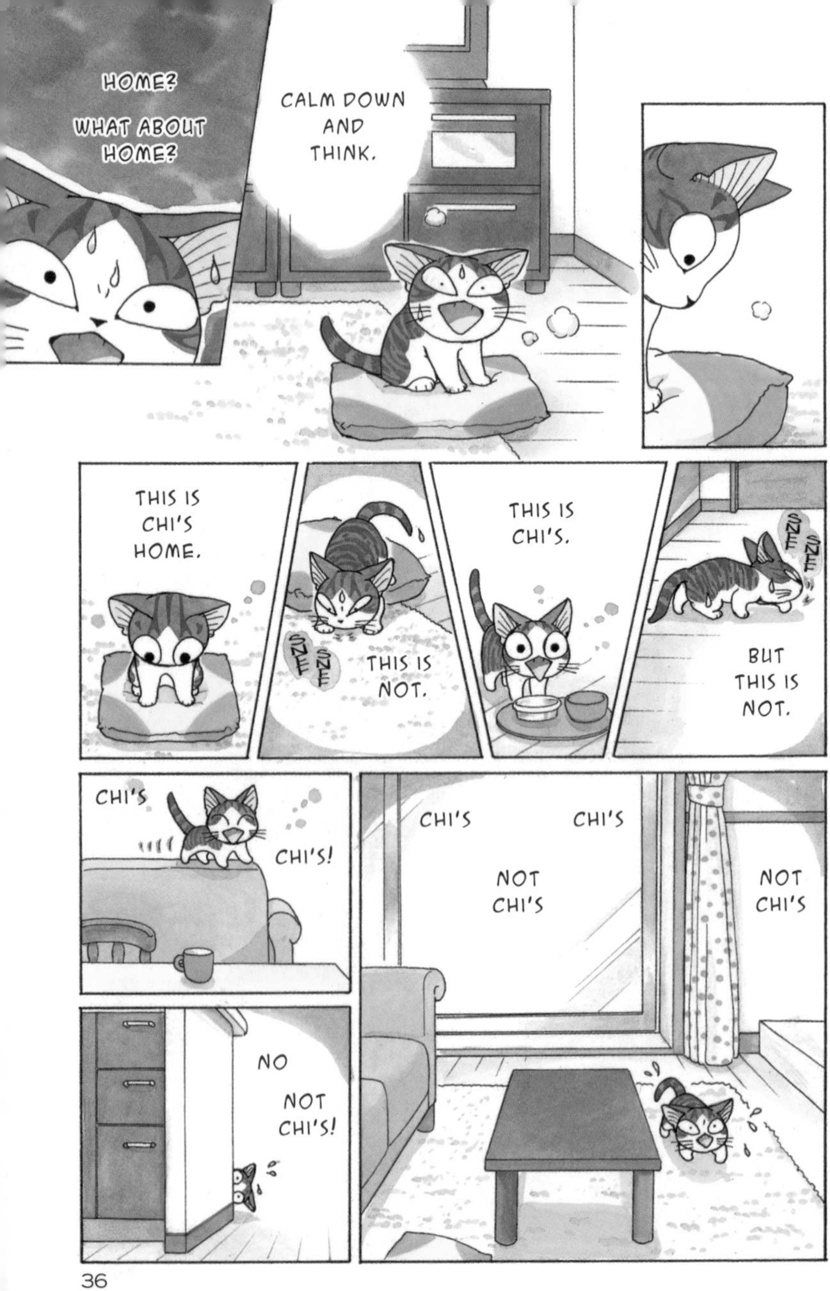
HOME?
WHAT ABOUT HOME?
CALM DOWN AND THINK.
THIS IS CHI'S HOME.
SNIF SNIF
THIS IS NOT.
THIS IS CHI'S.
SNIF SNIF
BUT THIS IS NOT.
CHI'S
CHI'S!
NO
NOT CHI'S!
CHI'S
CHI'S
NOT CHI'S
NOT CHI'S

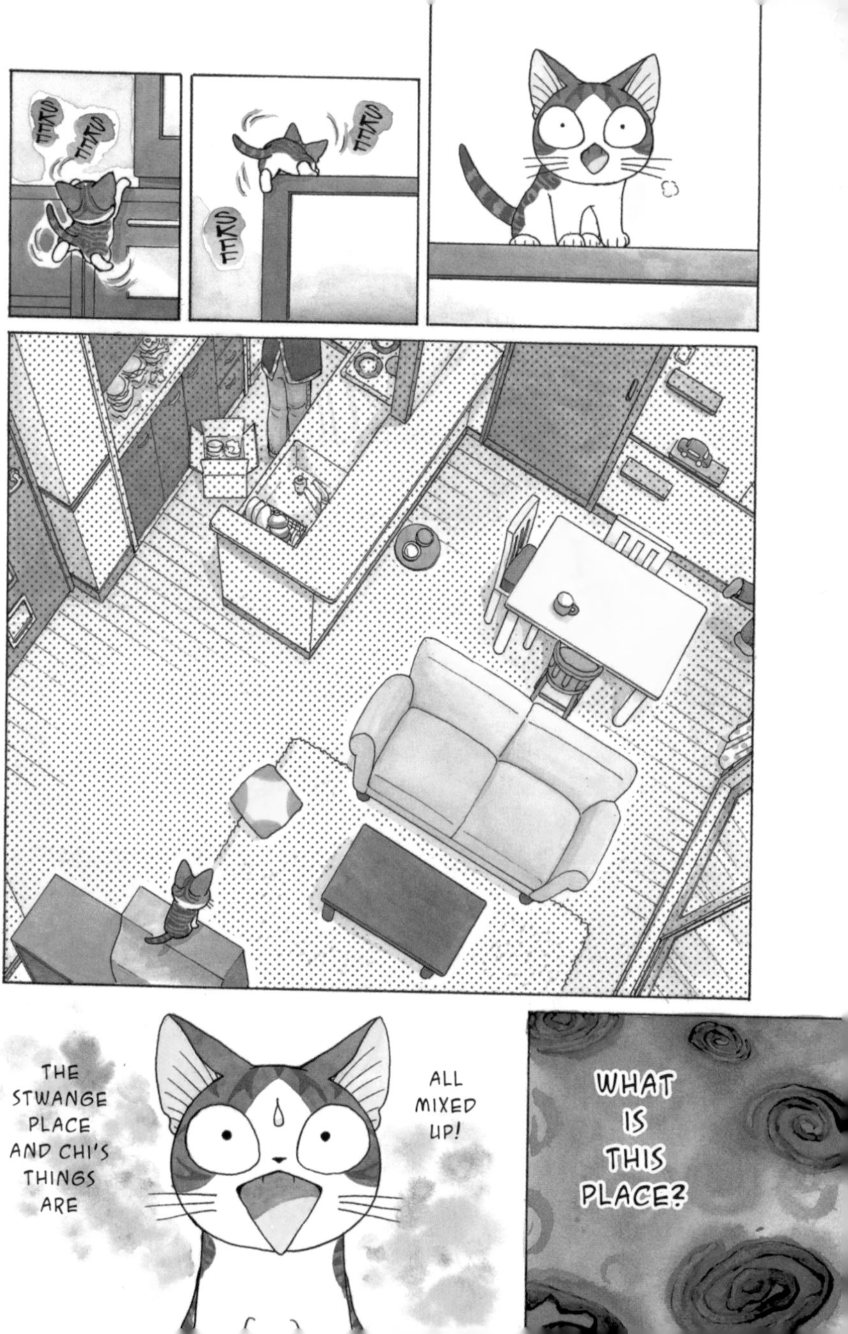
SKREET
SKREET
SKREET
SKREET
THE STWANGE PLACE AND CHI'S THINGS ARE
ALL MIXED UP!
WHAT IS THIS PLACE?

WHAT SHOULD CHI DO?

HRN?

HMM?

!

HO-HO

THIS IS MINE!

I'LL MAKE ALL THIS MINE!

TEEHEE

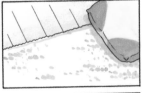

38

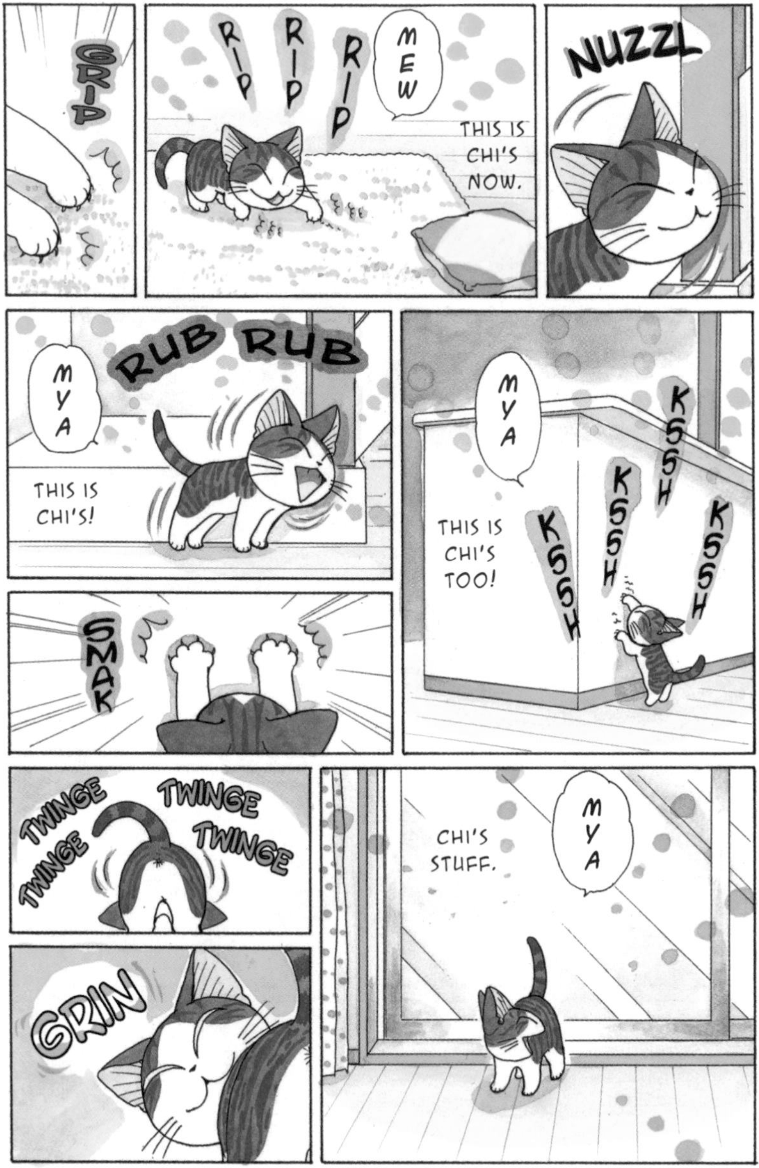
GRIP
RIP RIP RIP
MEW
THIS IS CHI'S NOW.
NUZZL
RUB RUB
MYA
THIS IS CHI'S!
SMAK
MYA
THIS IS CHI'S TOO!
KSSH KSSH KSSH KSSH
TWINGE TWINGE TWINGE TWINGE
GRIN
CHI'S STUFF.
MYA

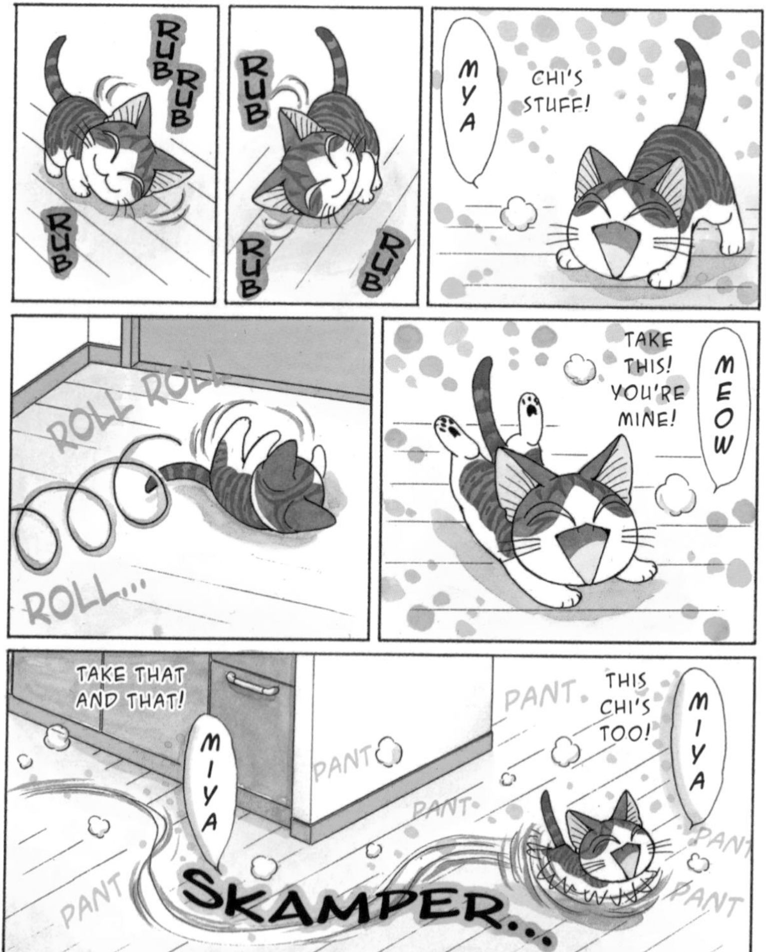
RUB RUB
RUB
RUB
RUB
RUB
MYA
CHI'S STUFF!
ROLL ROLL
ROLL...
TAKE THIS! YOU'RE MINE!
MEOW
TAKE THAT AND THAT!
MIYA
PANT
PANT
PANT
THIS CHI'S TOO!
MIYA
PANT
SKAMPER...
PANT
PANT
PANT
PANT
PANT
PANT
PANT

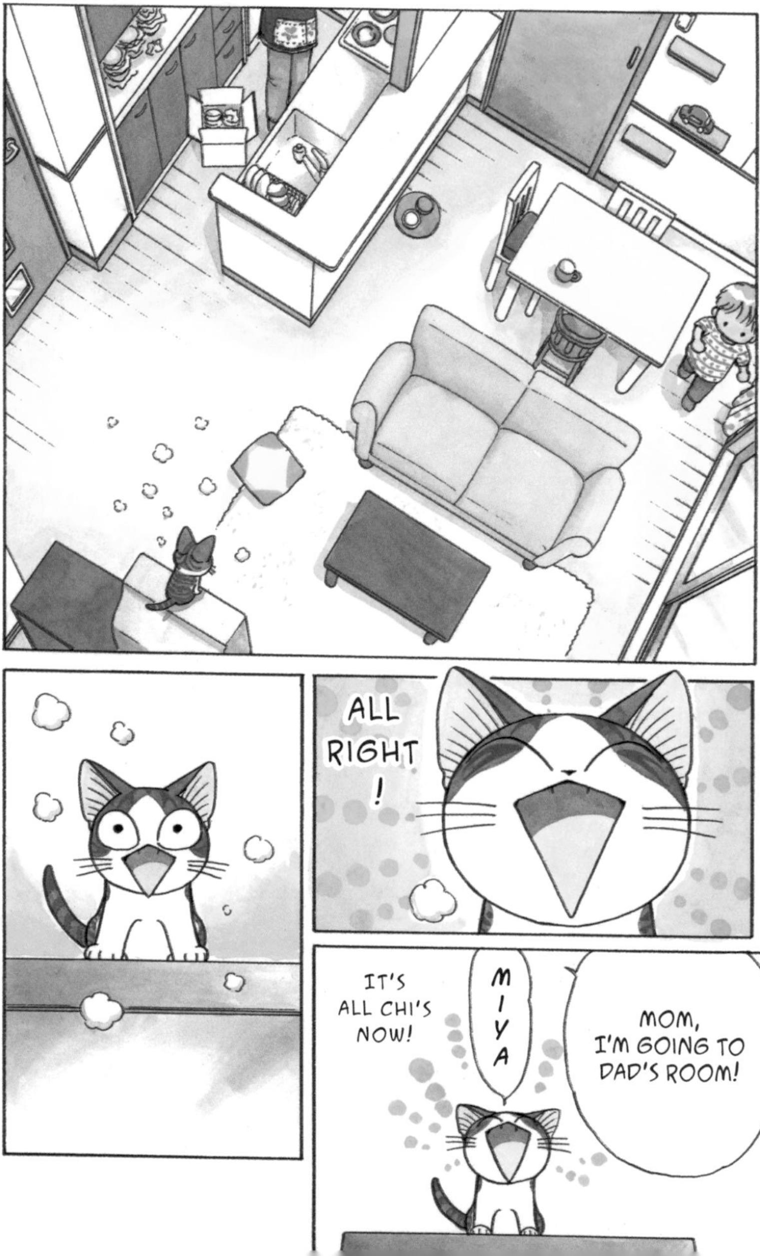
ALL RIGHT!
IT'S ALL CHI'S NOW!
MIYA
MOM, I'M GOING TO DAD'S ROOM!

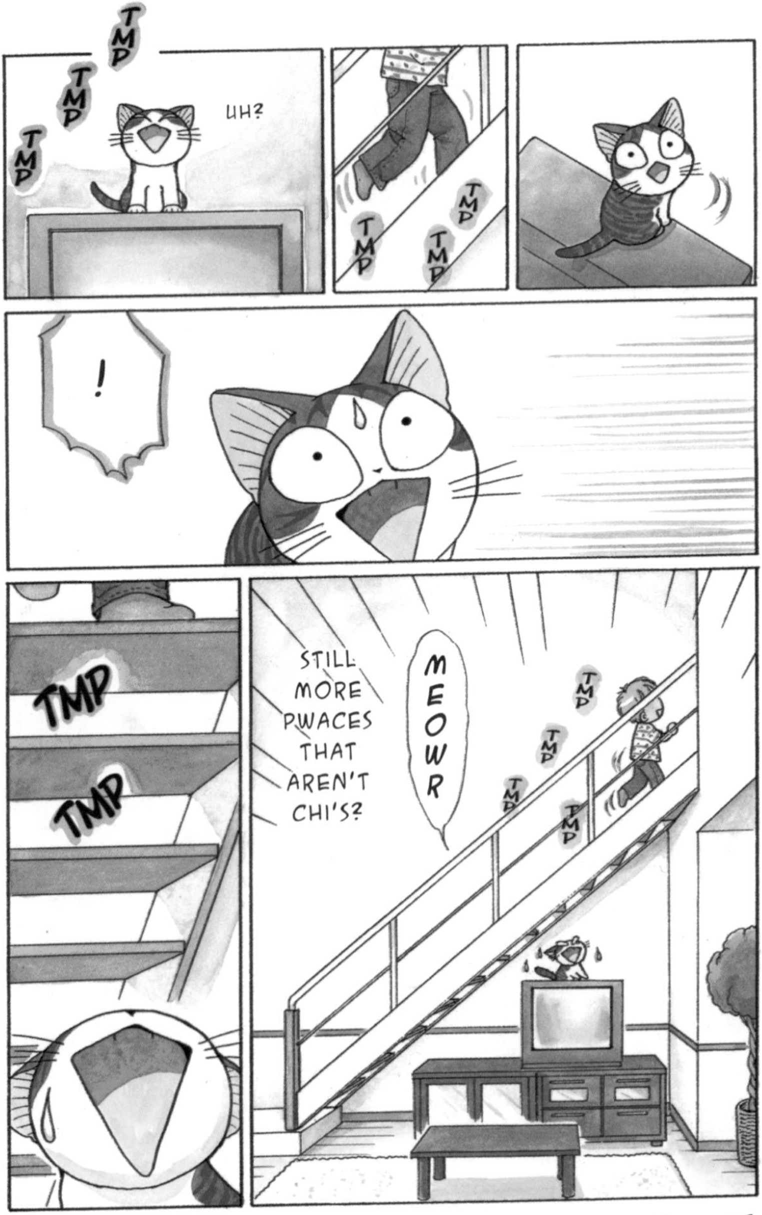
TMP
TMP
TMP
UH?
TMP
TMP
TMP
!
TMP
TMP
MEOWR
STILL MORE PWACES THAT AREN'T CHI'S?
TMP
TMP
TMP
TMP

the end

homemade 62: a cat climbs

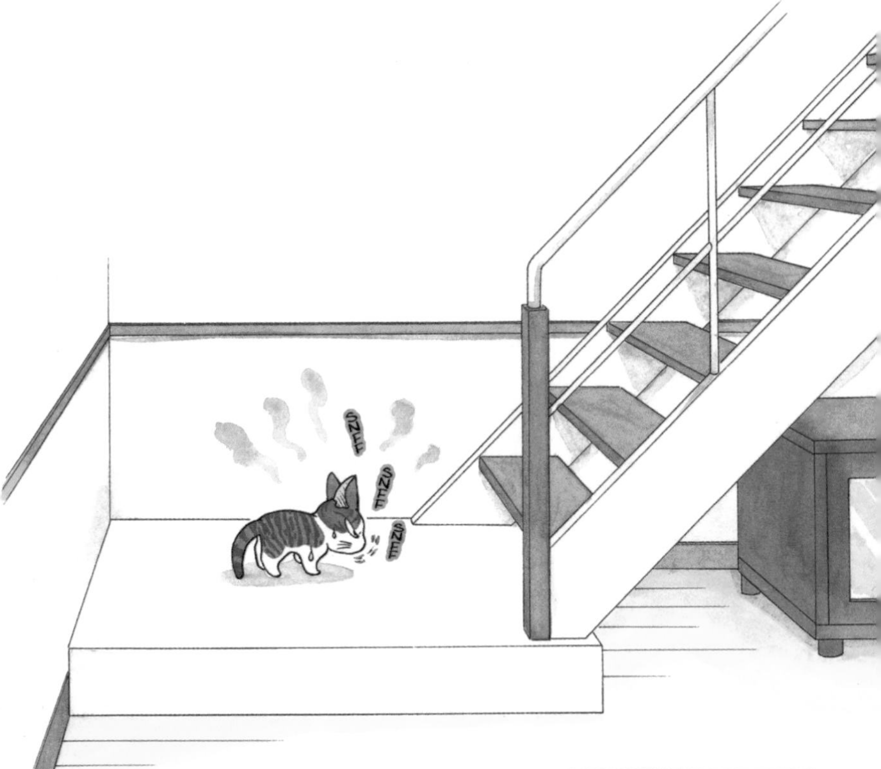
SNFF
SNFF
SNFF

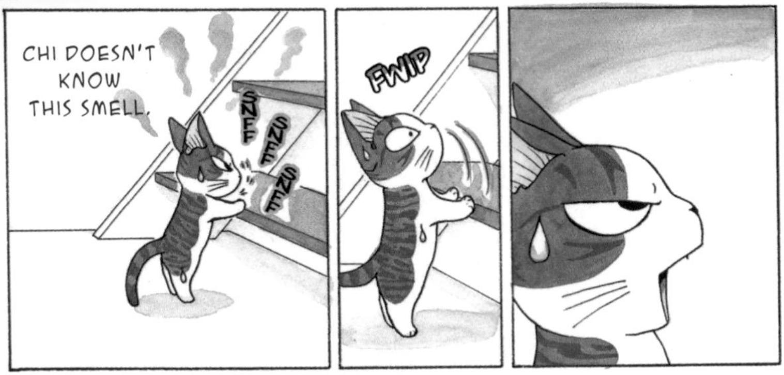
CHI DOESN'T KNOW THIS SMELL.
SNFF
SNFF
SNFF
FWIP

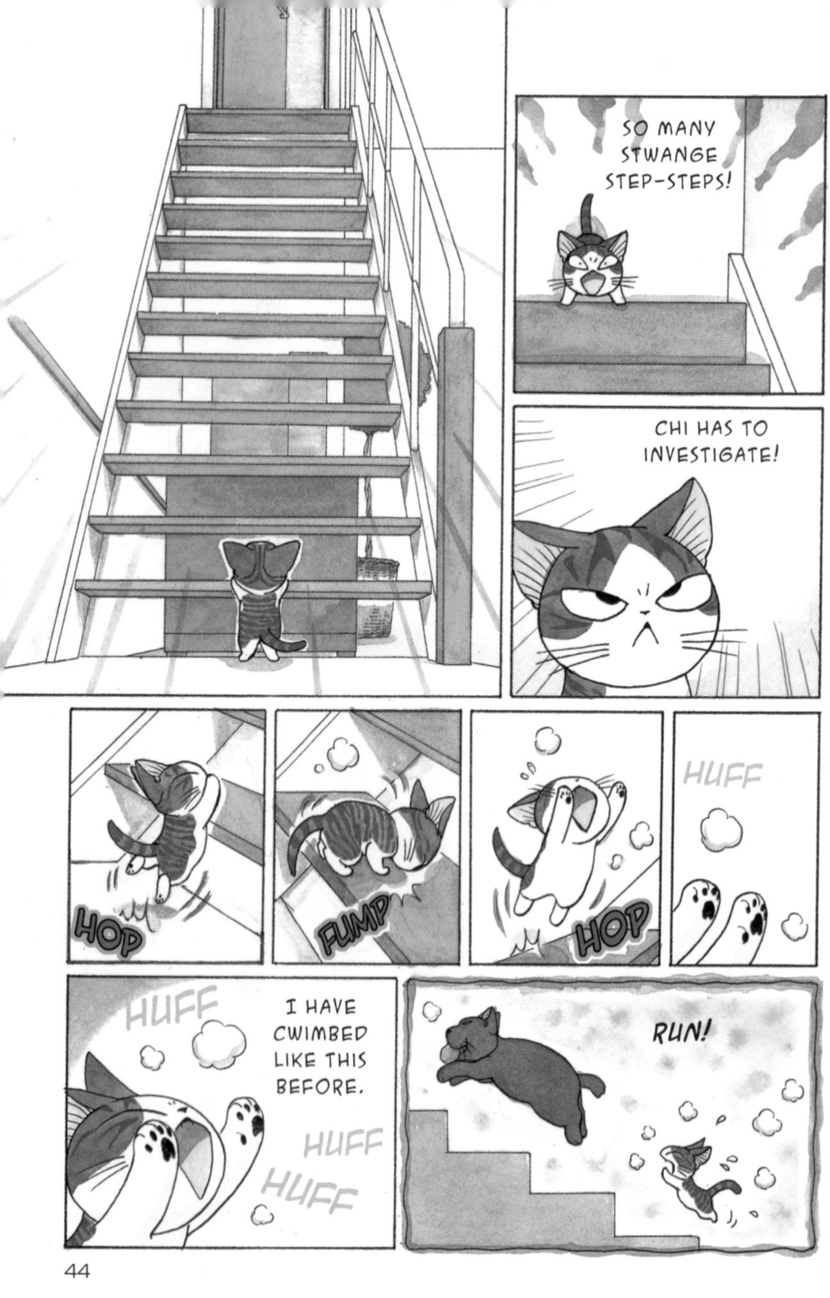
SO MANY STWANGE STEP-STEPS!
CHI HAS TO INVESTIGATE!
HOP
FUMP
HOP
HUFF
HUFF
I HAVE CWIMBED LIKE THIS BEFORE.
HUFF
HUFF
RUN!

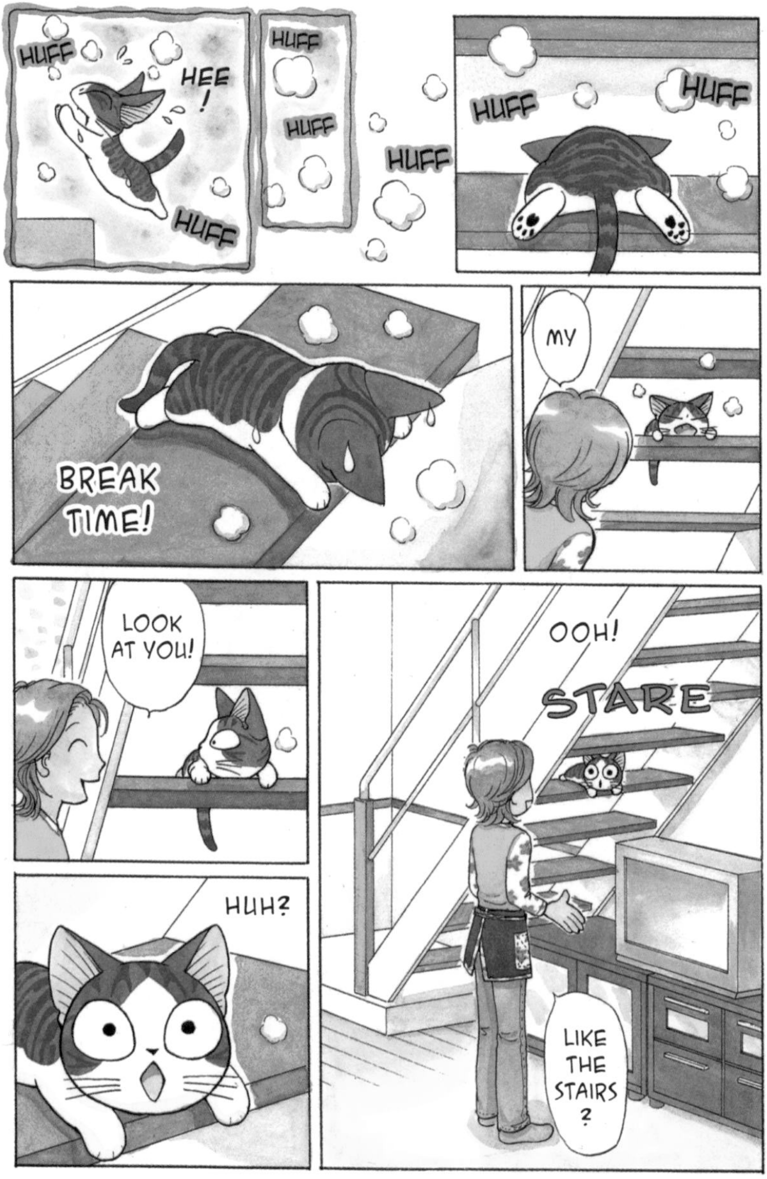
HUFF
HEE!
HUFF
HUFF
HUFF
HUFF
HUFF
HUFF
BREAK TIME!
MY
LOOK AT YOU!
HUH?
OOH!
STARE
LIKE THE STAIRS?

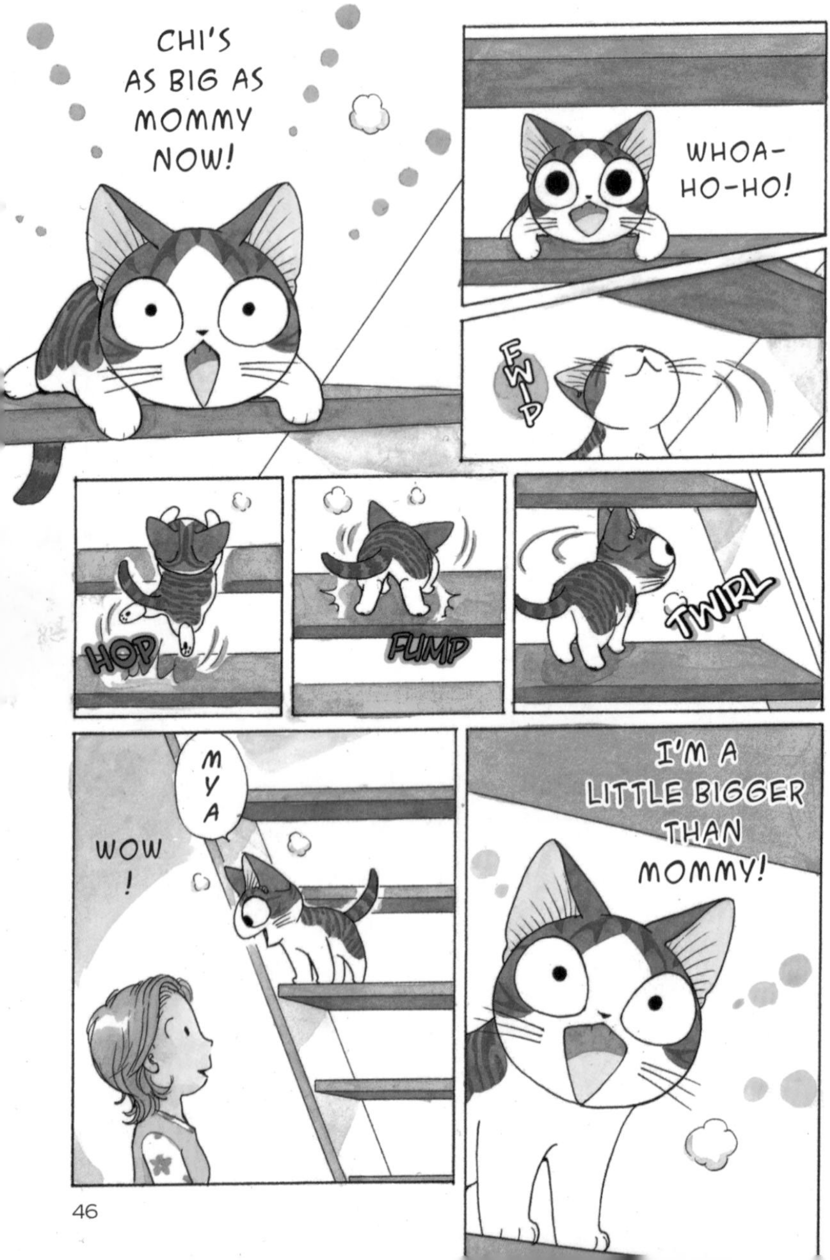
CHI'S AS BIG AS MOMMY NOW!
WHOA-HO-HO!
FWIP
HOP
FUMP
TWIRL
MYA
WOW!
I'M A LITTLE BIGGER THAN MOMMY!

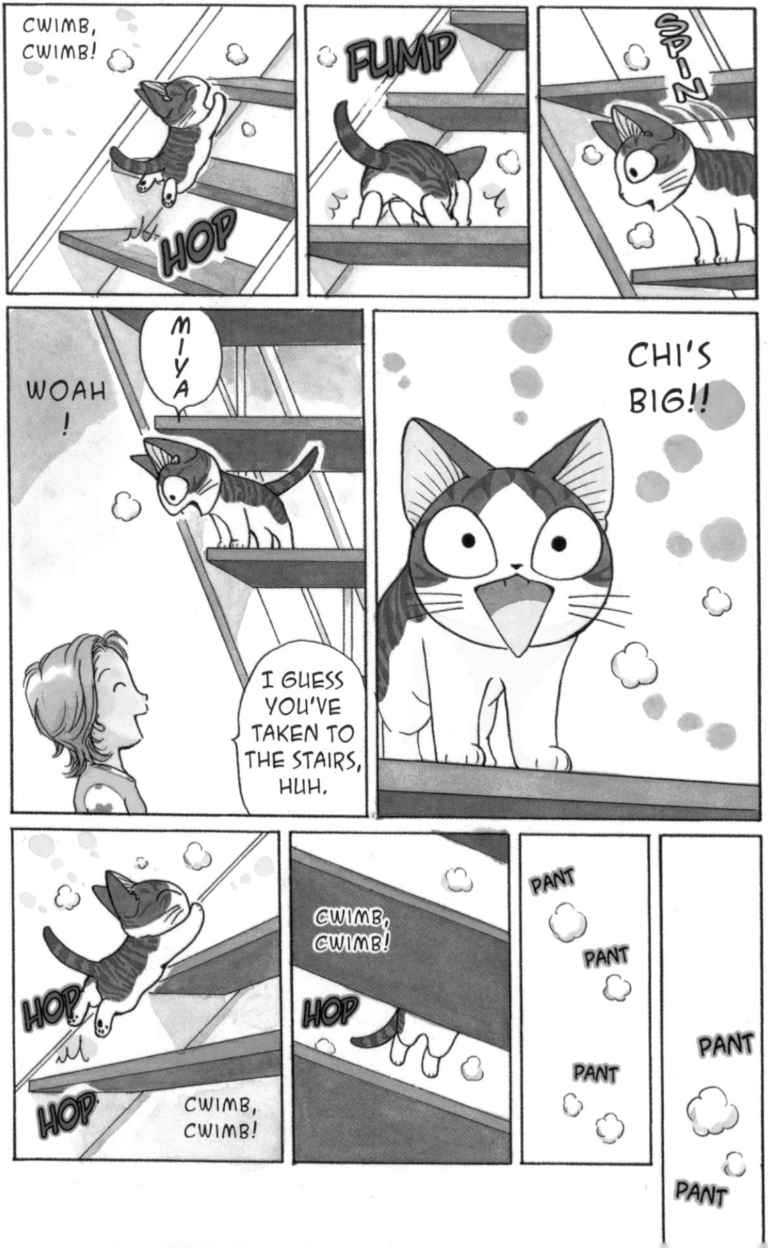
CWIMB, CWIMB!
HOP
FUMP
SPIN
WOAH!
MIYA
I GUESS YOU'VE TAKEN TO THE STAIRS, HUH.
CHI'S BIG!!
HOP
HOP
CWIMB, CWIMB!
CWIMB, CWIMB!
HOP
PANT
PANT
PANT
PANT
PANT

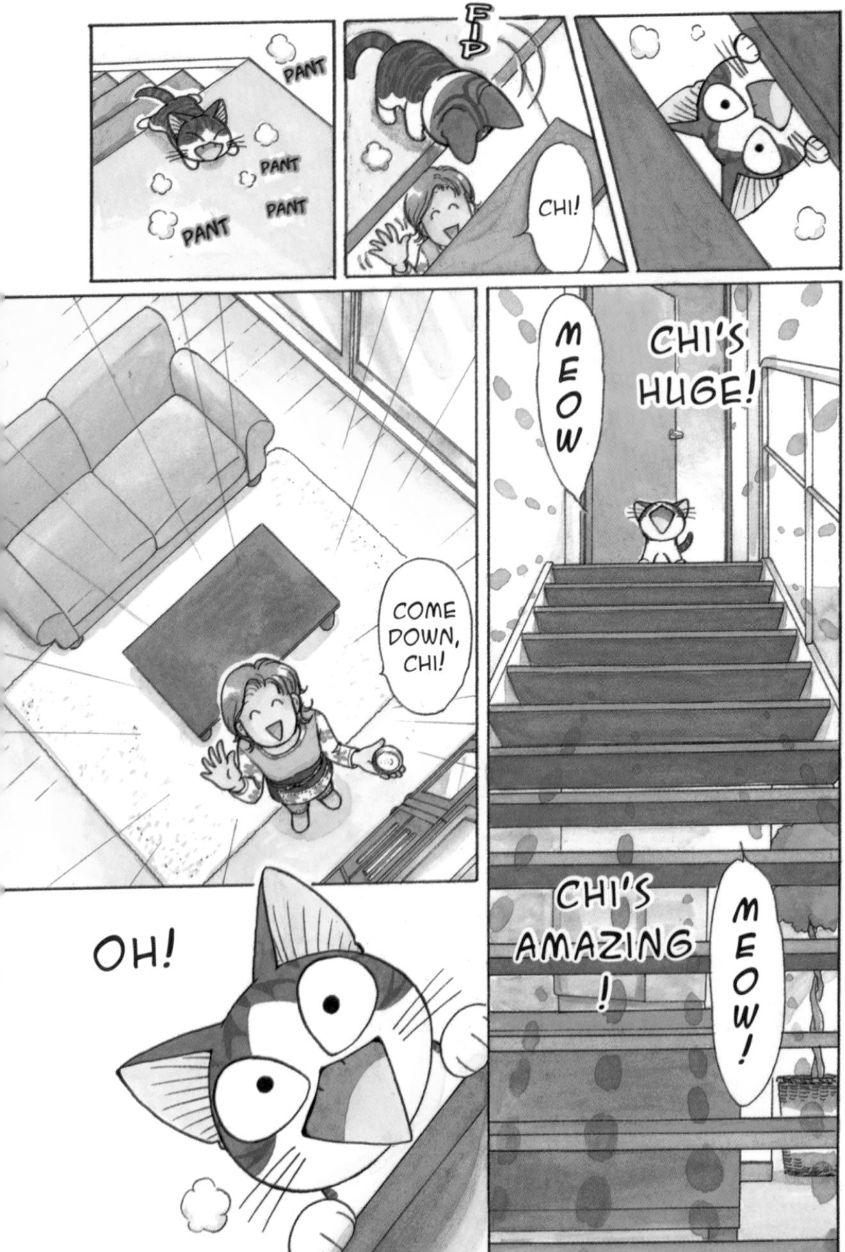
PANT
PANT
PANT
PANT
FIP
CHI!
COME DOWN, CHI!
MEOW
CHI'S HUGE!
CHI'S AMAZING!
MEOW!
OH!

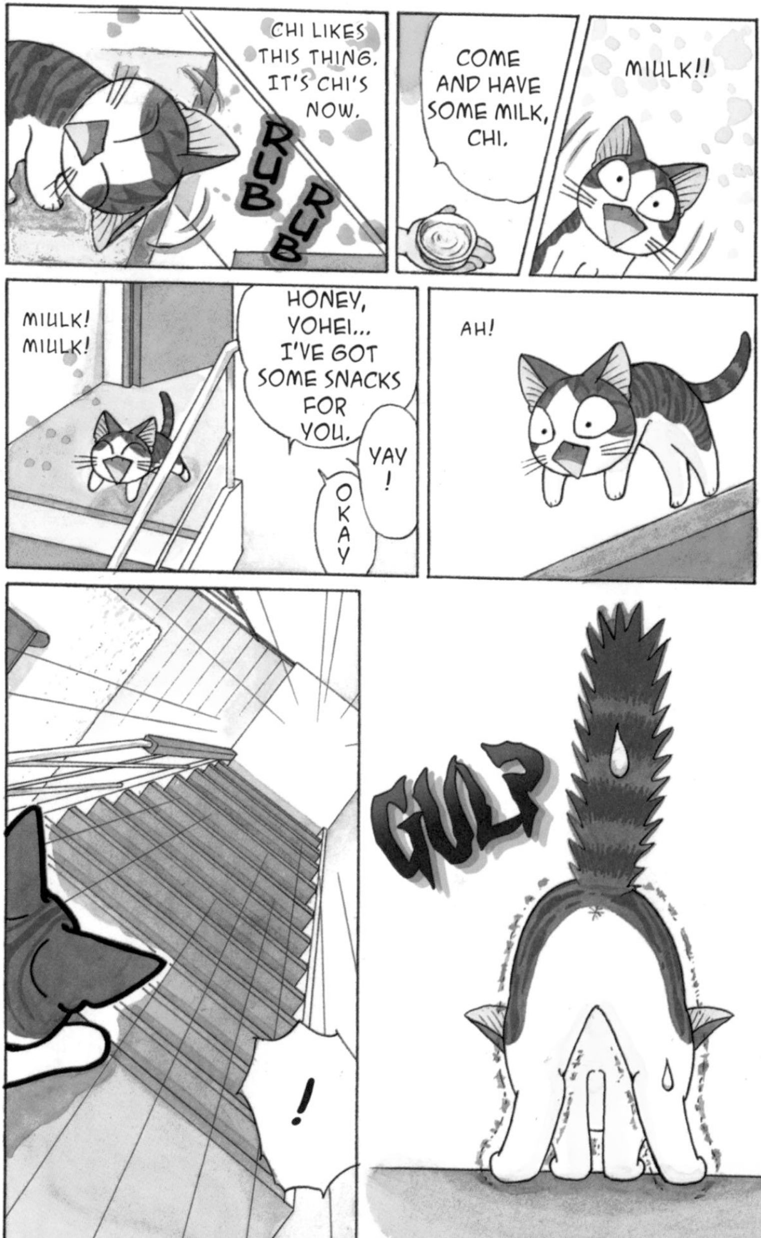
CHI LIKES THIS THING. IT'S CHI'S NOW.
RUB RUB
COME AND HAVE SOME MILK, CHI.
MIULK!!
MIULK! MIULK!
HONEY, YOHEI... I'VE GOT SOME SNACKS FOR YOU.
YAY!
OKAY
AH!
!
GULP

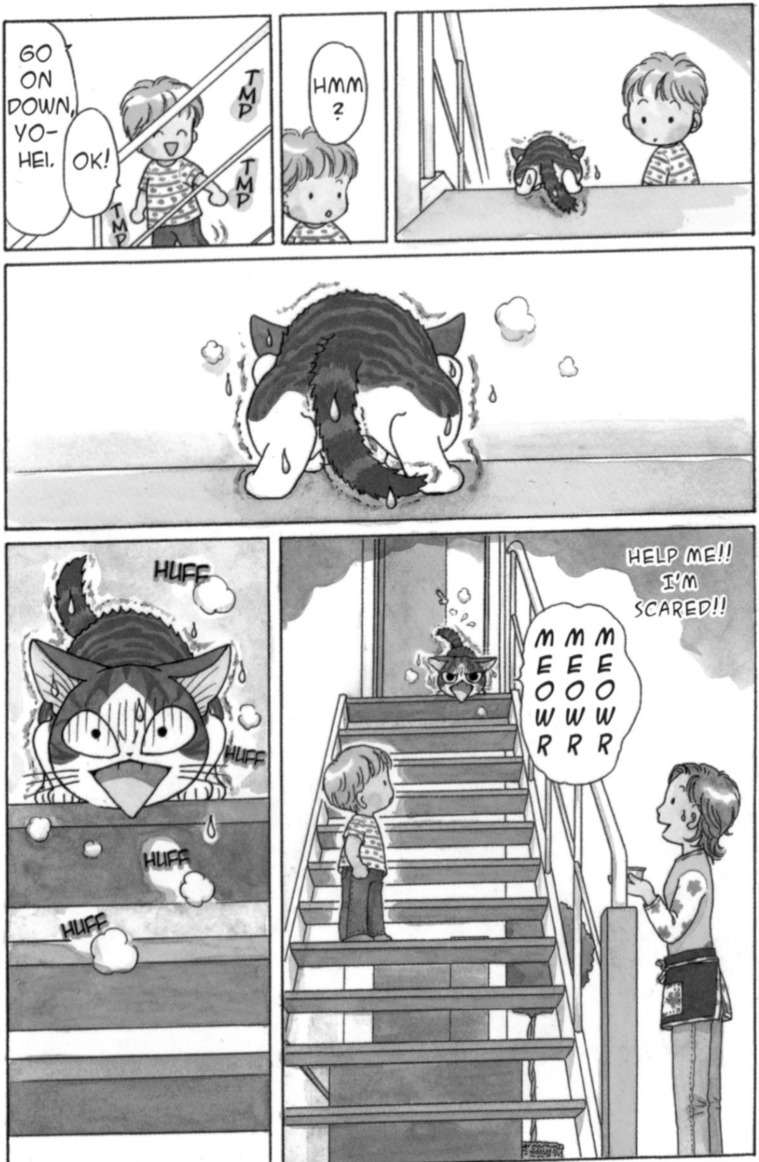
GO ON DOWN, YO-HEI.
OK!
TMP TMP TMP
HMM?
HUFF
HUFF
HUFF
HUFF
HELP ME!! I'M SCARED!!
MEOWR MEOWR MEOWR

the end

homemade 63: a cat greets

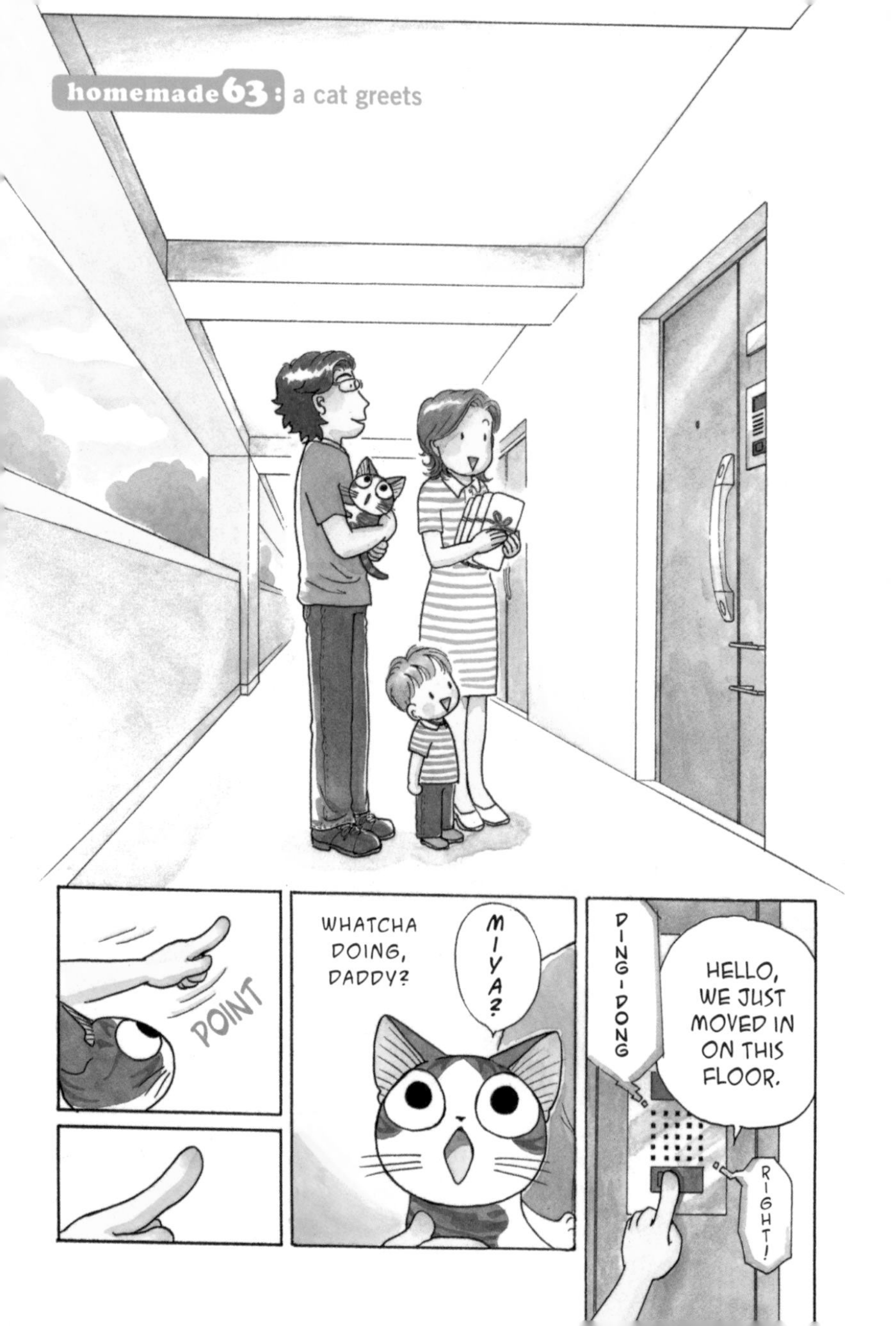
POINT
WHATCHA DOING, DADDY?
MIYA?
DING-DONG
HELLO, WE JUST MOVED IN ON THIS FLOOR.
RIGHT!

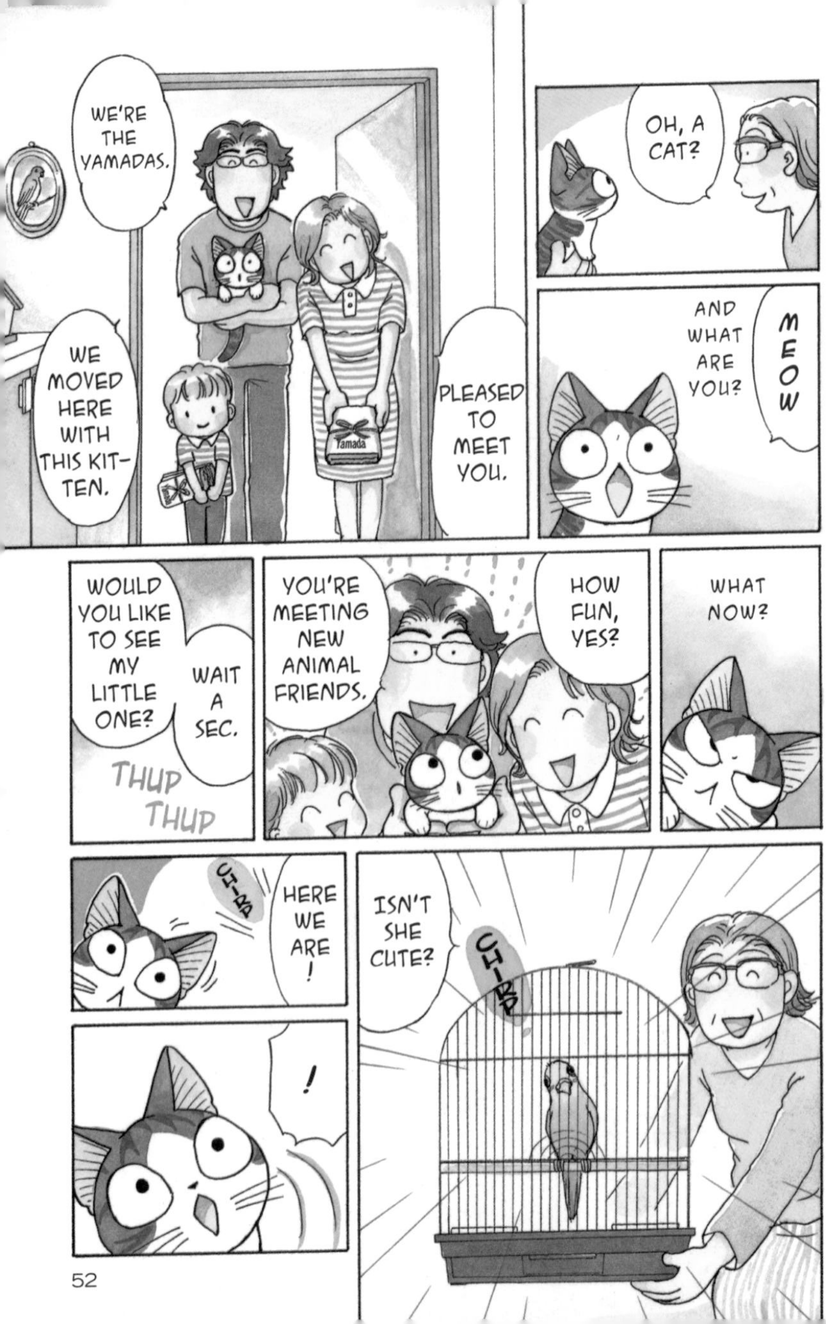
WE'RE THE YAMADAS.
WE MOVED HERE WITH THIS KIT-TEN.
Yamada
PLEASED TO MEET YOU.
OH, A CAT?
AND WHAT ARE YOU?
MEOW
WOULD YOU LIKE TO SEE MY LITTLE ONE?
WAIT A SEC.
THUP THUP
YOU'RE MEETING NEW ANIMAL FRIENDS.
HOW FUN, YES?
WHAT NOW?
CHIRP
HERE WE ARE!
!
ISN'T SHE CUTE?
CHIRP

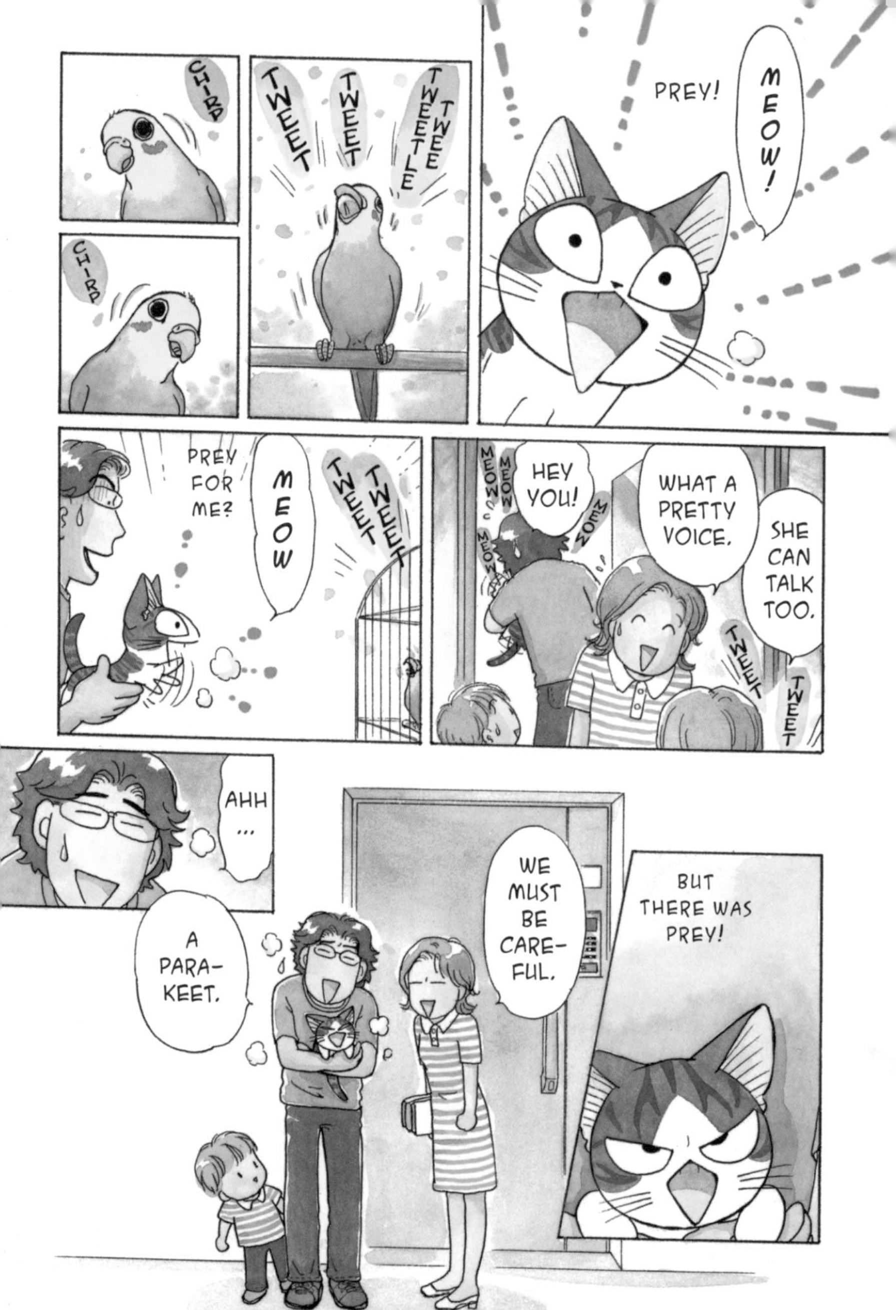
CHIRP
CHIRP
TWEET
TWEET
TWEETLE
TWEE
PREY!
MEOW!
PREY FOR ME?
MEOW
TWEET
TWEET
MEOW
MEOW
HEY YOU!
MEOW
MEOW
WHAT A PRETTY VOICE.
SHE CAN TALK TOO.
TWEET
TWEET
AHH ...
A PARA-KEET.
WE MUST BE CARE-FUL.
BUT THERE WAS PREY!

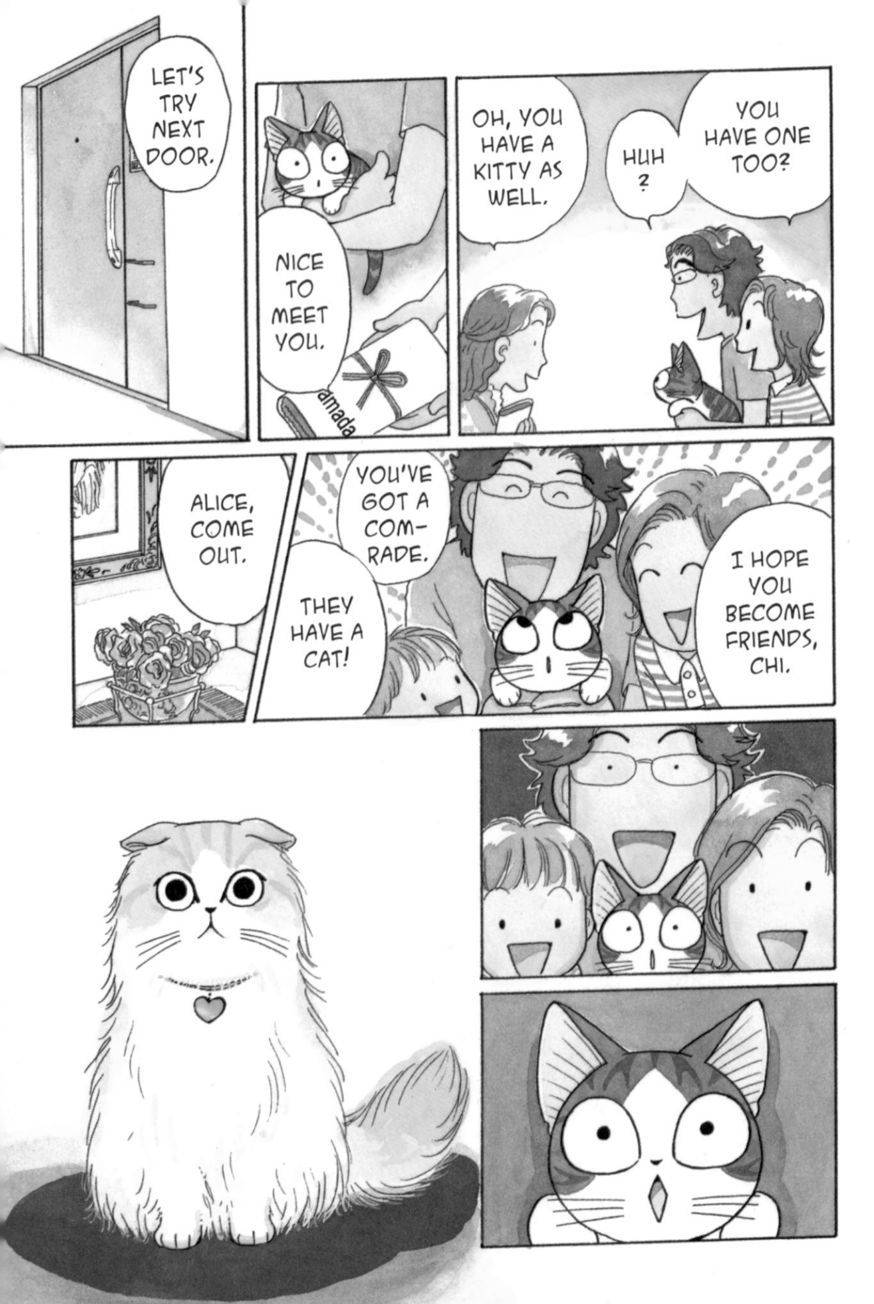
LET'S TRY NEXT DOOR.
NICE TO MEET YOU.
amada
OH, YOU HAVE A KITTY AS WELL.
HUH?
YOU HAVE ONE TOO?
ALICE, COME OUT.
YOU'VE GOT A COM-RADE.
THEY HAVE A CAT!
I HOPE YOU BECOME FRIENDS, CHI.

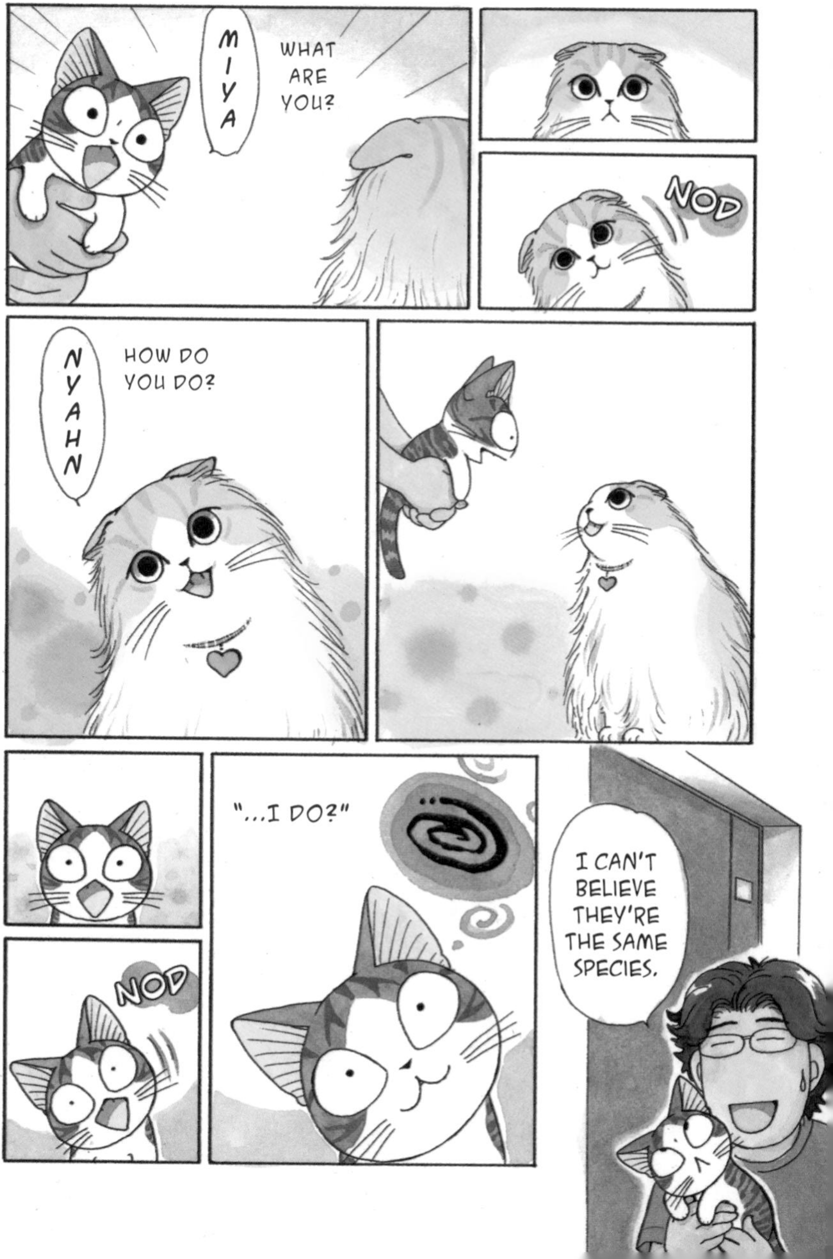
MIYA
WHAT ARE YOU?
NOD
NYAHN
HOW DO YOU DO?
NOD
"...I DO?"
I CAN'T BELIEVE THEY'RE THE SAME SPECIES.

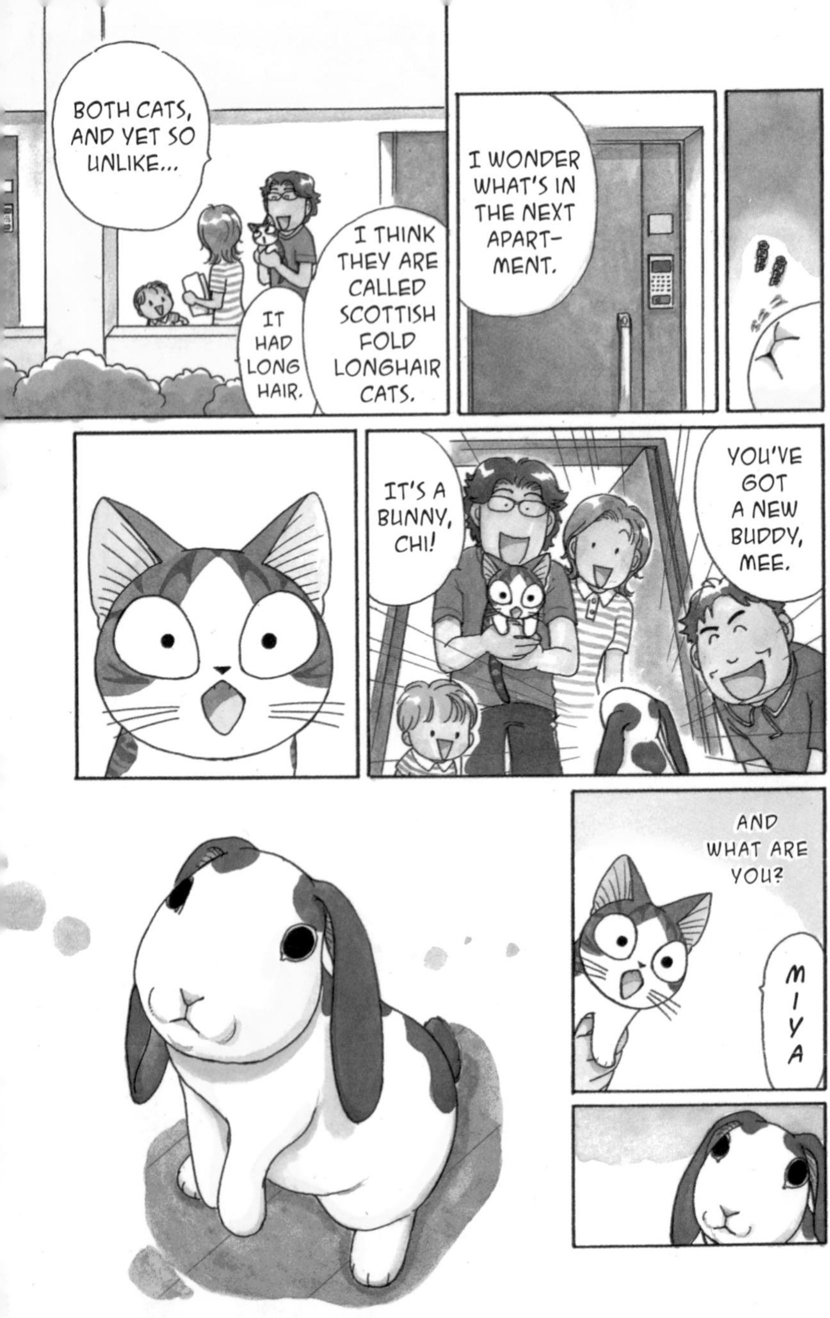
BOTH CATS, AND YET SO UNLIKE...
I THINK THEY ARE CALLED SCOTTISH FOLD LONGHAIR CATS.
IT HAD LONG HAIR.
I WONDER WHAT'S IN THE NEXT APARTMENT.
IT'S A BUNNY, CHI!
YOU'VE GOT A NEW BUDDY, MEE.
AND WHAT ARE YOU?
MIYA

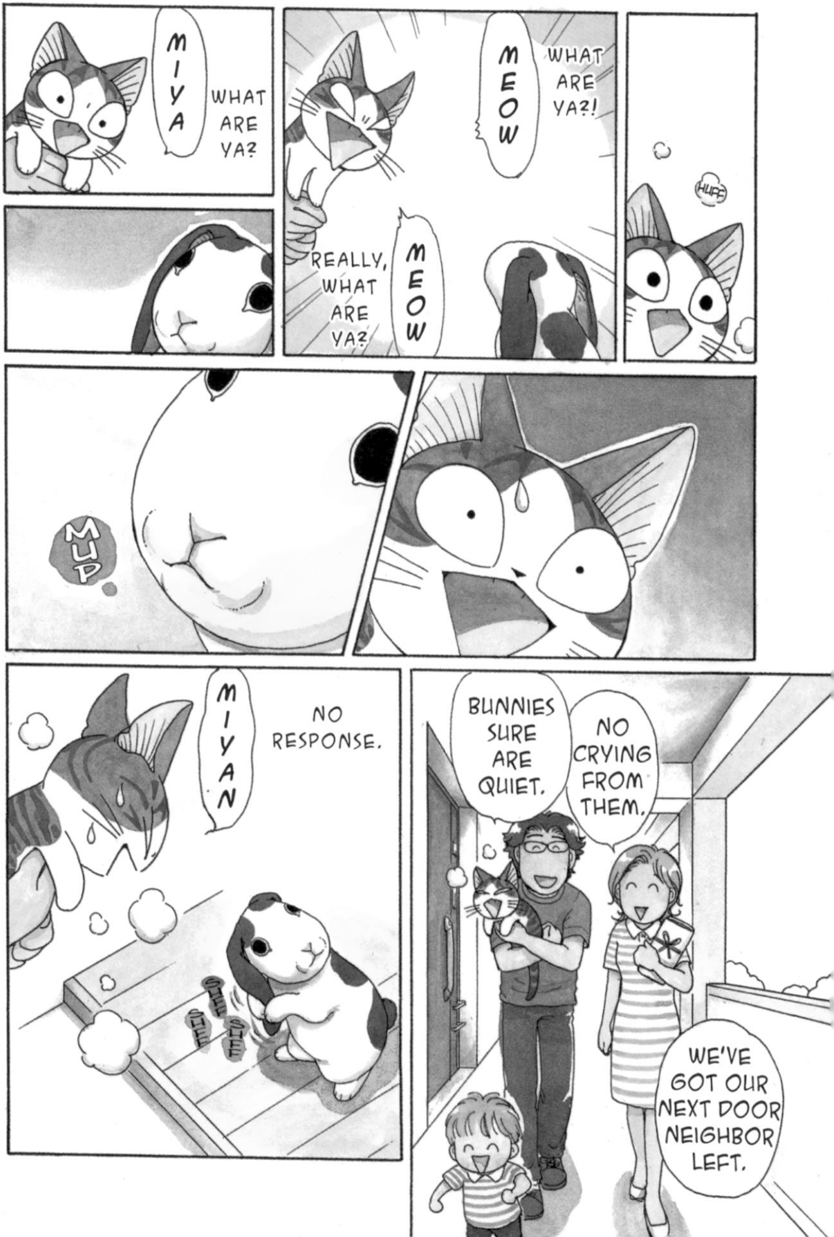
MIYA
WHAT ARE YA?
MEOW
WHAT ARE YA?!
REALLY, WHAT ARE YA?
MEOW
HUFF
MUP
MIYAN
NO RESPONSE.
SHEF SHEF SHEF
BUNNIES SURE ARE QUIET.
NO CRYING FROM THEM.
WE'VE GOT OUR NEXT DOOR NEIGHBOR LEFT.

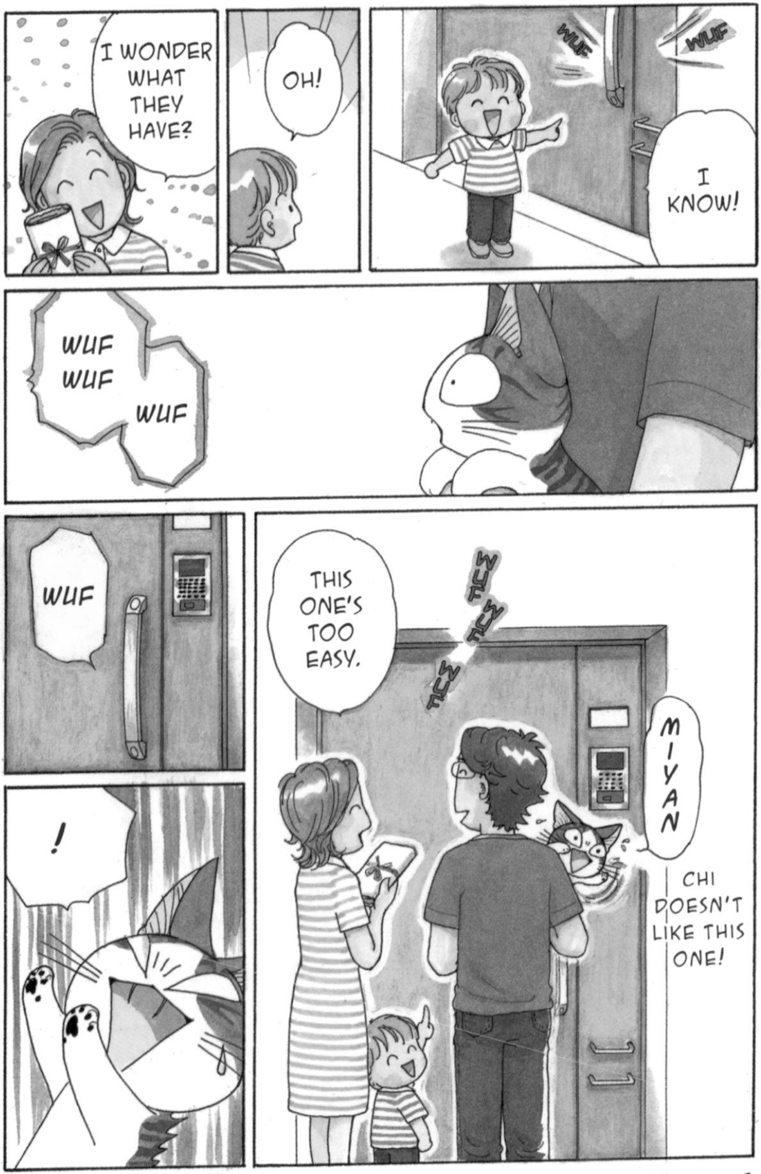
I WONDER WHAT THEY HAVE?
OH!
WUF
WUF
I KNOW!
WUF WUF WUF
WUF
!
THIS ONE'S TOO EASY.
WUF WUF WUF
MIYAN
CHI DOESN'T LIKE THIS ONE!

the end

homemade 64: a cat-challenges

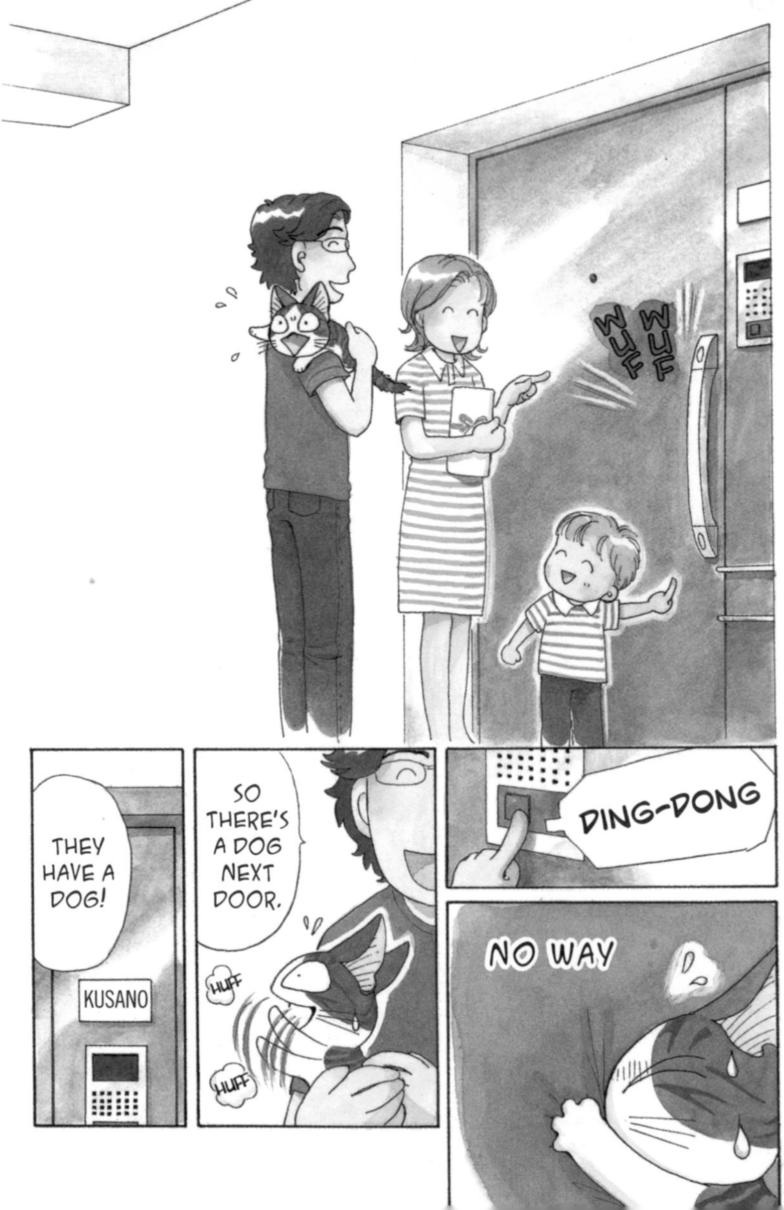

WUF WUF
THEY HAVE A DOG!
KUSANO
SO THERE'S A DOG NEXT DOOR.
HUFF
HUFF
DING-DONG
NO WAY

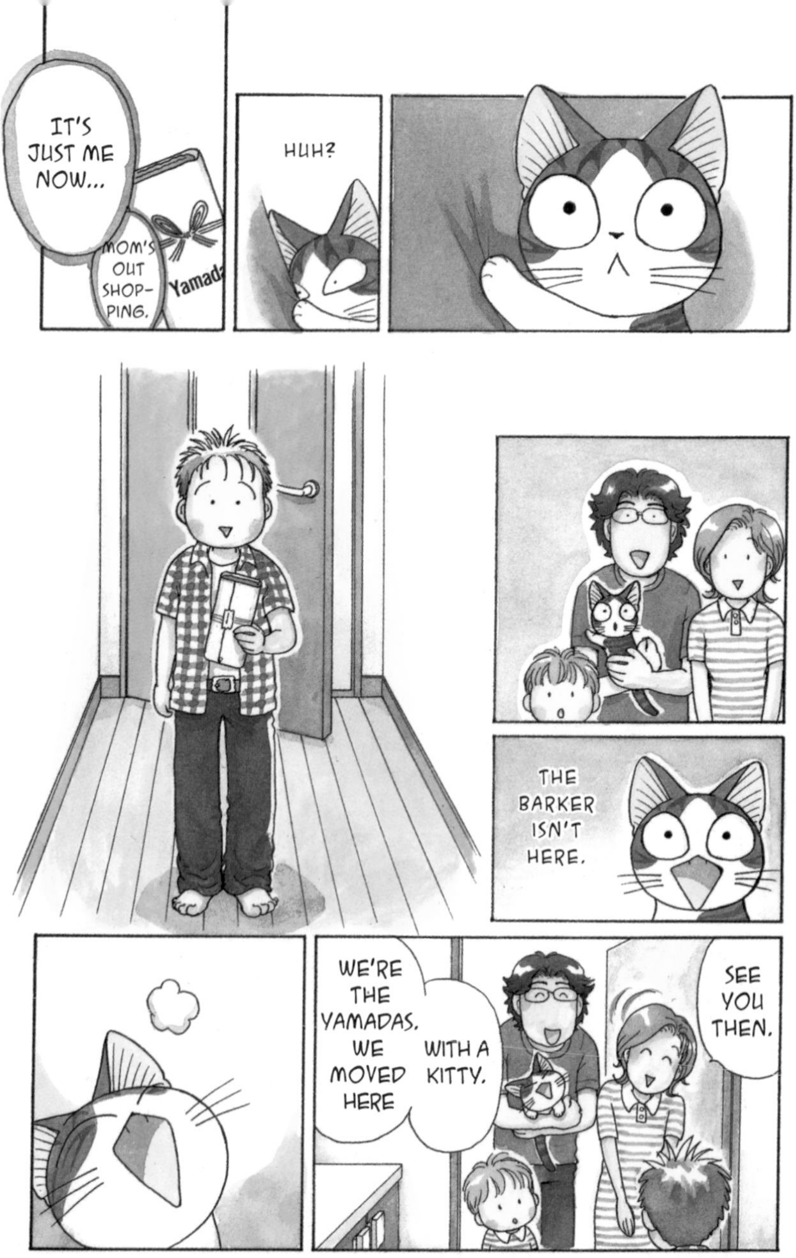

IT'S JUST ME NOW...
MOM'S OUT SHOP-PING.
Yamada
HUH?
THE BARKER ISN'T HERE.
WE'RE THE YAMADAS. WE MOVED HERE
WITH A KITTY.
SEE YOU THEN.

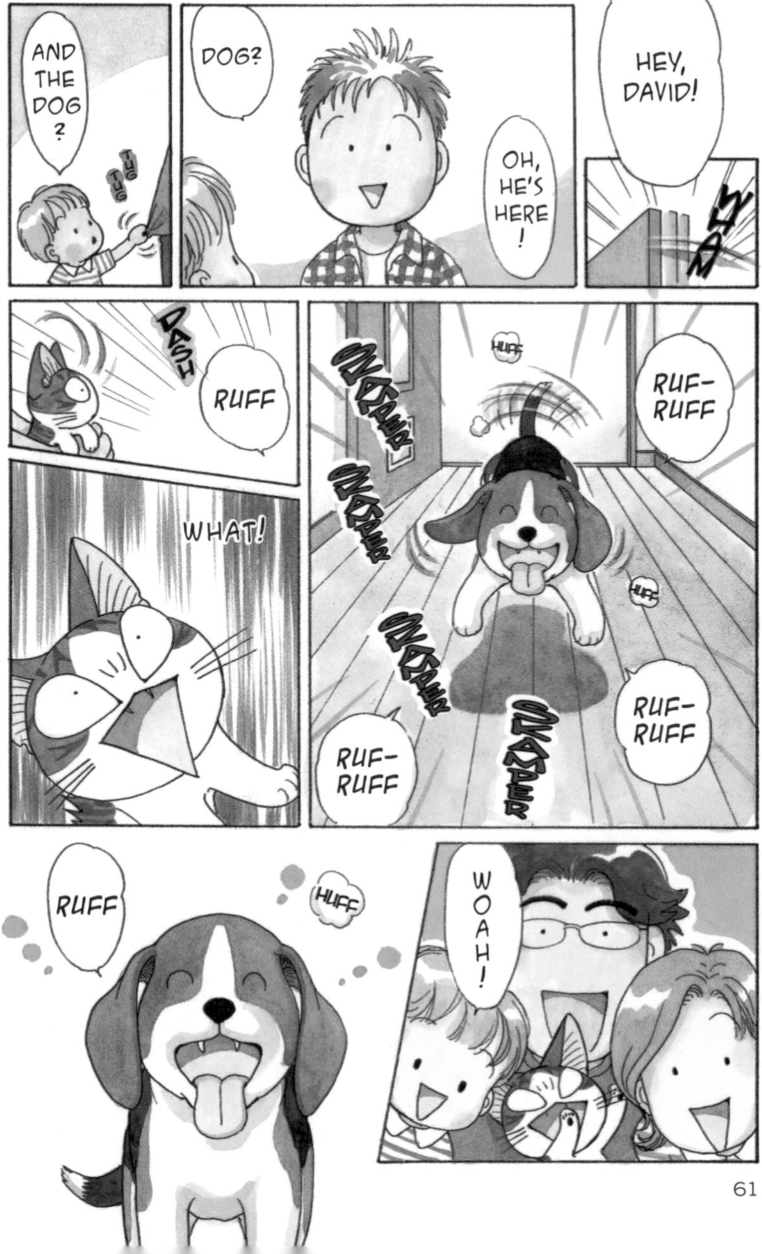
AND THE DOG?
TUG TUG
DOG?
OH, HE'S HERE!
HEY, DAVID!
WHAM
DASH
RUFF
WHAT!
HUFF
SCAMPER
SCAMPER
RUF-RUFF
HUFF
SCAMPER
RUF-RUFF
RUF-RUFF
SCAMPER
RUFF
HUFF
WOAH!

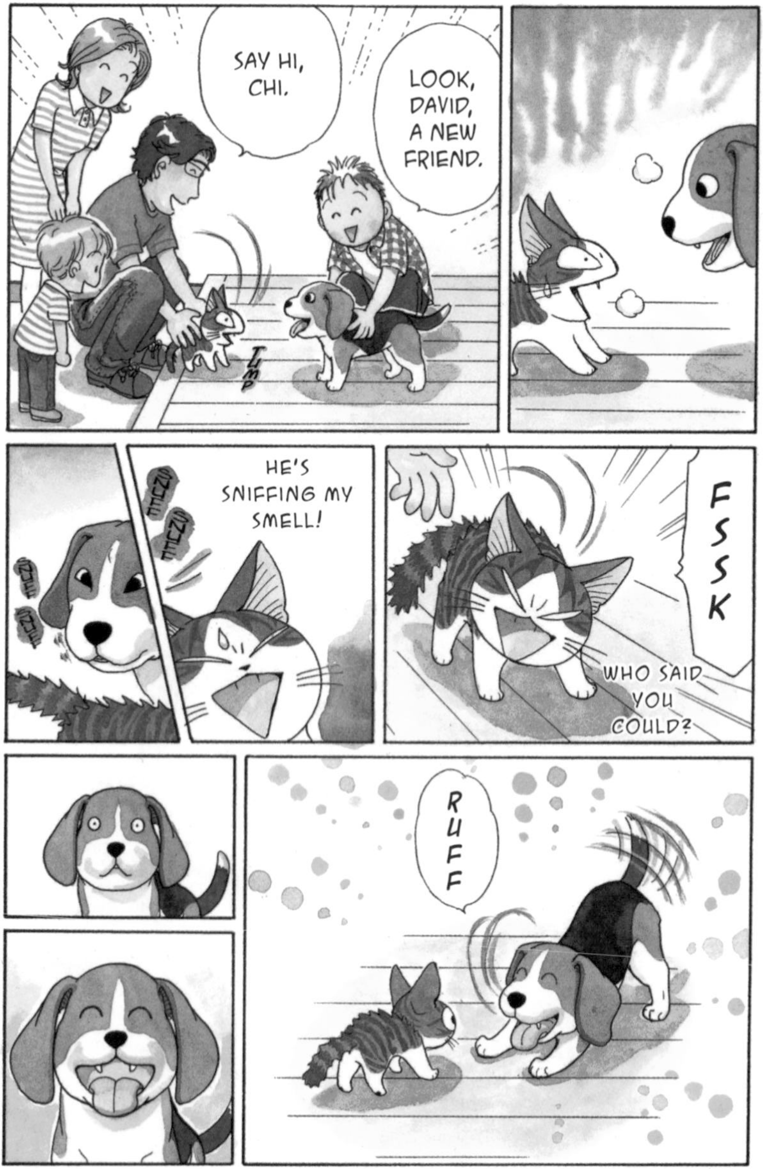
SAY HI, CHI.
LOOK, DAVID, A NEW FRIEND.
TUMP
SNUF
SNUF
SNUFF
SNUFF
HE'S SNIFFING MY SMELL!
FSSK
WHO SAID YOU COULD?
RUFF

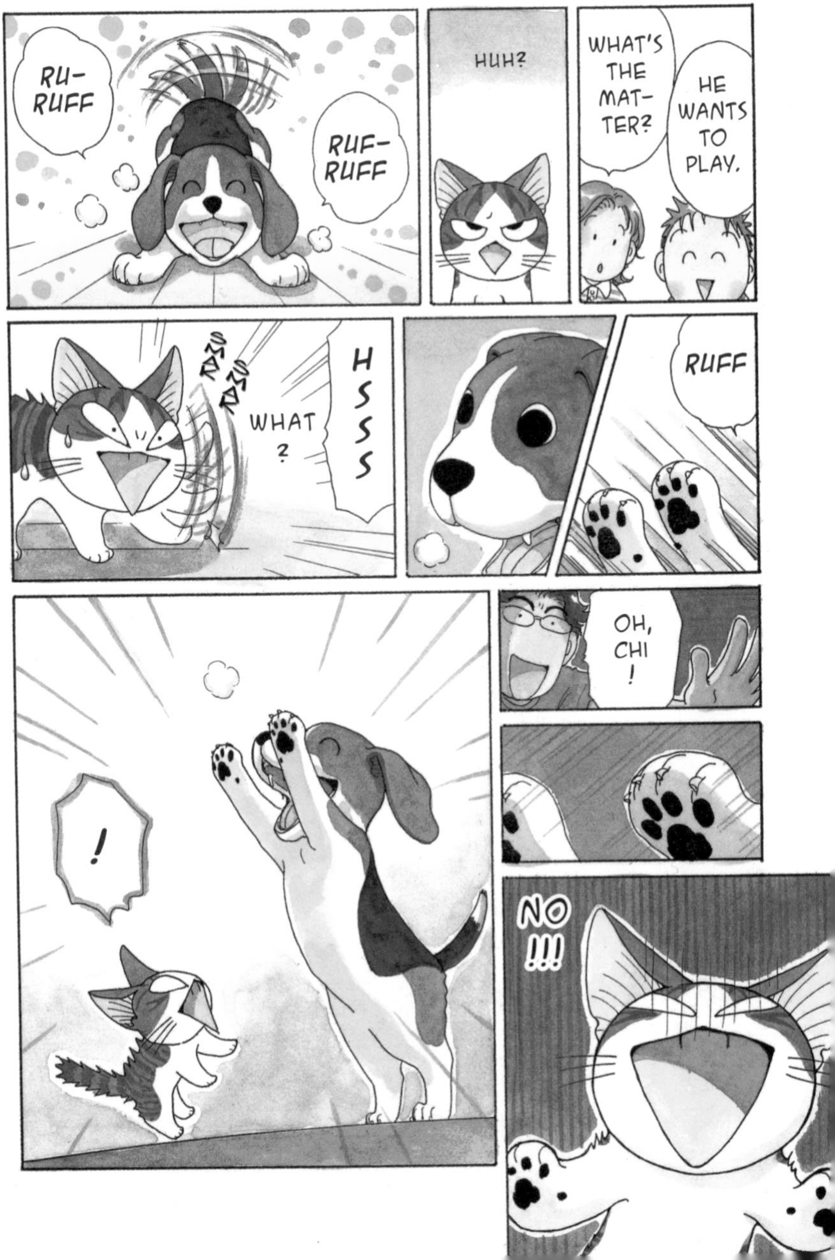
RU-RUFF
RUF-RUFF
HUH?
WHAT'S THE MAT-TER?
HE WANTS TO PLAY.
SMAR SMAR
WHAT?
HSSS
RUFF
!
OH, CHI!
NO!!!

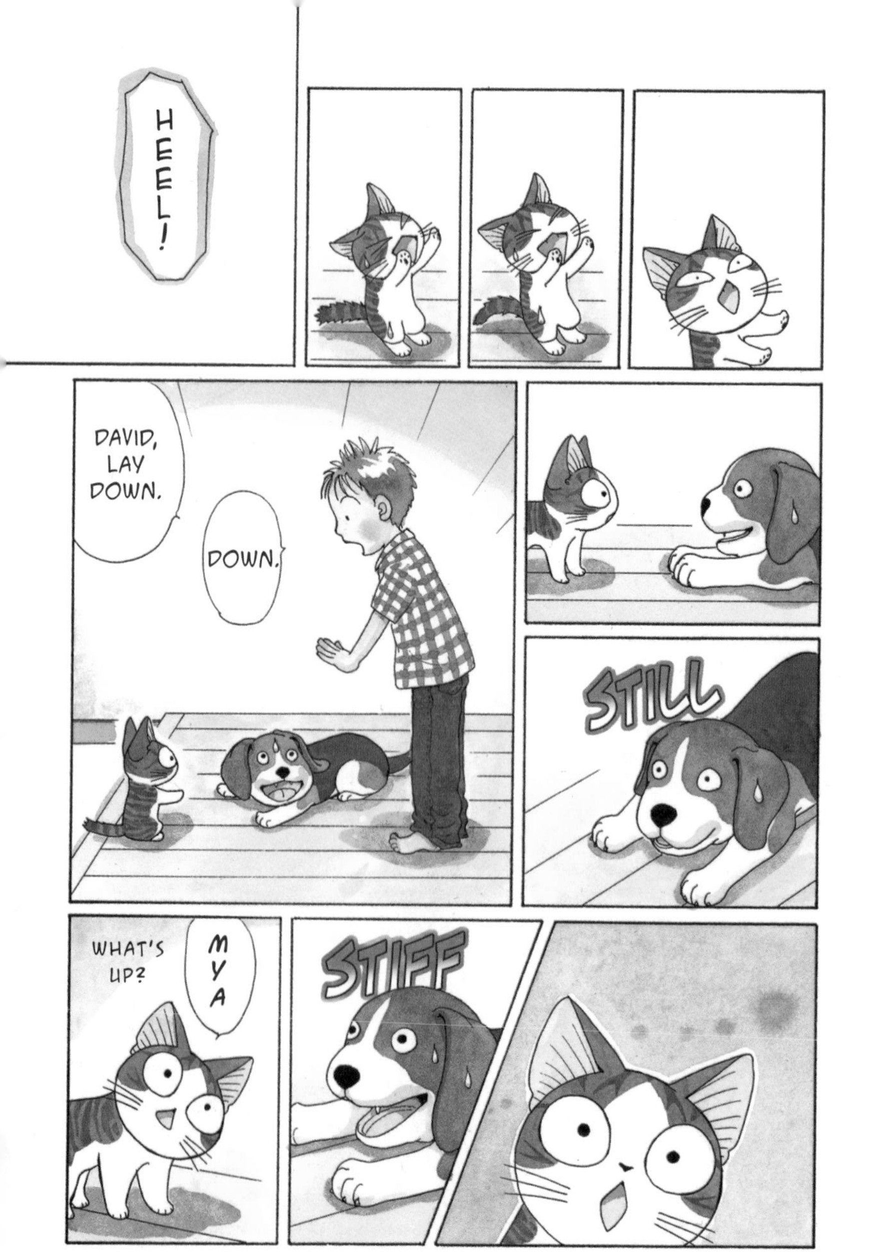
HEEL!
DAVID, LAY DOWN.
DOWN.
STILL
WHAT'S UP?
MYA
STIFF

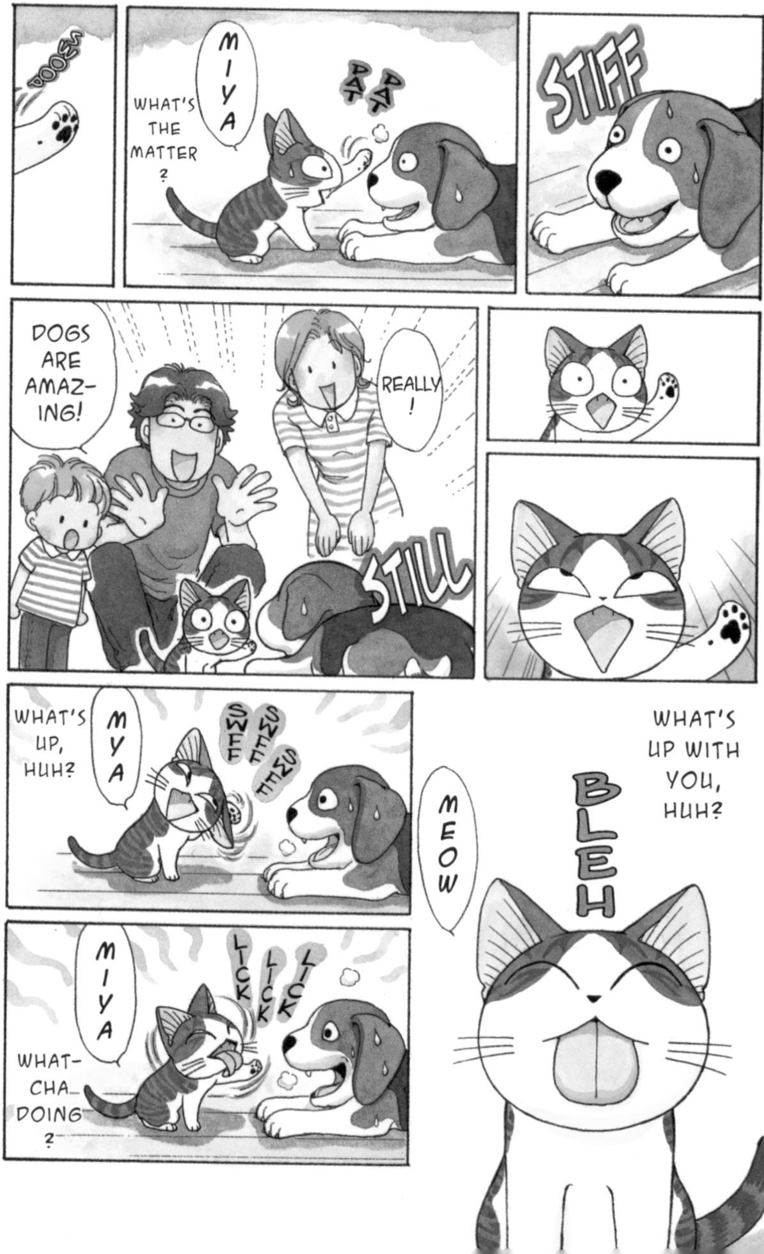
SWOOP
MIYA
WHAT'S THE MATTER?
PAT PAT
STIFF
DOGS ARE AMAZ-ING!
REALLY!
STILL
MYA
WHAT'S UP, HUH?
SWFF SWFF SWFF
MIYA
WHAT-CHA DOING?
LICK LICK LICK
MEOW
WHAT'S UP WITH YOU, HUH?
BLEH

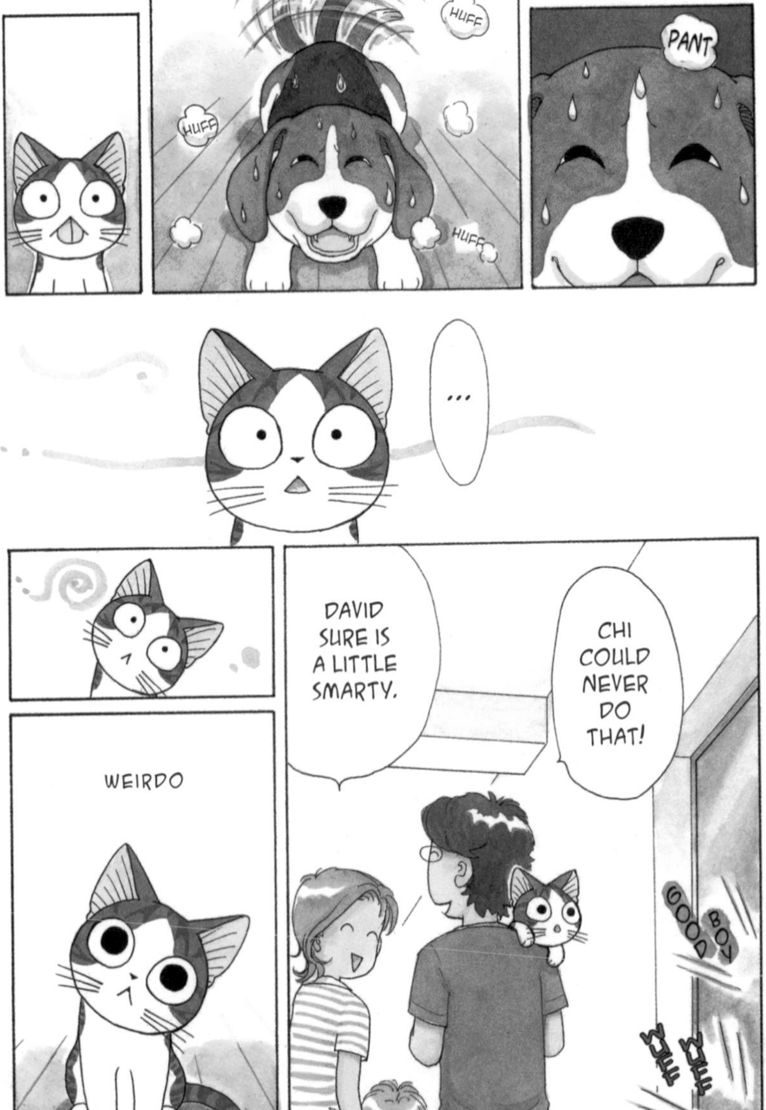
HUFF
HUFF
HUFF
PANT
...
WEIRDO
DAVID SURE IS A LITTLE SMARTY.
CHI COULD NEVER DO THAT!
GOOD BOY
WUFF WUFF

the end

homemade 65: a cat worries

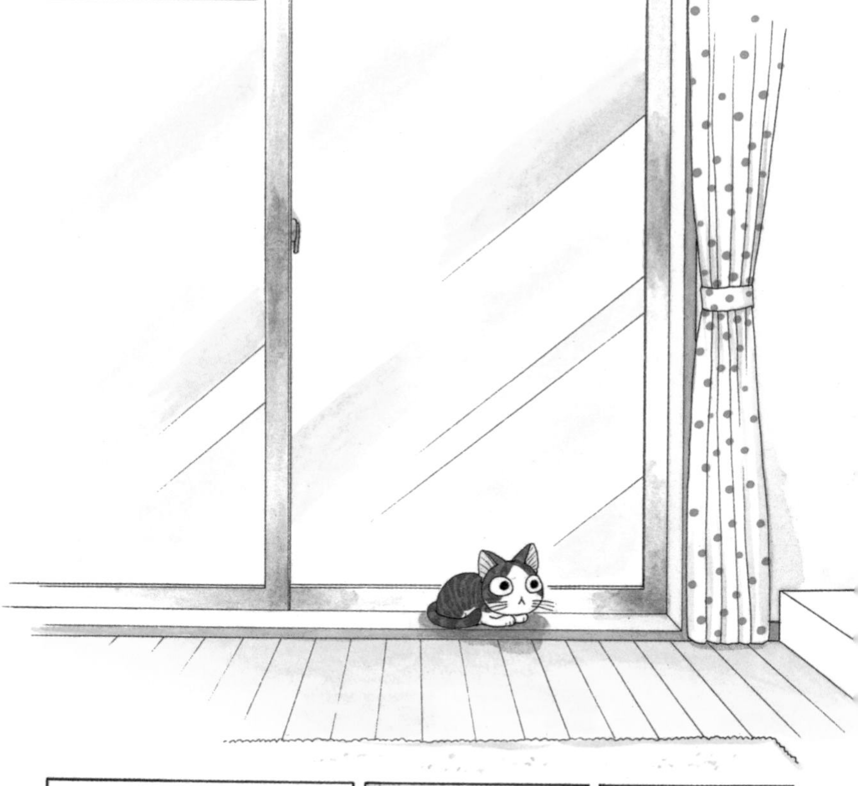

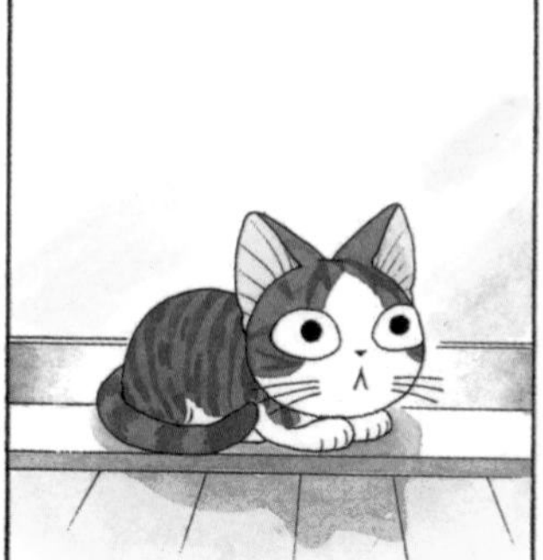

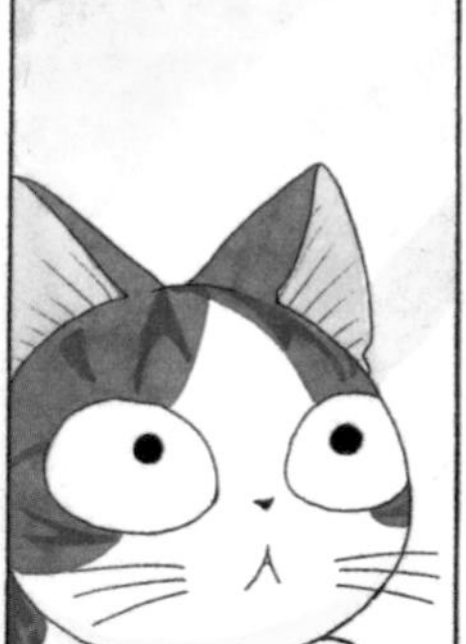

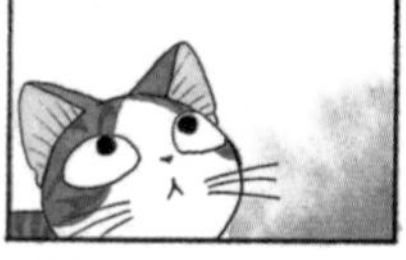

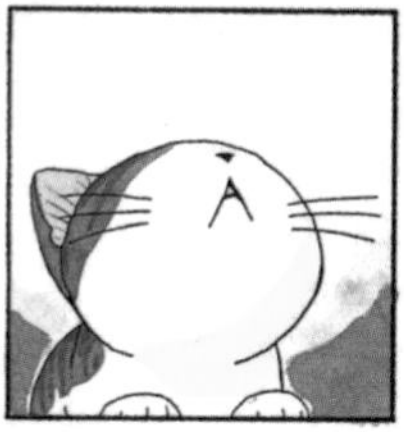

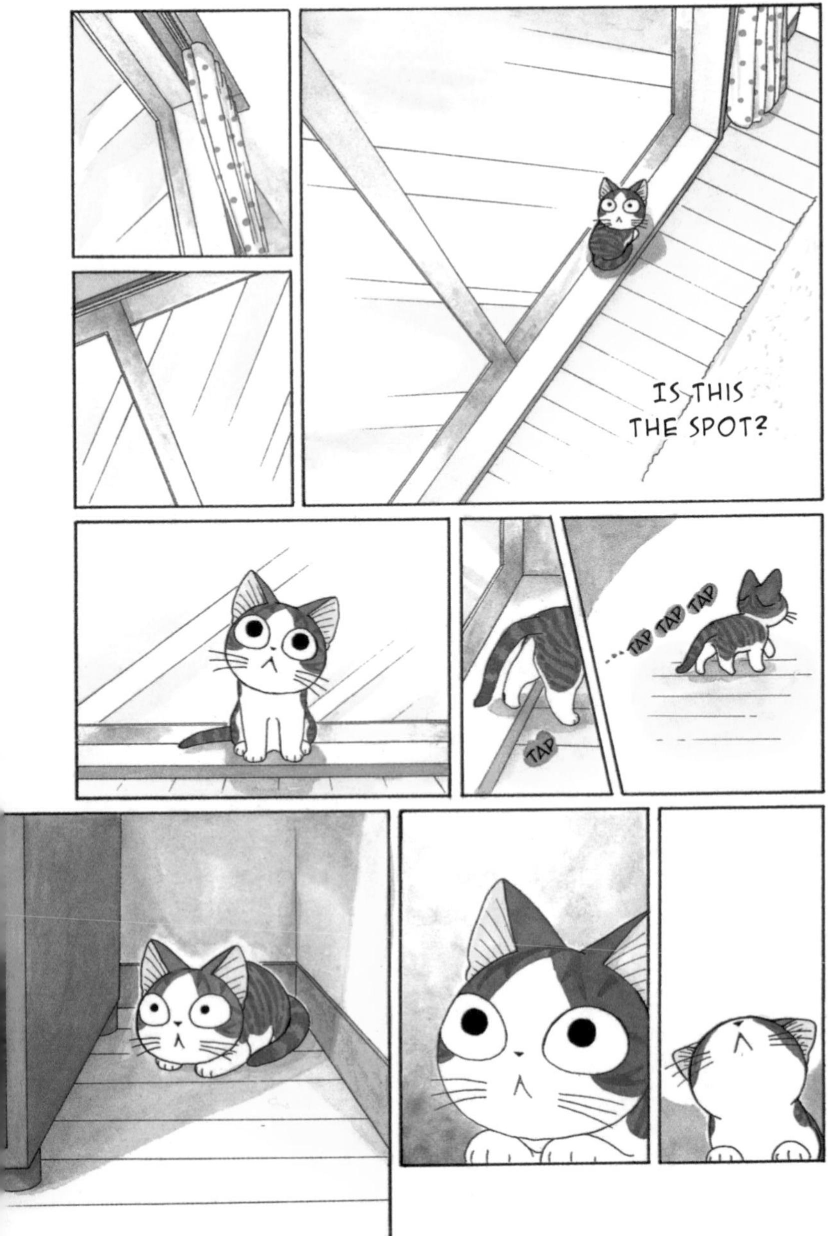
IS THIS THE SPOT?
TAP
TAP TAP TAP

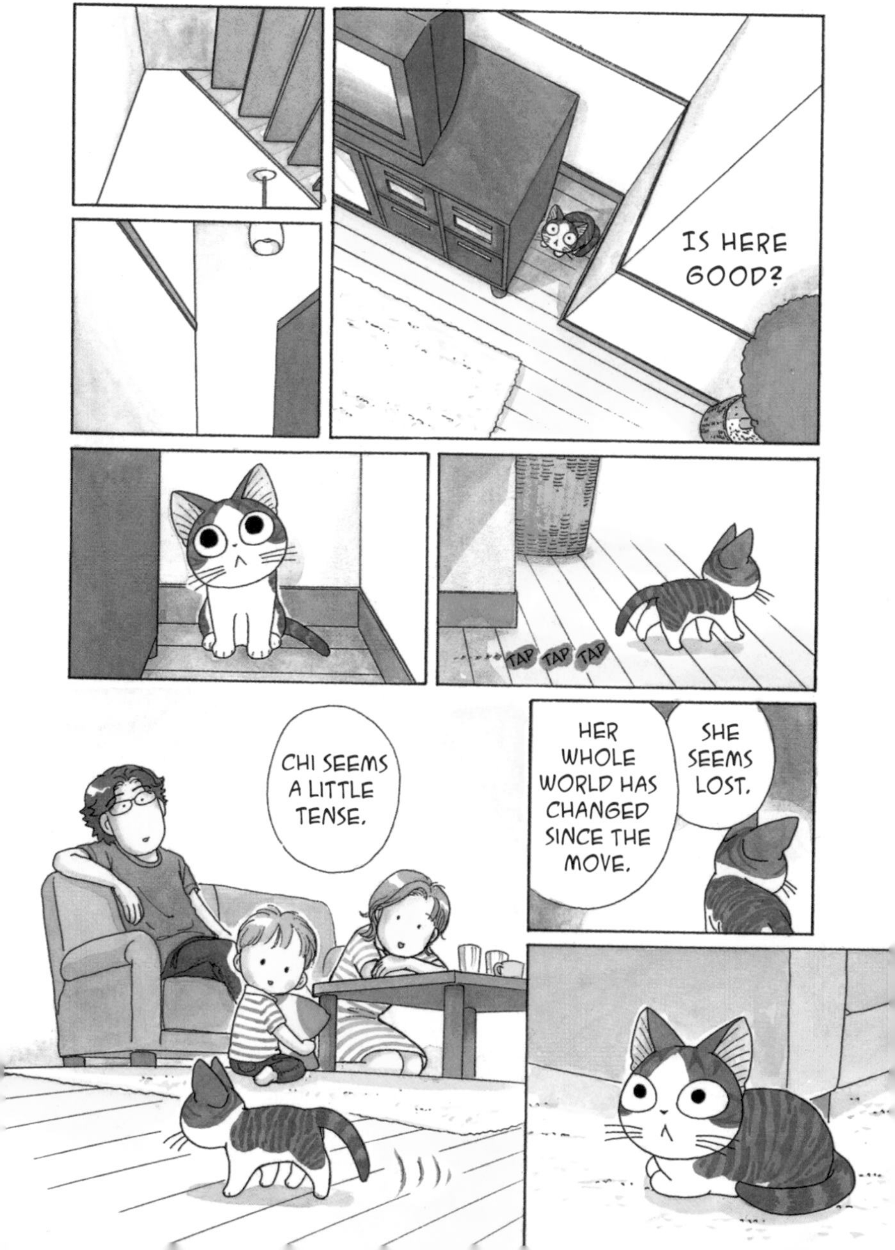
IS HERE GOOD?
TAP TAP TAP
CHI SEEMS A LITTLE TENSE.
HER WHOLE WORLD HAS CHANGED SINCE THE MOVE.
SHE SEEMS LOST.

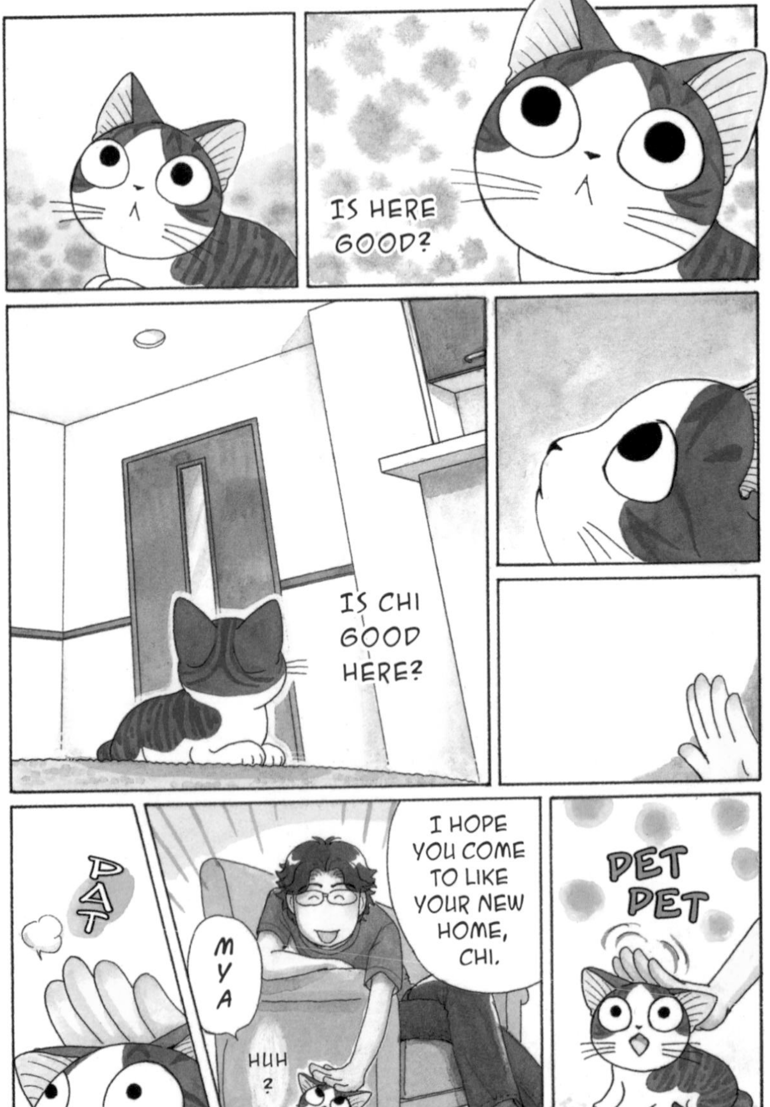
IS HERE GOOD?
IS CHI GOOD HERE?
PAT
MYA
HUH?
I HOPE YOU COME TO LIKE YOUR NEW HOME, CHI.
PET PET

PET
PET

PET
PET

PRRR
PRRR

PRRR
PRRR

OH?

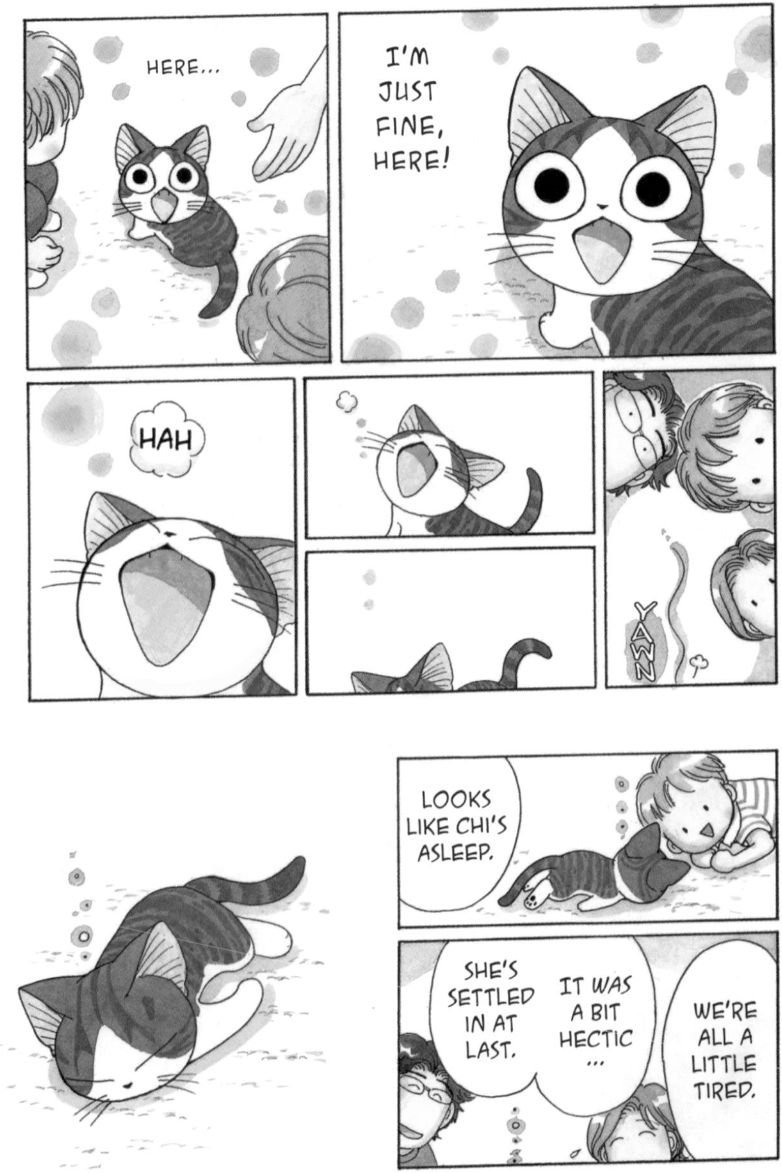

HERE...
I'M JUST FINE, HERE!
HAH
YAWN
LOOKS LIKE CHI'S ASLEEP.
SHE'S SETTLED IN AT LAST.
IT WAS A BIT HECTIC ...
WE'RE ALL A LITTLE TIRED.

YAWN

WATCHING CHI SLEEP WITHOUT A CARE'S SO RELAXING.

YEAH

AH... I'M TIRED.

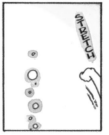

STRETCH

HERE IS FINE.

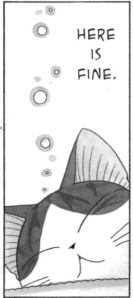

HERE IS FINE.

SHUV

HEY?

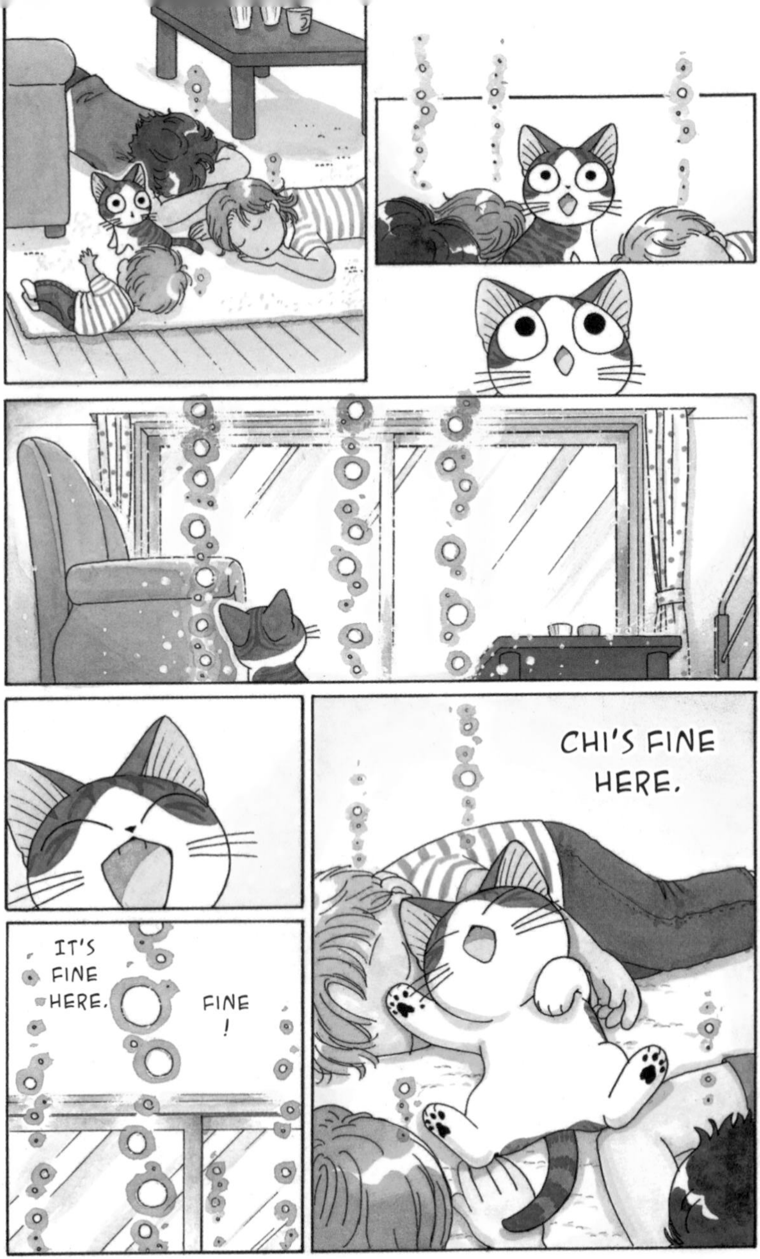
CHI'S FINE HERE.
IT'S FINE HERE.
FINE !

the end

homemade 66: a cat is mistaken

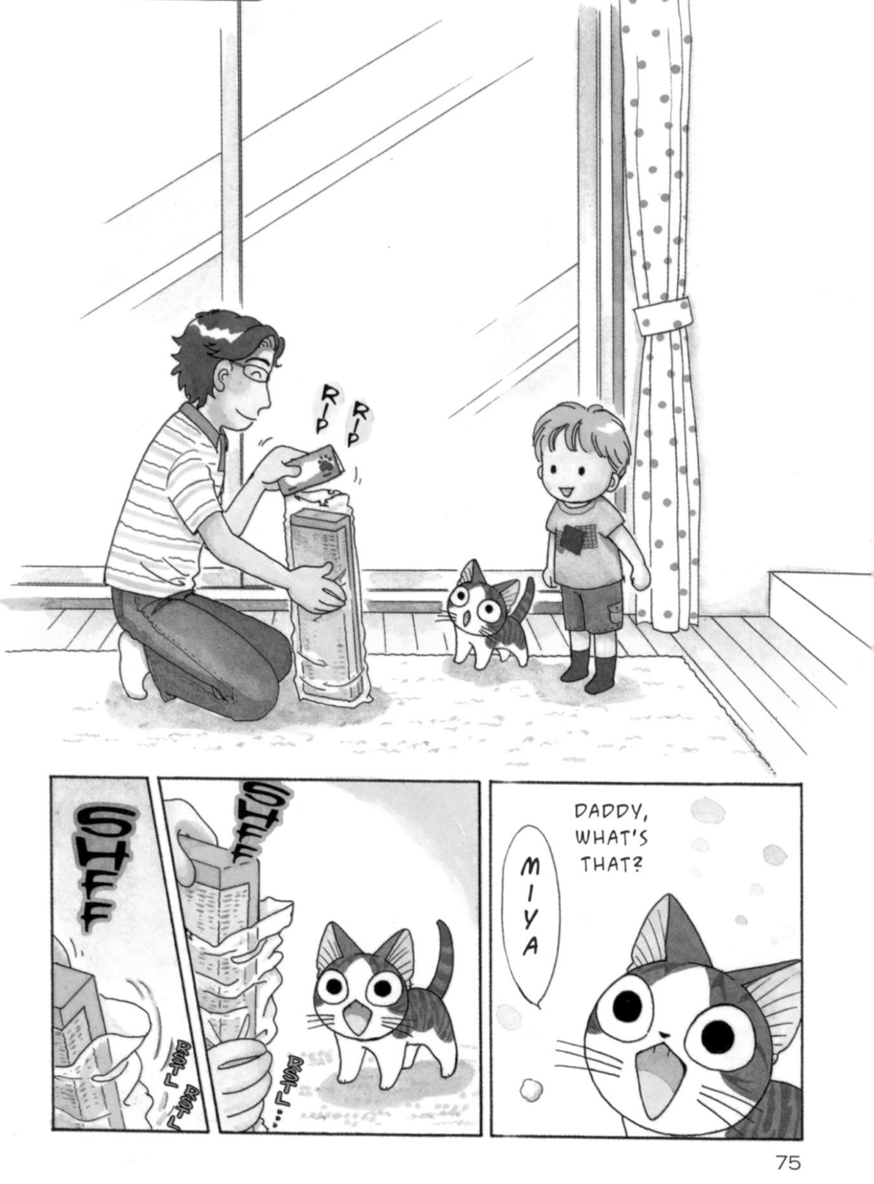

RIP RIP
SHFF
SHFF
RSTL RSTL
RSTL...
MIYA
DADDY, WHAT'S THAT?

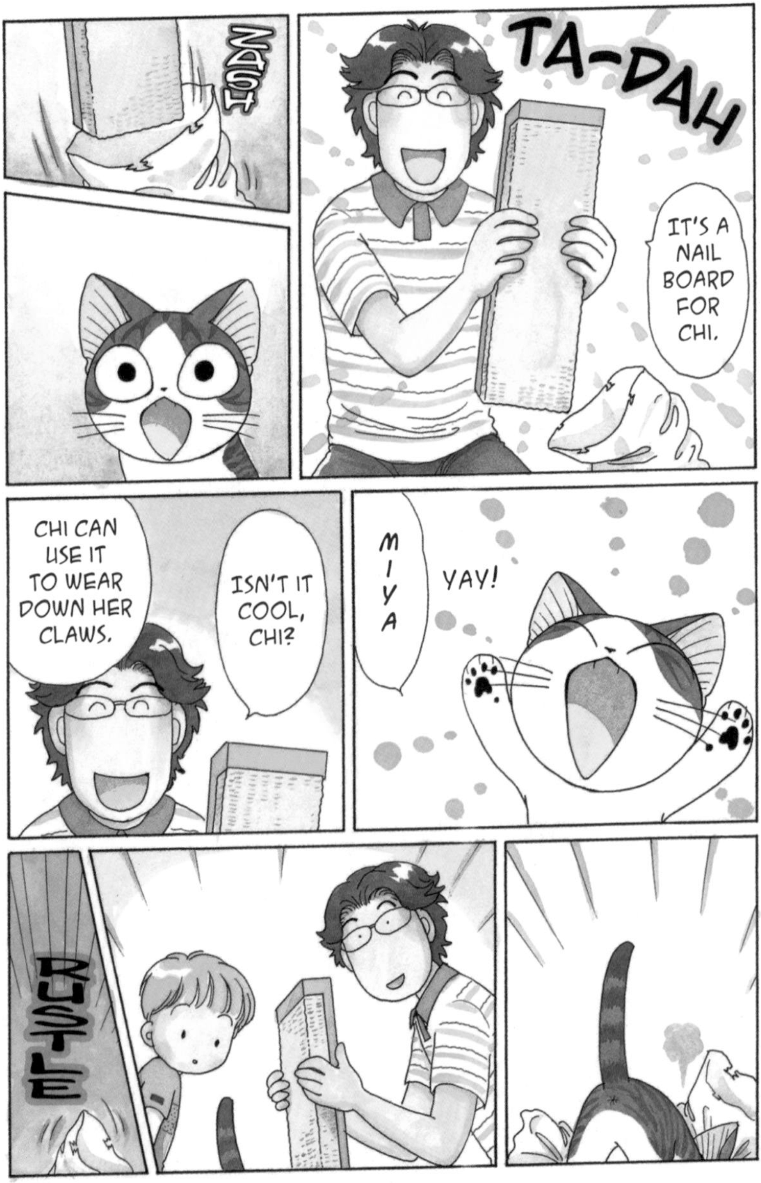
ZASH
TA-DAH
IT'S A NAIL BOARD FOR CHI.
CHI CAN USE IT TO WEAR DOWN HER CLAWS.
ISN'T IT COOL, CHI?
MIYA
YAY!
RUSTLE

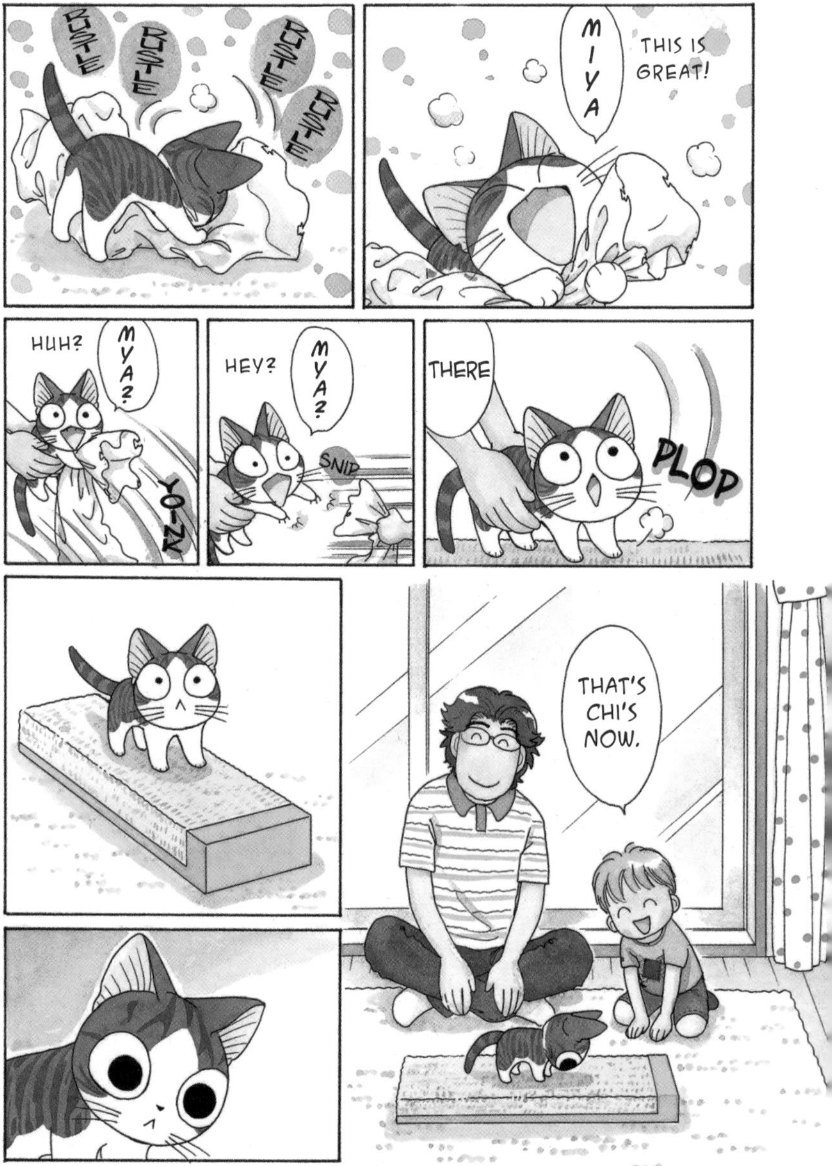
RUSTLE
RUSTLE
RUSTLE
RUSTLE
MIYA
THIS IS GREAT!
HUH?
MYA?
YOINK
HEY?
MYA?
SNIP
THERE
PLOP
THAT'S CHI'S NOW.

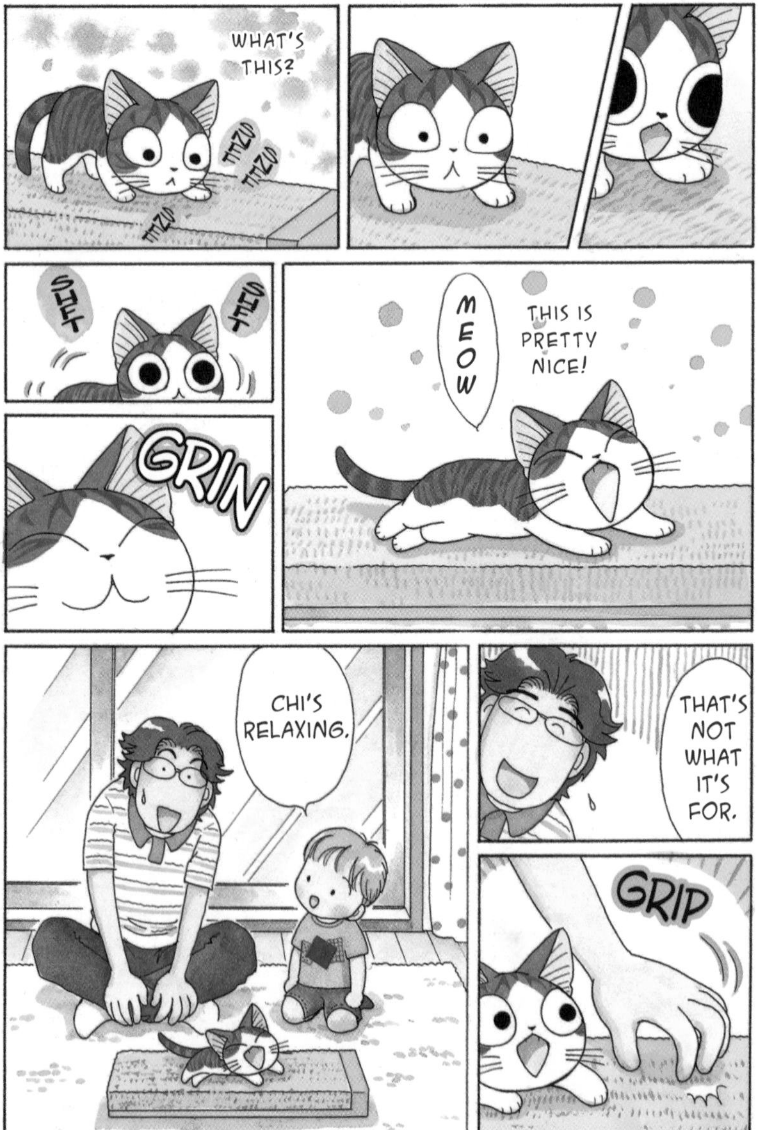
WHAT'S THIS?
SHFT
SHFT
GRIN
MEOW
THIS IS PRETTY NICE!
CHI'S RELAXING.
THAT'S NOT WHAT IT'S FOR.
GRIP

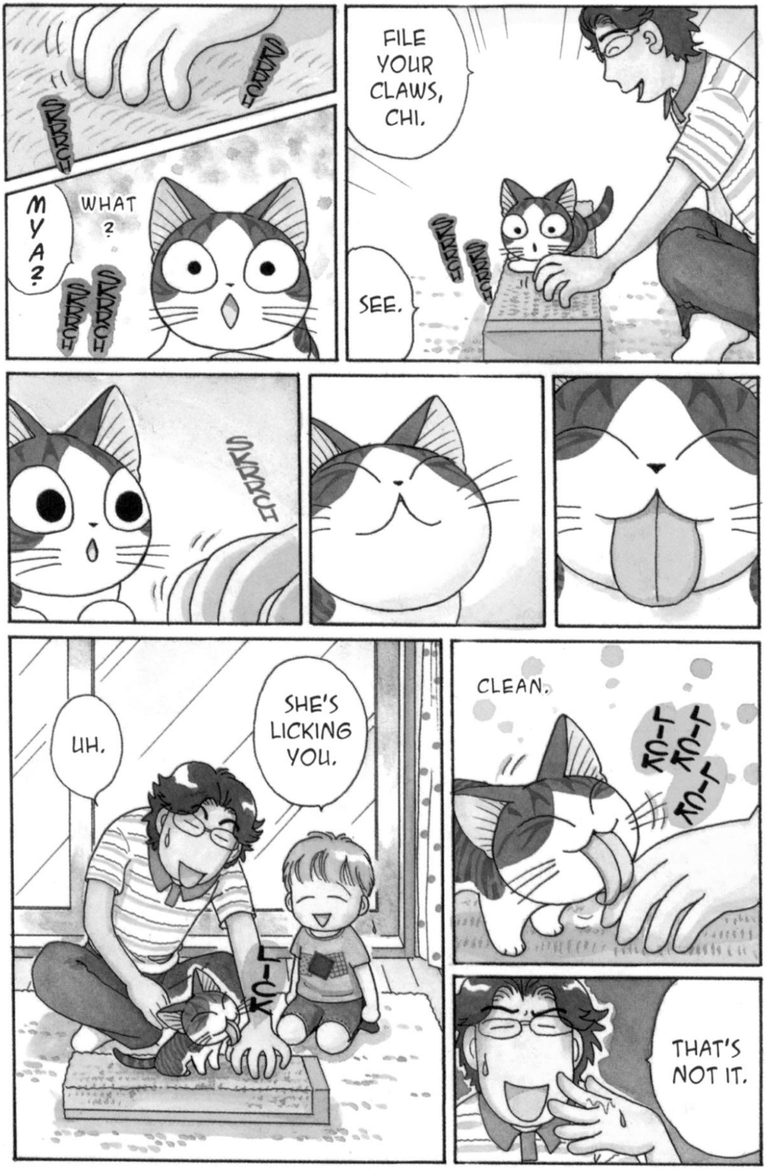
SKRRCH
SKRRCH
MYA?
WHAT?
SKRRCH
SKRRCH
FILE YOUR CLAWS, CHI.
SEE.
SKRRCH
SKRRCH
SKRRCH
UH.
SHE'S LICKING YOU.
LICK
CLEAN.
LICK LICK
LICK LICK
THAT'S NOT IT.

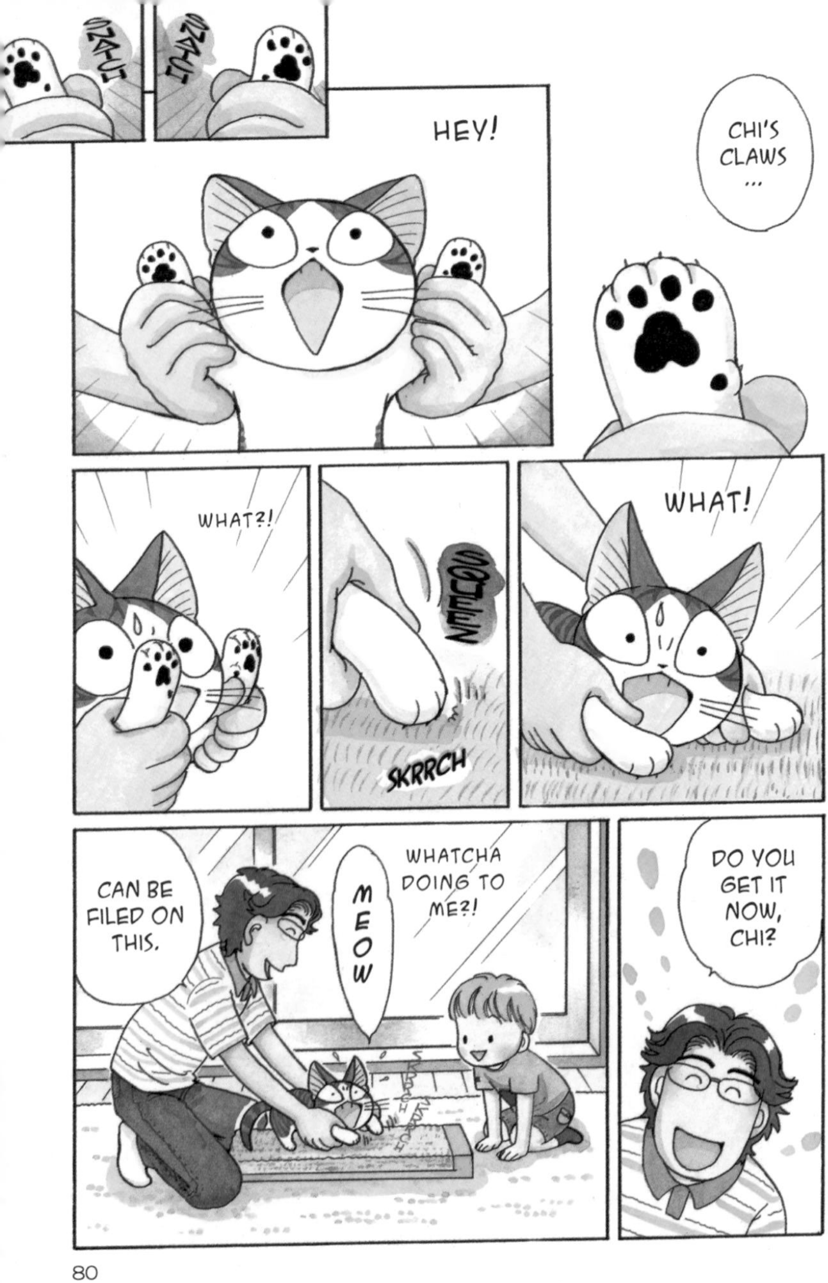
SNATCH
SNATCH
HEY!
CHI'S CLAWS ...
WHAT?!
SQUEEN
SKRRCH
WHAT!
CAN BE FILED ON THIS.
MEOW
WHATCHA DOING TO ME?!
SKRRCH
SKRRCH
DO YOU GET IT NOW, CHI?

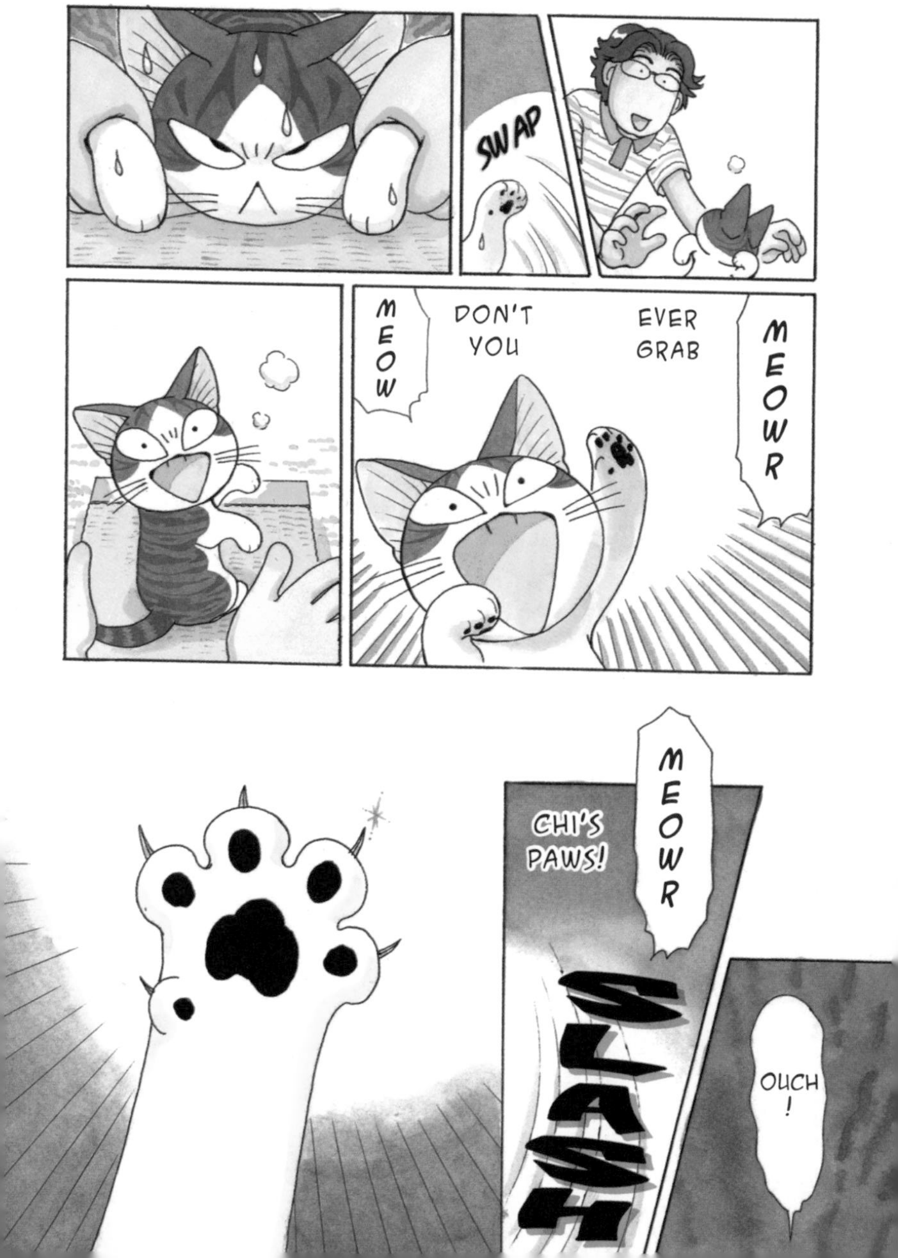
SWAP
MEOW
DON'T YOU
EVER GRAB
MEOWR
CHI'S PAWS!
MEOWR
SLASH
OUCH!

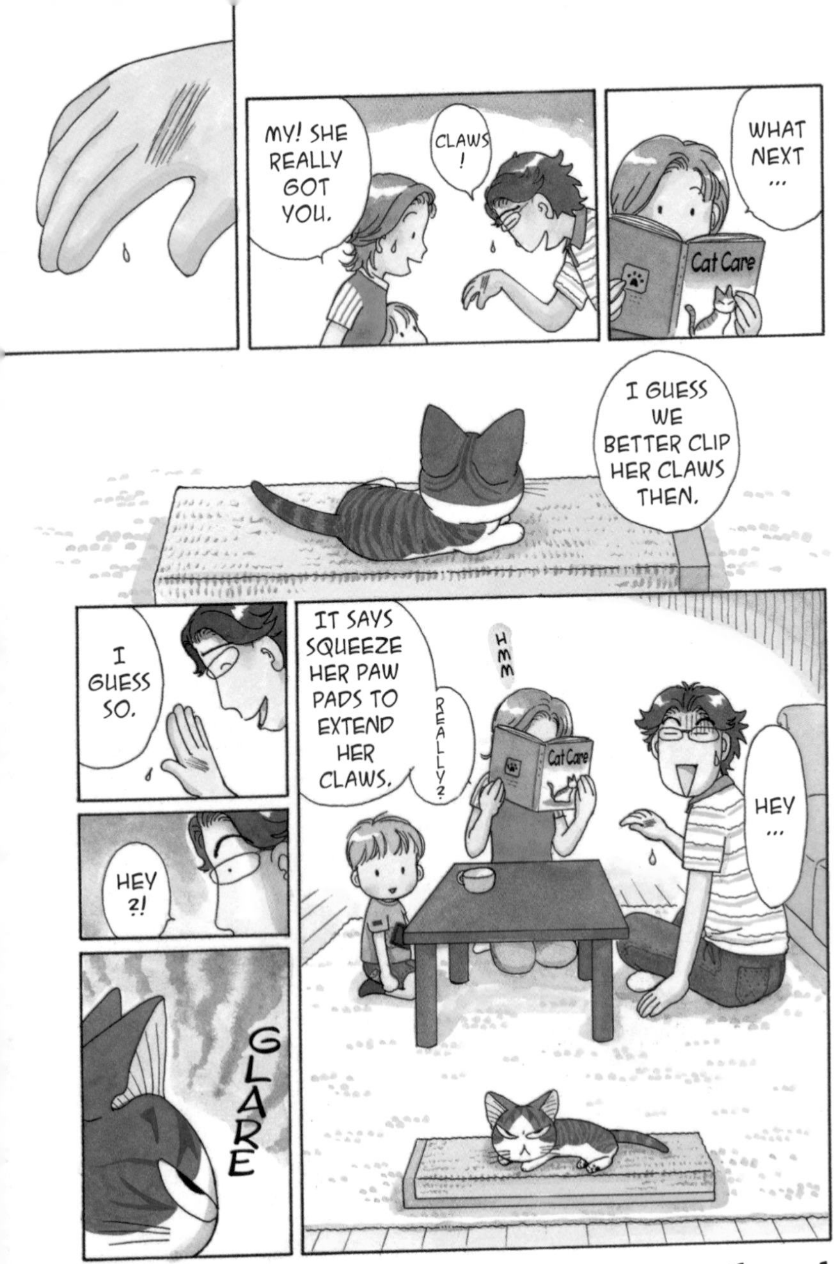
MY! SHE REALLY GOT YOU.
CLAWS!
WHAT NEXT...
Cat Care
I GUESS WE BETTER CLIP HER CLAWS THEN.
I GUESS SO.
HEY?!
GLARE
IT SAYS SQUEEZE HER PAW PADS TO EXTEND HER CLAWS.
HMM
REALLY?
Cat Care
HEY...

the end

homemade 67: a cat has her claws trimmed

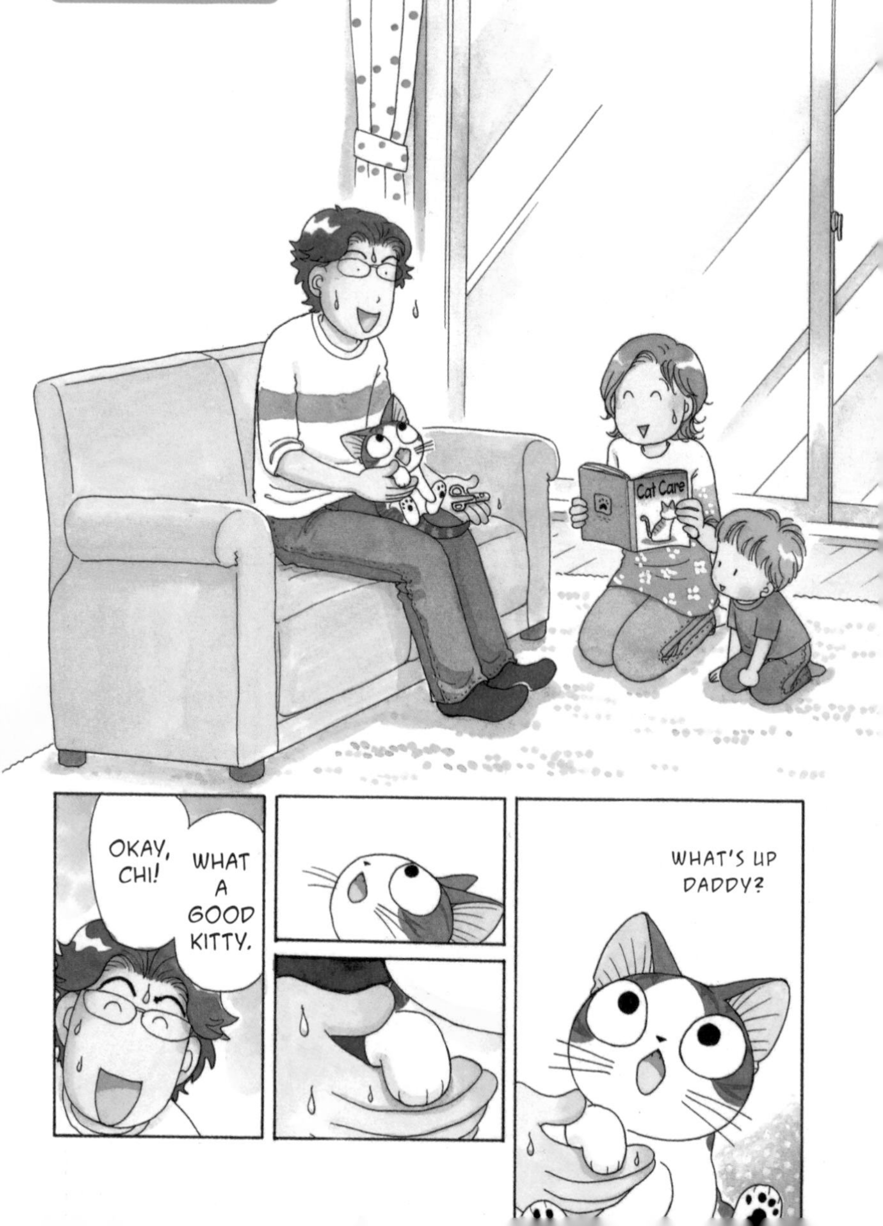
Cat Care
OKAY, CHI!
WHAT A GOOD KITTY.
WHAT'S UP DADDY?

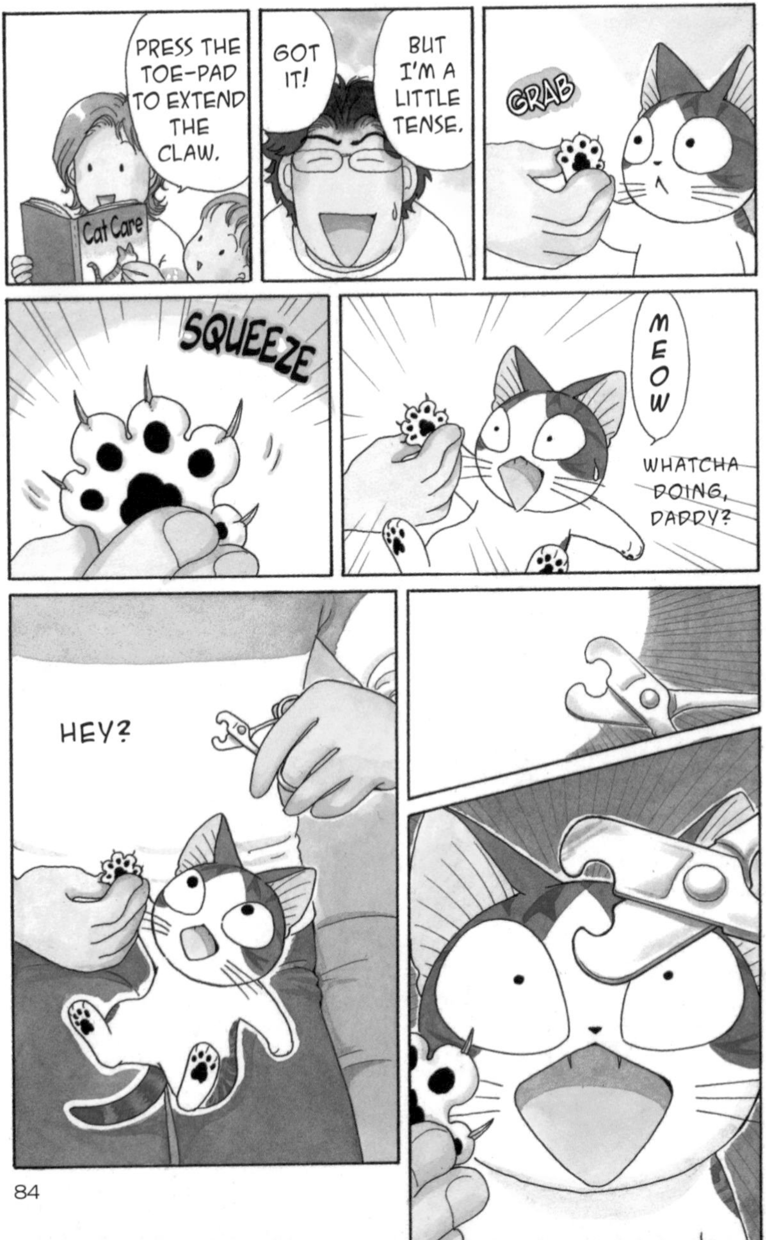

PRESS THE TOE-PAD TO EXTEND THE CLAW.
Cat Care
GOT IT!
BUT I'M A LITTLE TENSE.
GRAB
SQUEEZE
MEOW
WHATCHA DOING, DADDY?
HEY?

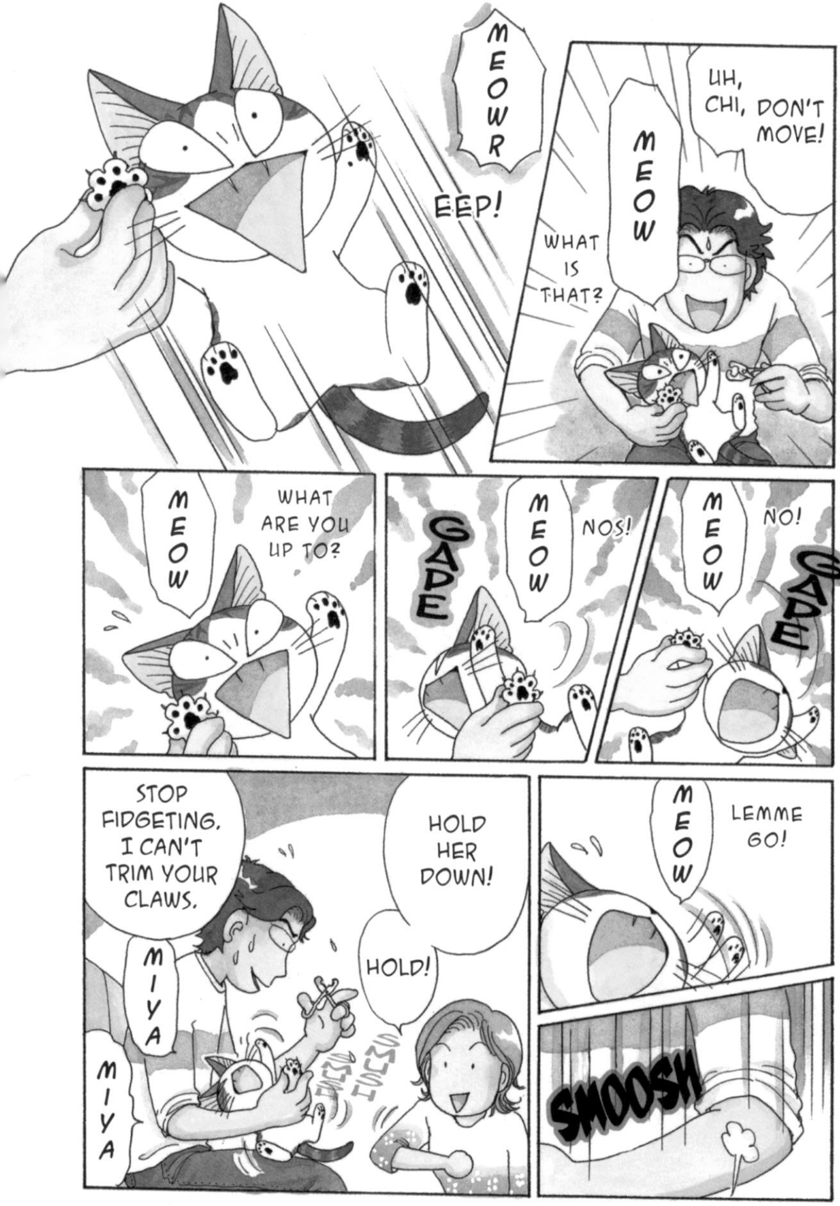
MEOWR
EEP!
UH, CHI, DON'T MOVE!
MEOW
WHAT IS THAT?
MEOW
WHAT ARE YOU UP TO?
GADE
MEOW
NOS!
MEOW
NO!
GADE
STOP FIDGETING. I CAN'T TRIM YOUR CLAWS.
HOLD HER DOWN!
MIYA
MIYA
HOLD!
SMUSH SMUSH
MEOW
LEMME GO!
SMOOSH

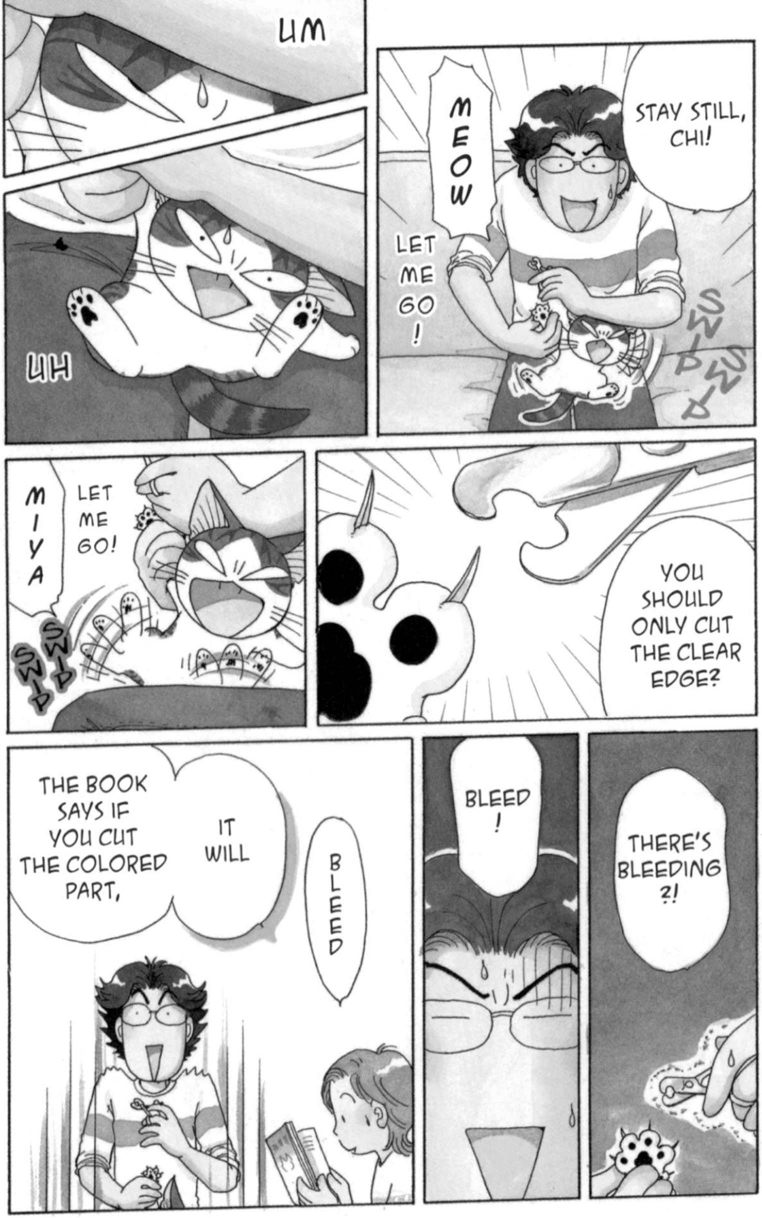
UM
UH
MEOW
LET ME GO!
STAY STILL, CHI!
SWIP
SWIP
MIYA
LET ME GO!
SWIP
SWIP
YOU SHOULD ONLY CUT THE CLEAR EDGE?
THE BOOK SAYS IF YOU CUT THE COLORED PART,
IT WILL
BLEED
BLEED!
THERE'S BLEEDING?!

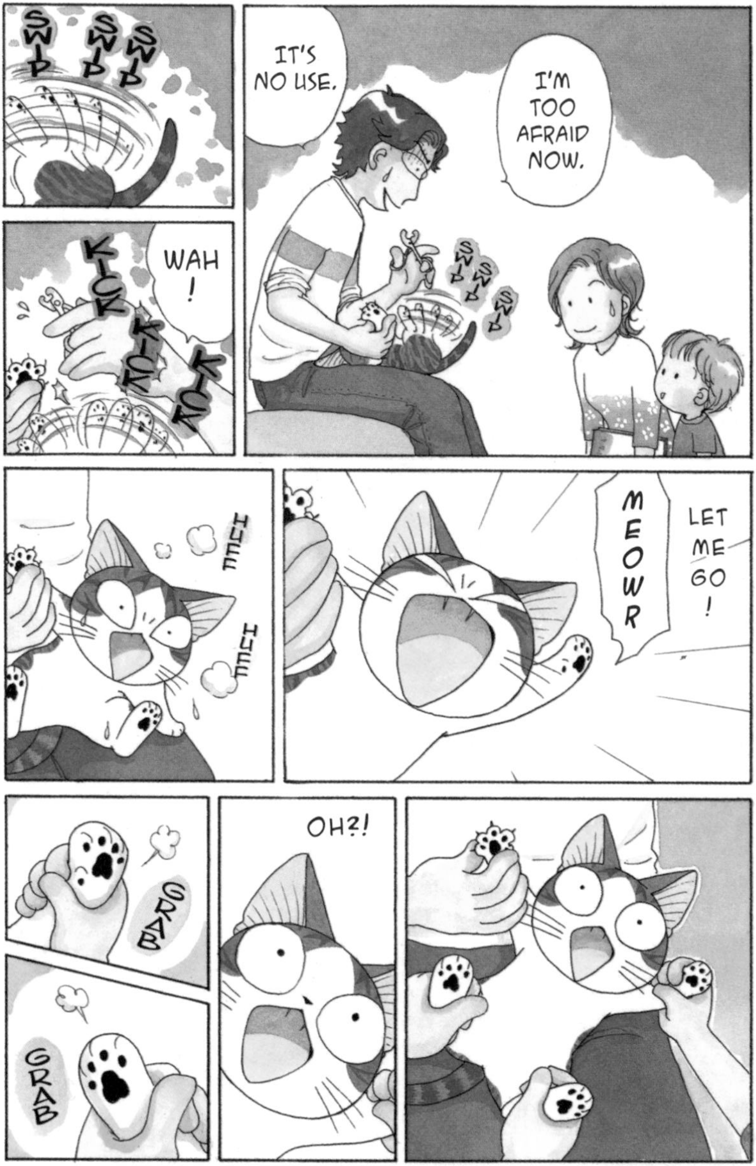
SWIP SWIP SWIP
KICK KICK KICK
WAH!
IT'S NO USE.
I'M TOO AFRAID NOW.
SWIP SWIP SWIP
HUFF HUFF
MEOWR
LET ME GO!
GRAB
GRAB
OH?!

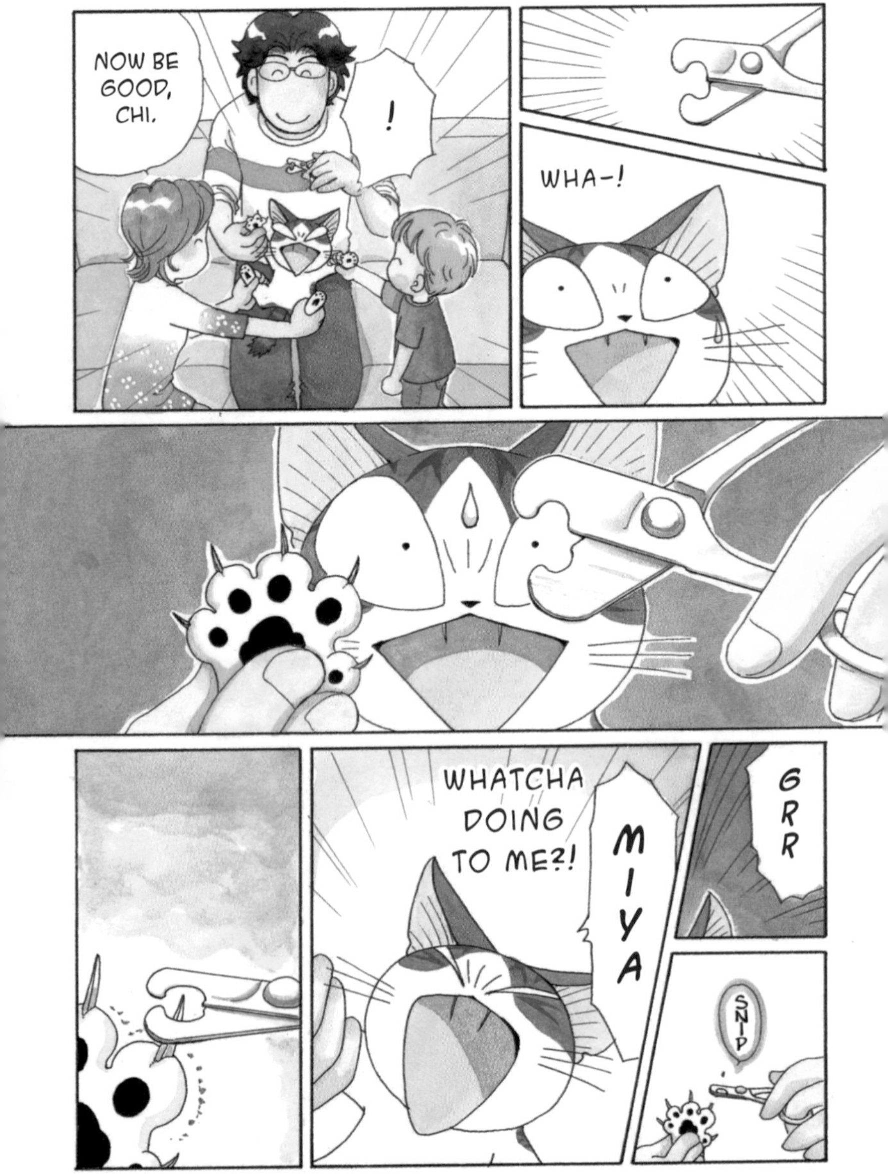
NOW BE GOOD, CHI.
!
WHA-!
WHATCHA DOING TO ME?!
MIYA
GRR
SNIP

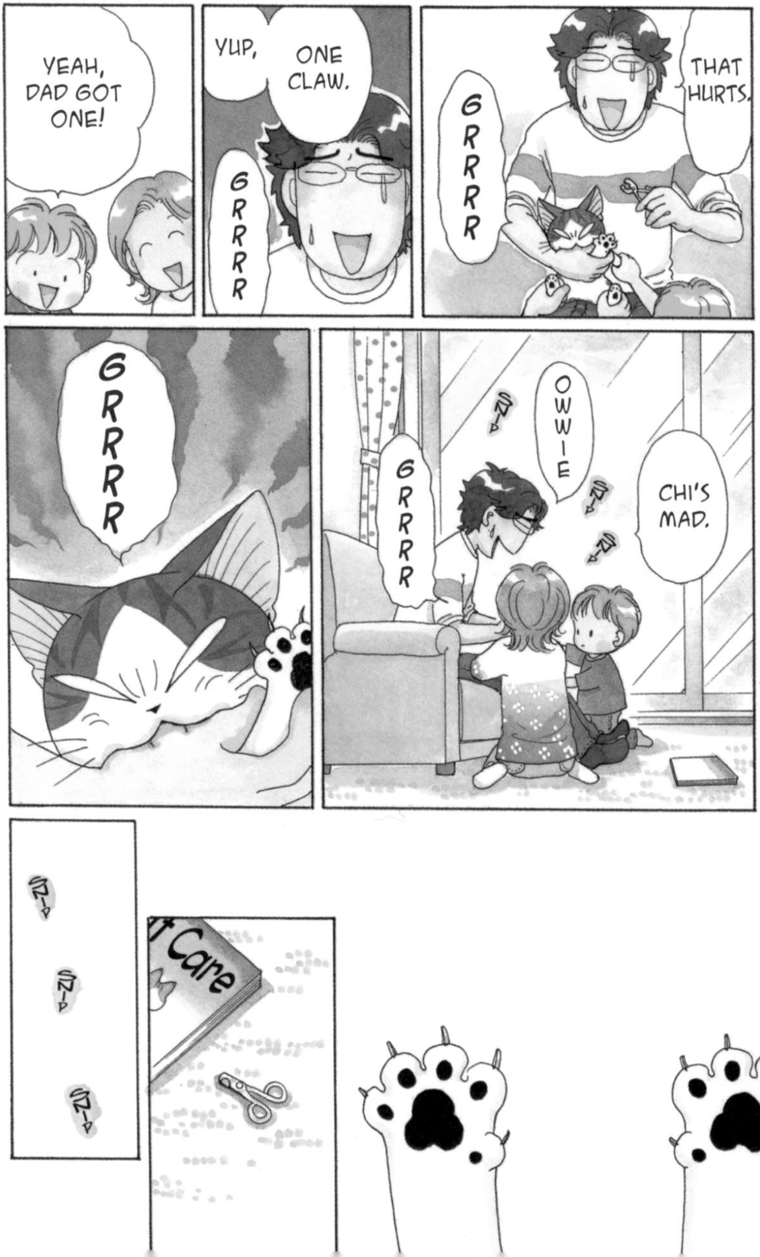

YEAH, DAD GOT ONE!
YUP,
ONE CLAW.
GRRRR
GRRRR
THAT HURTS.
GRRRR
SNIP
OWWIE
GRRRR
SNIP
SNIP
CHI'S MAD.
SNIP
SNIP
SNIP

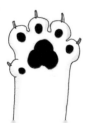

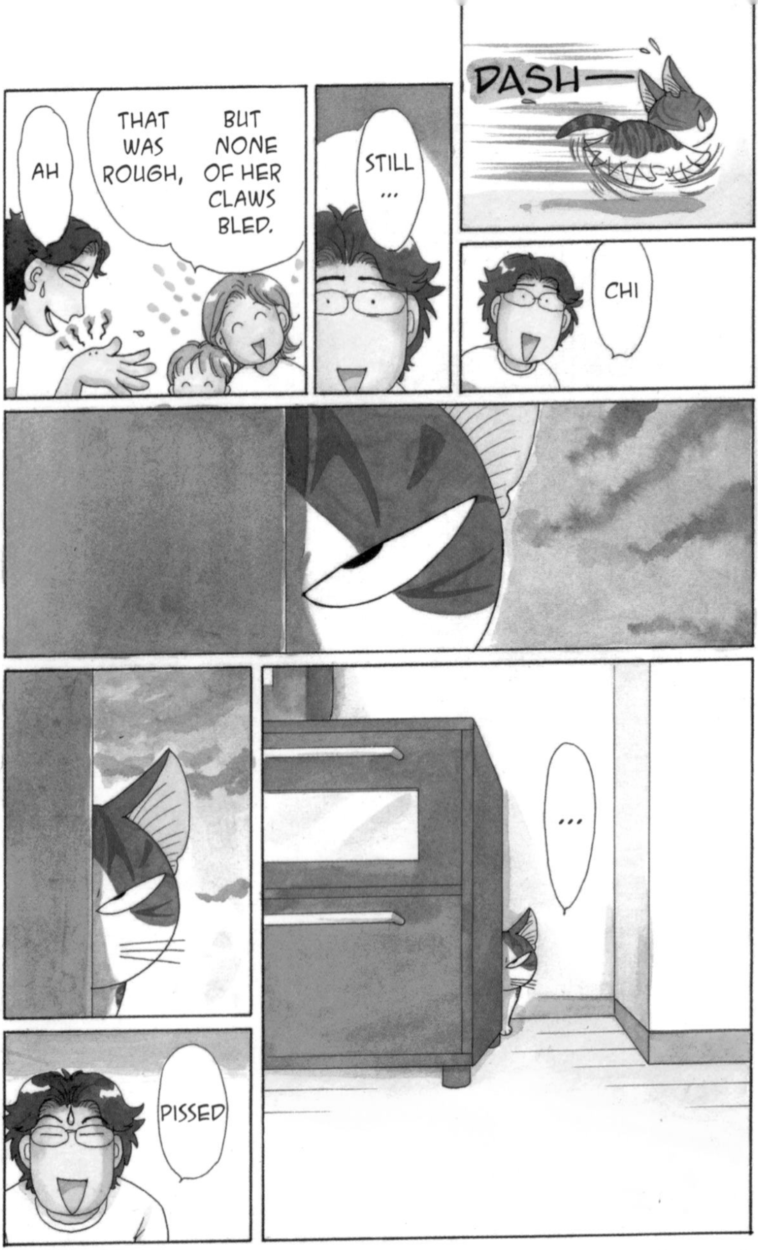
AH
THAT WAS ROUGH, BUT NONE OF HER CLAWS BLED.
STILL ...
DASH—
CHI
PISSED
...

the end

homemade 68: a cat joins in

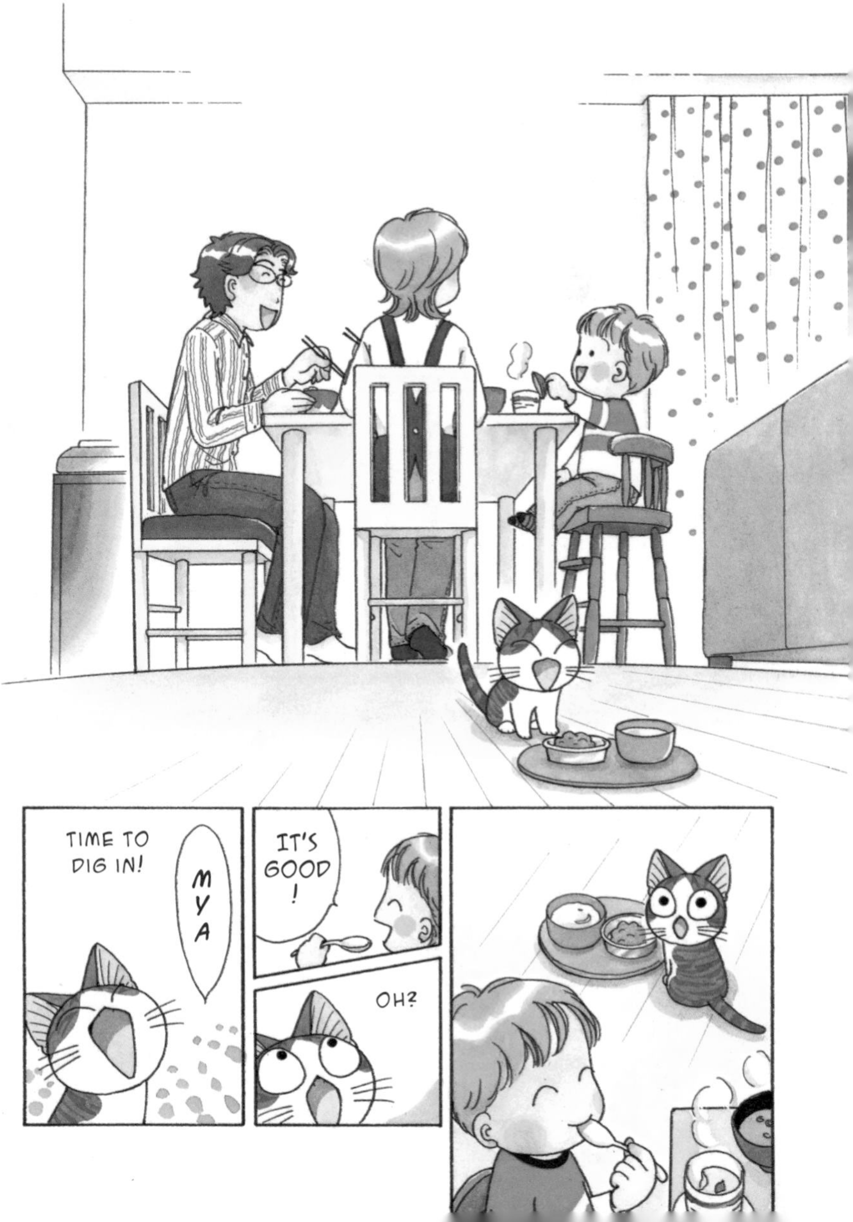
TIME TO DIG IN!
MYA
IT'S GOOD!
OH?

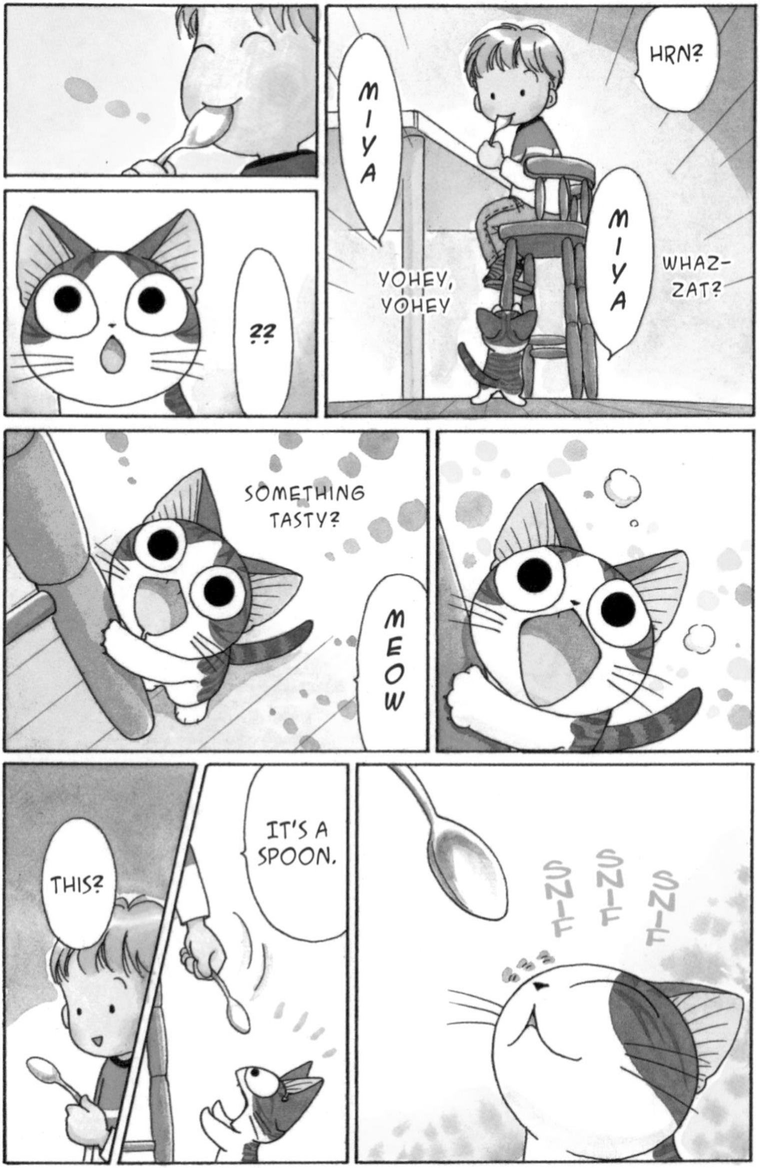
??
MIYA
HRN?
YOHEY, YOHEY
MIYA
WHAZ-ZAT?
SOMETHING TASTY?
MEOW
THIS?
IT'S A SPOON.
SNIF SNIF SNIF

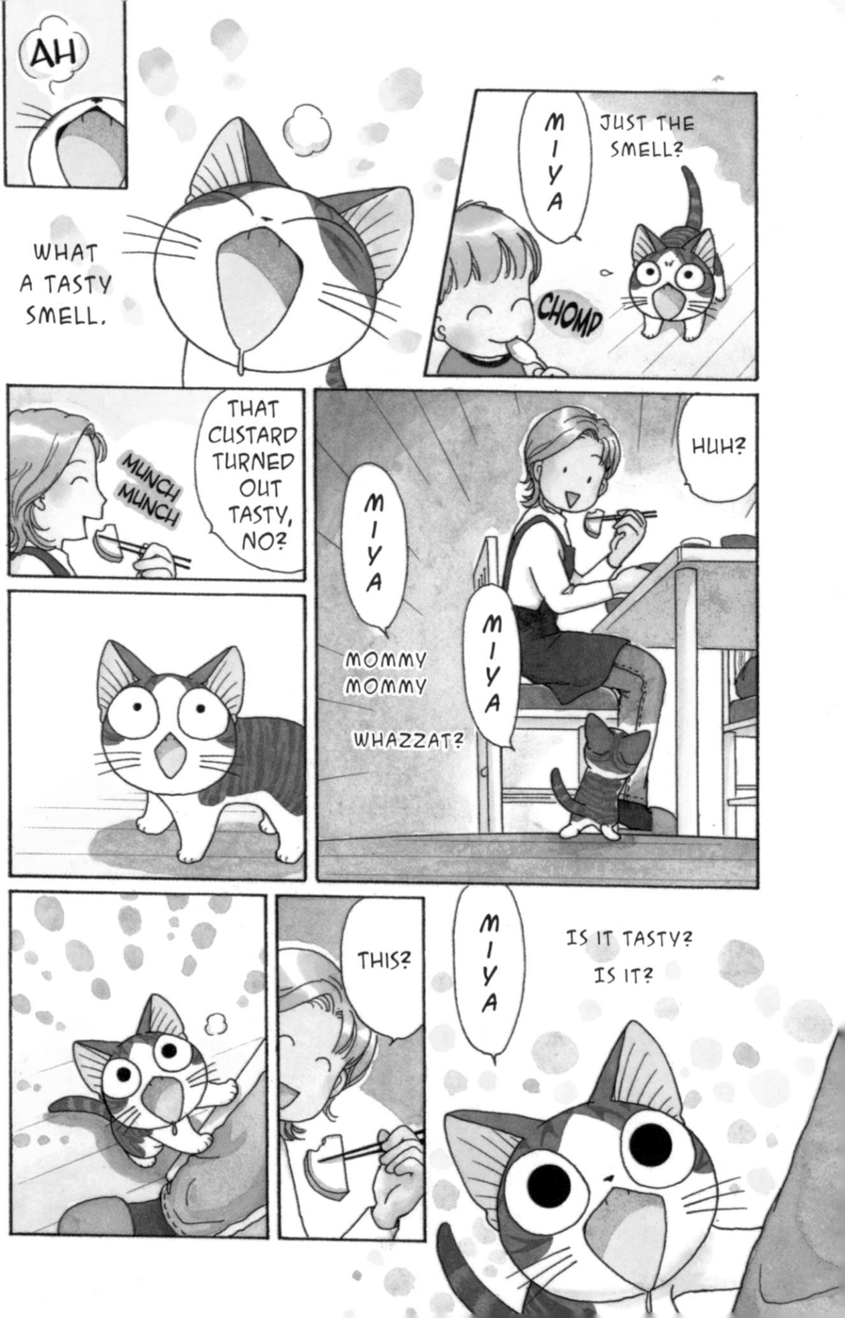
AH
WHAT A TASTY SMELL.
MIYA
JUST THE SMELL?
CHOMP
MUNCH MUNCH
THAT CUSTARD TURNED OUT TASTY, NO?
HUH?
MIYA
MOMMY MOMMY
MIYA
WHAZZAT?
THIS?
MIYA
IS IT TASTY? IS IT?

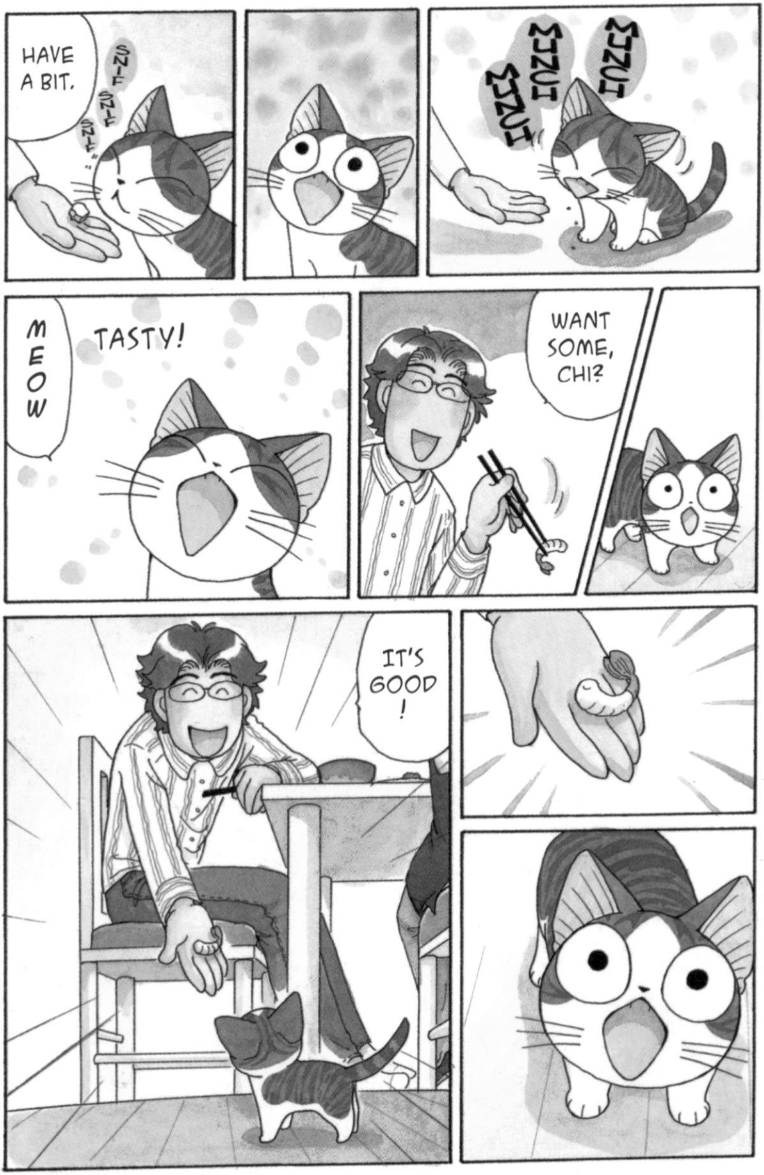
HAVE A BIT.
SNIF SNIF SNIF
MUNCH MUNCH MUNCH
MEOW
TASTY!
WANT SOME, CHI?
IT'S GOOD!

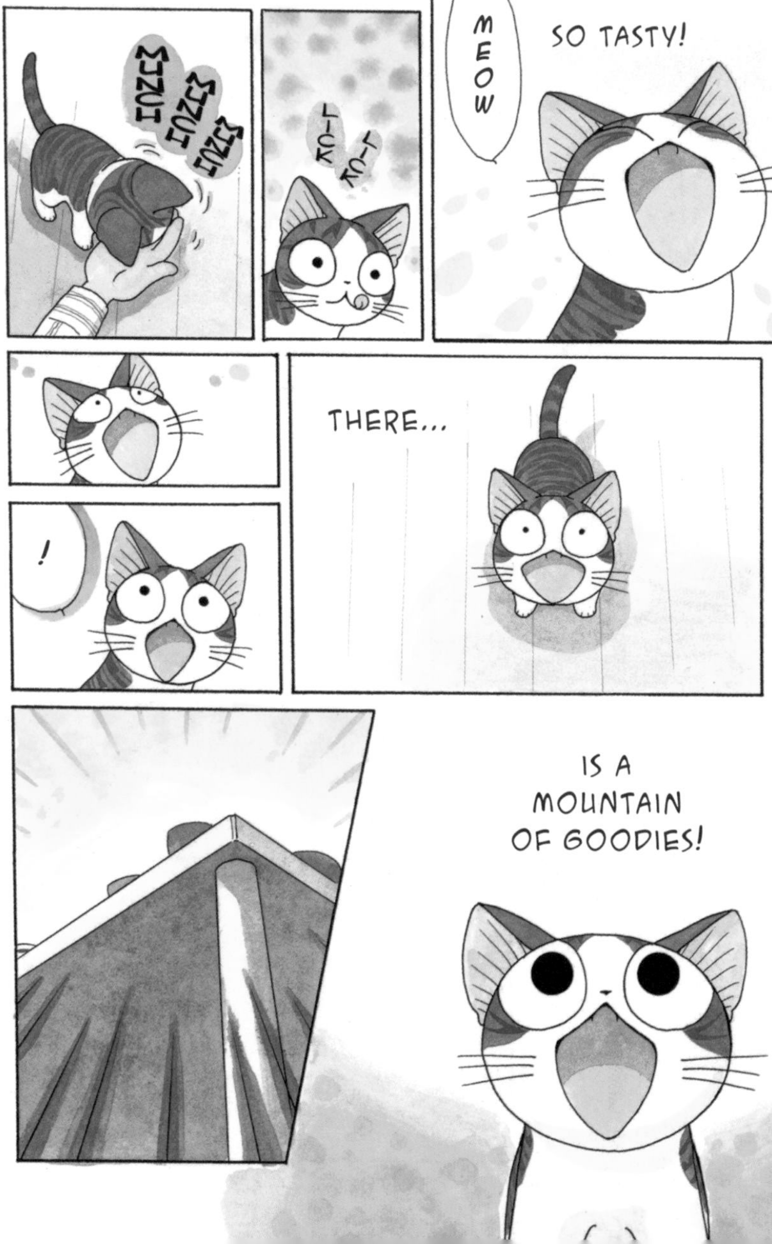
MUNCH MUNCH MUNCH
LICK LICK
MEOW
SO TASTY!
!
THERE...
IS A MOUNTAIN OF GOODIES!

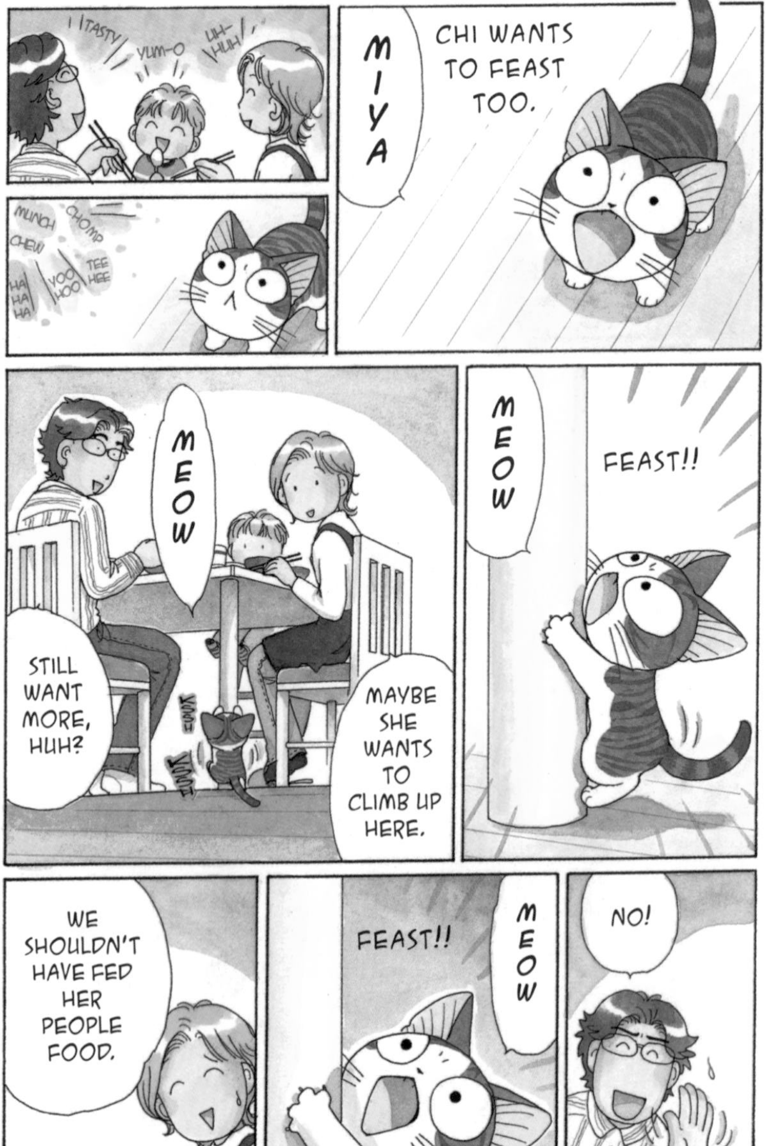
TASTY
YUM-O
UH-HUH
MUNCH
CHOMP
CHEW
HA HA HA
YOO HOO
TEE HEE
MIYA
CHI WANTS TO FEAST TOO.
MEOW
STILL WANT MORE, HUH?
MAYBE SHE WANTS TO CLIMB UP HERE.
MEOW
FEAST!!
WE SHOULDN'T HAVE FED HER PEOPLE FOOD.
FEAST!!
MEOW
NO!

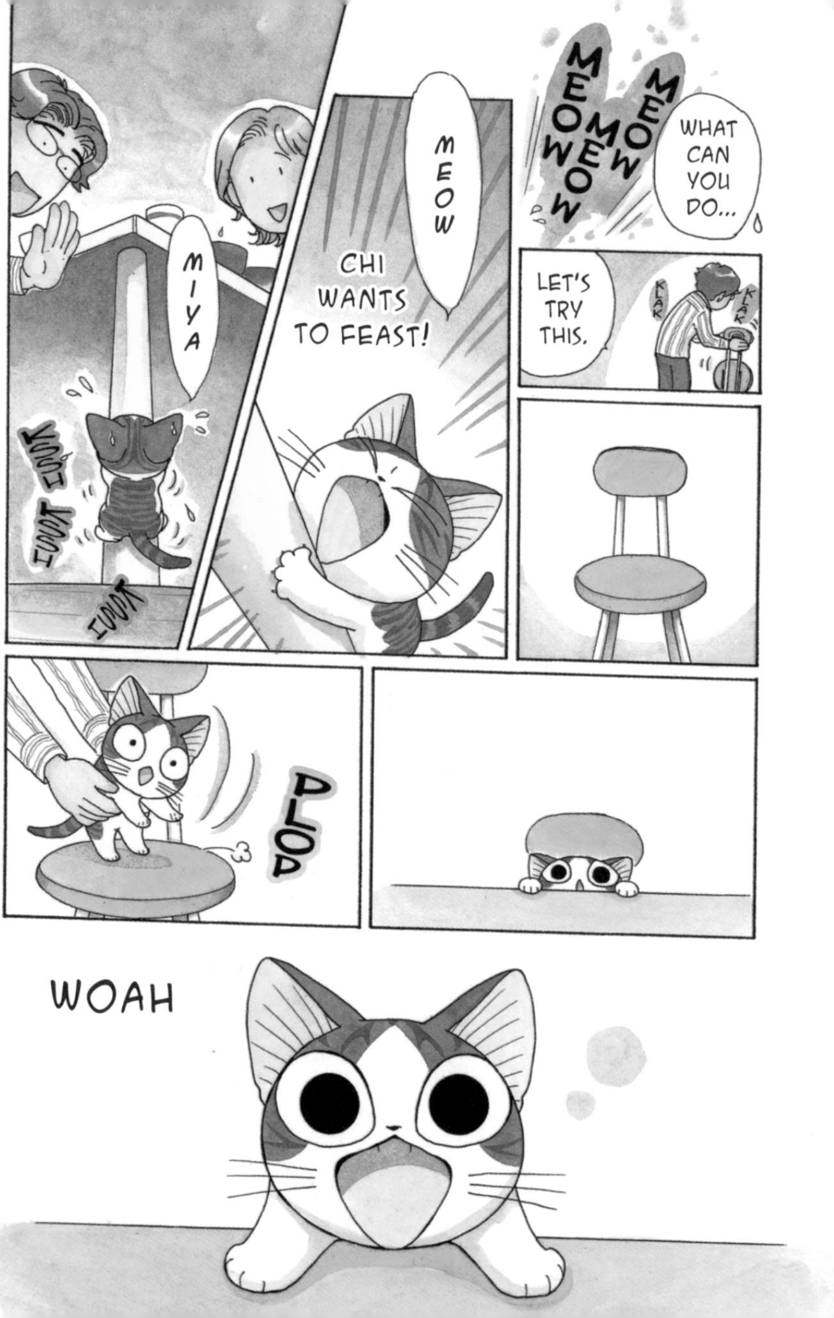
MIYA
MEOW
CHI WANTS TO FEAST!
MEOW MEOW MEOW MEOW
WHAT CAN YOU DO...
LET'S TRY THIS.
KLAK
KLAK
PLOP
WOAH

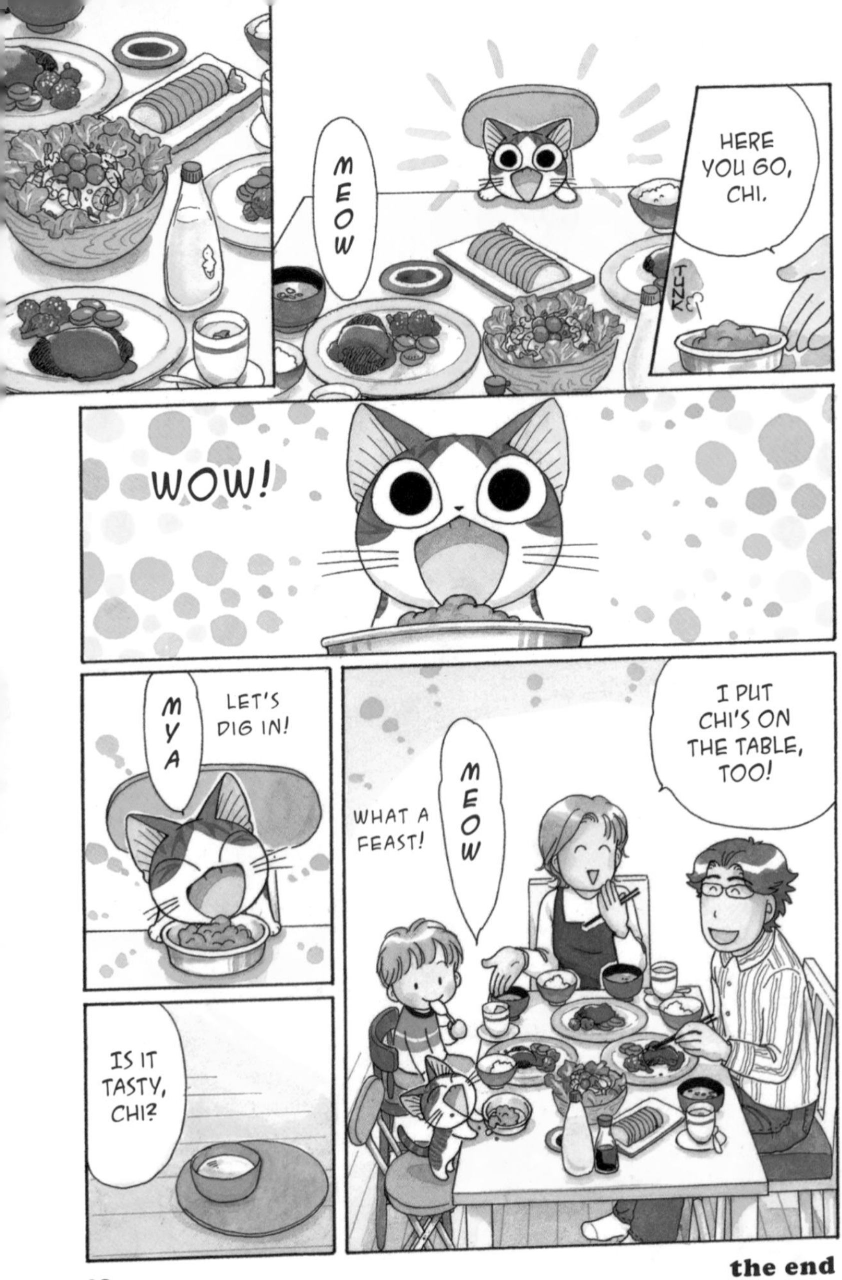
MEOW
HERE YOU GO, CHI.
TUNK
WOW!
MYA
LET'S DIG IN!
IS IT TASTY, CHI?
I PUT CHI'S ON THE TABLE, TOO!
MEOW
WHAT A FEAST!

the end

homemade 69: a cat plays in the yard

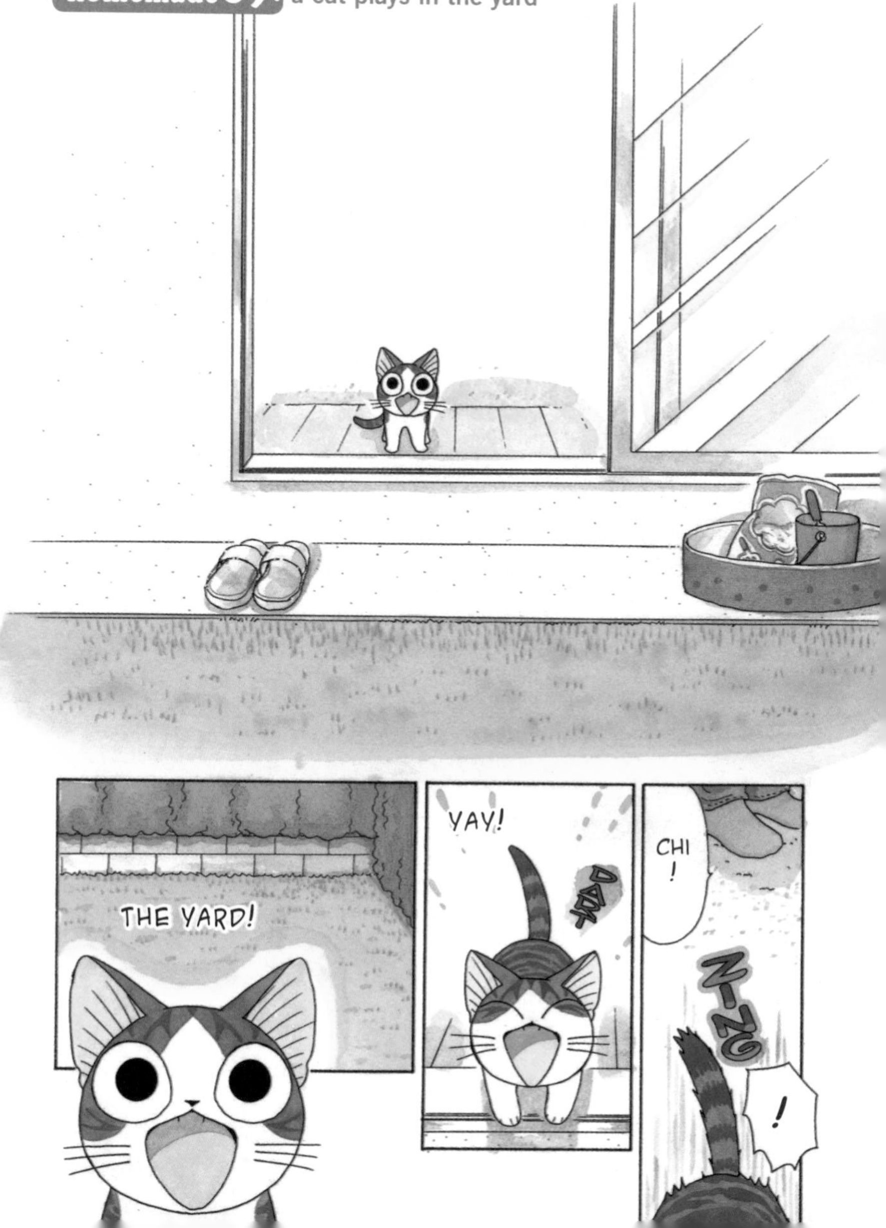
THE YARD!
YAY!
CHI!
ZING
!

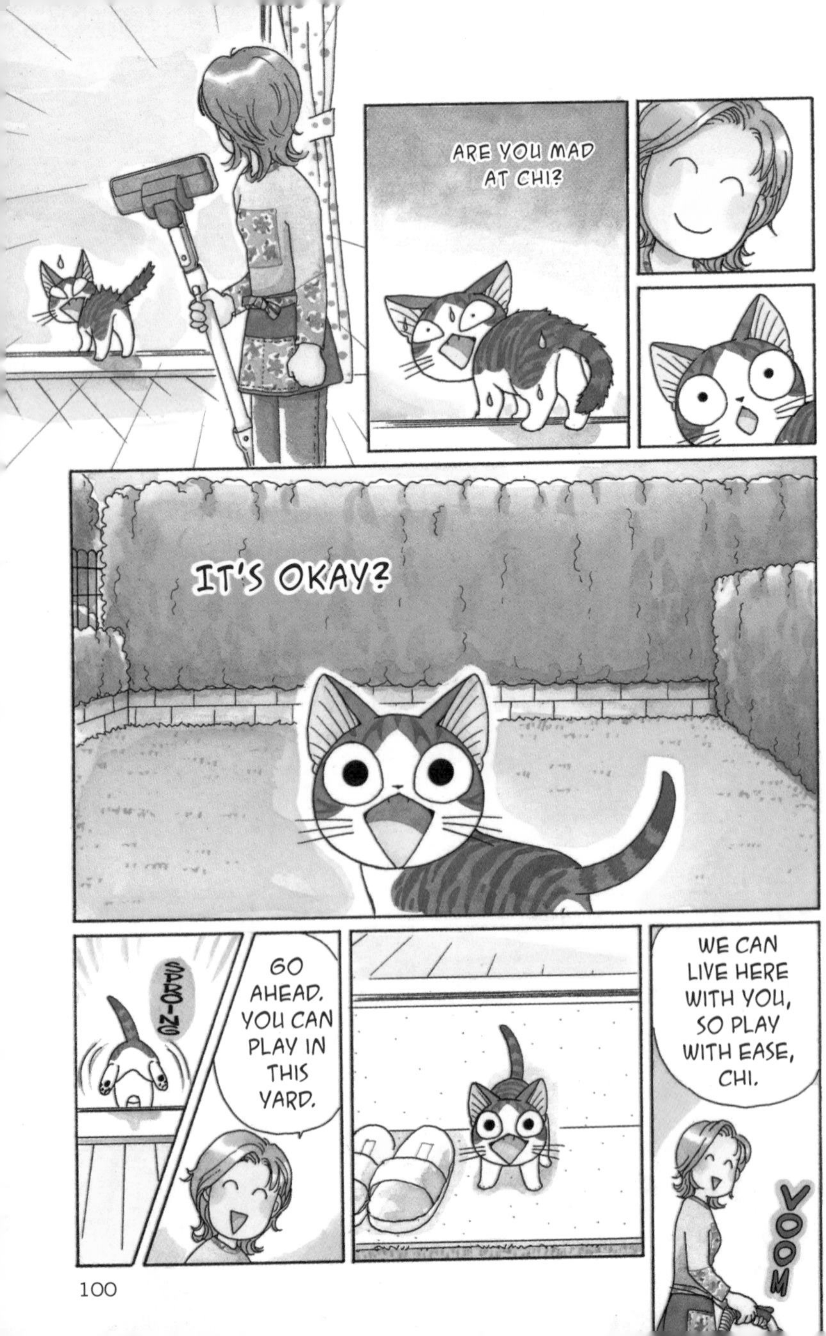
ARE YOU MAD AT CHI?
IT'S OKAY?
SPROING
GO AHEAD. YOU CAN PLAY IN THIS YARD.
WE CAN LIVE HERE WITH YOU, SO PLAY WITH EASE, CHI.
VOOM

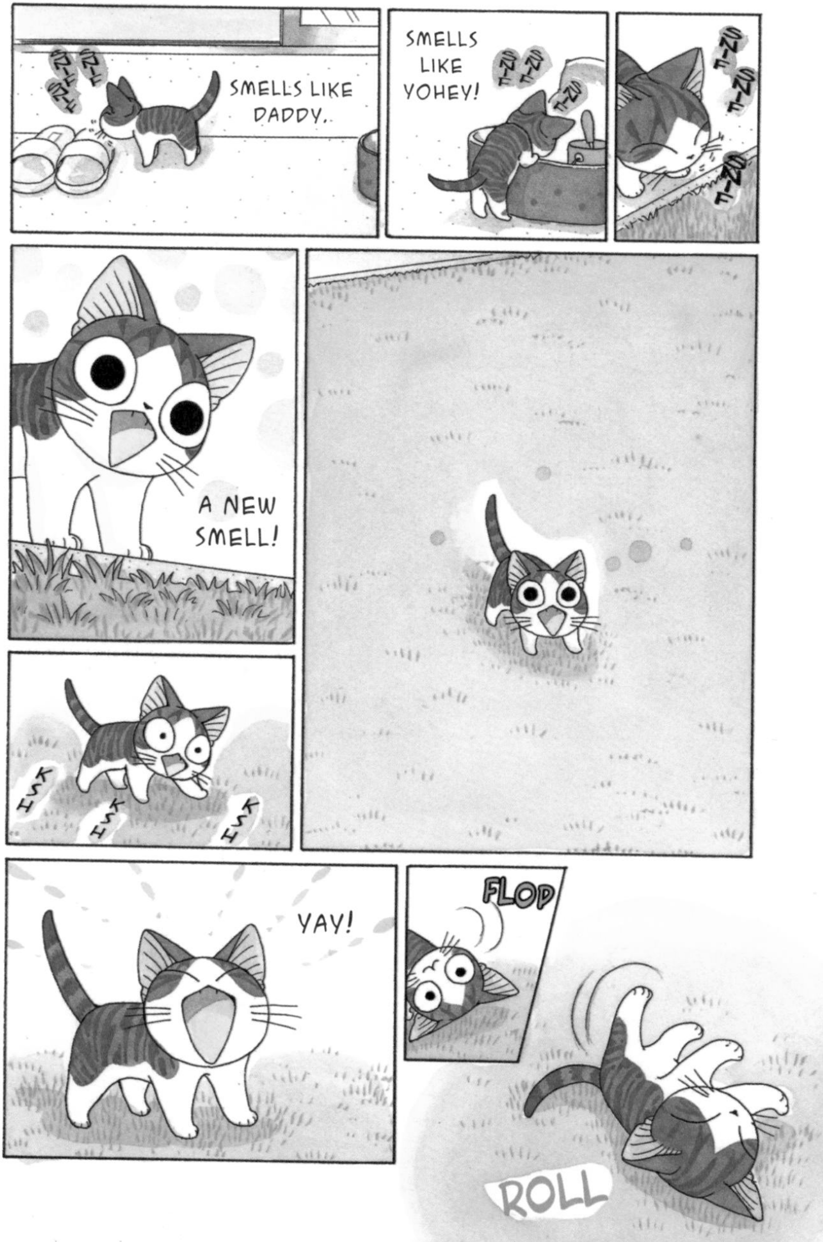
SNIF SNIF SNIF
SMELLS LIKE DADDY..
SMELLS LIKE YOHEY!
SNIF SNIF
SNIF SNIF SNIF
A NEW SMELL!
KSH KSH KSH
YAY!
FLOP
ROLL

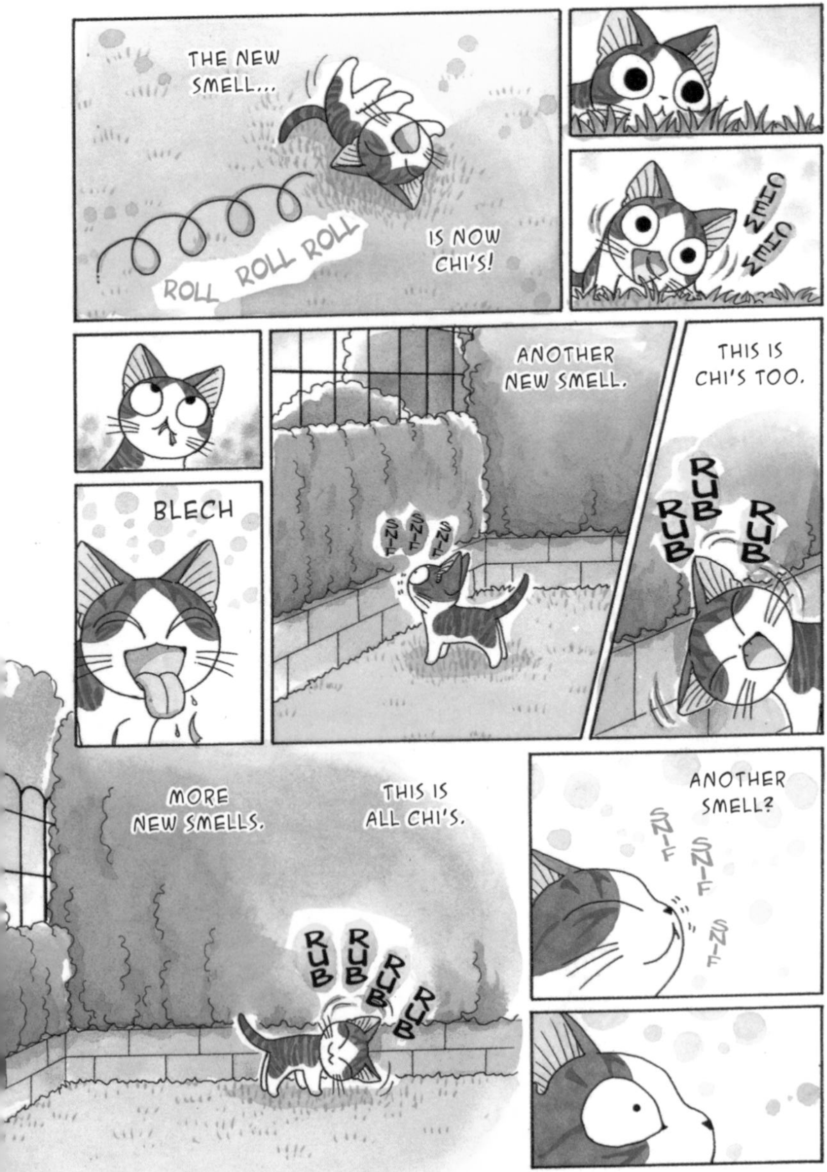
THE NEW SMELL...
ROLL ROLL ROLL
IS NOW CHI'S!
CHEW CHEW
BLECH
ANOTHER NEW SMELL.
SNIF SNIF SNIF
THIS IS CHI'S TOO.
RUB RUB RUB
MORE NEW SMELLS.
THIS IS ALL CHI'S.
RUB RUB RUB RUB
ANOTHER SMELL?
SNIF SNIF SNIF

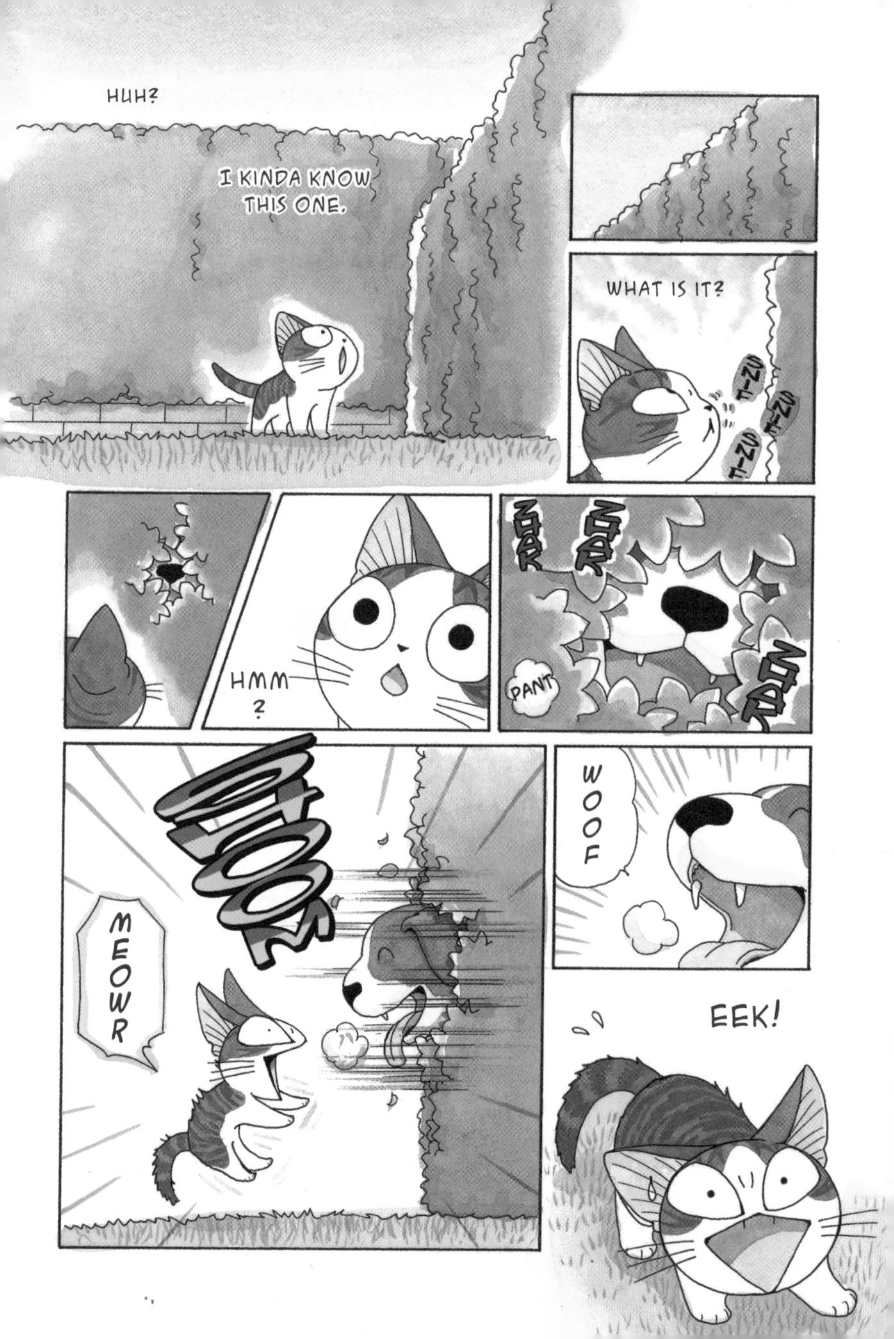
HUH?
I KINDA KNOW THIS ONE.
WHAT IS IT?
SNIF
SNIF
SNIF
HMM?
PANT
MEOWR
WOOF
EEK!

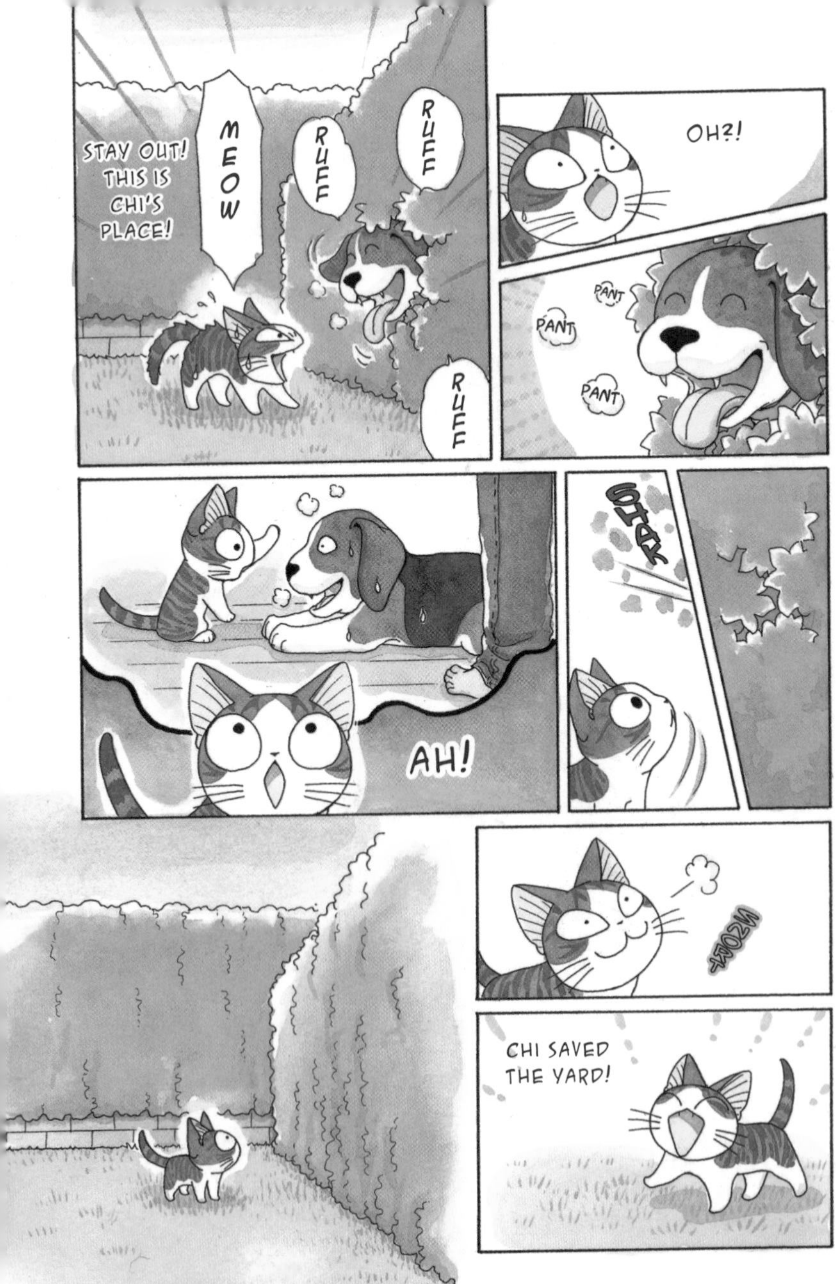
STAY OUT! THIS IS CHI'S PLACE!
MEOW
RUFF
RUFF
RUFF
OH?!
PANT
PANT
PANT
AH!
SHAK
CHI SAVED THE YARD!

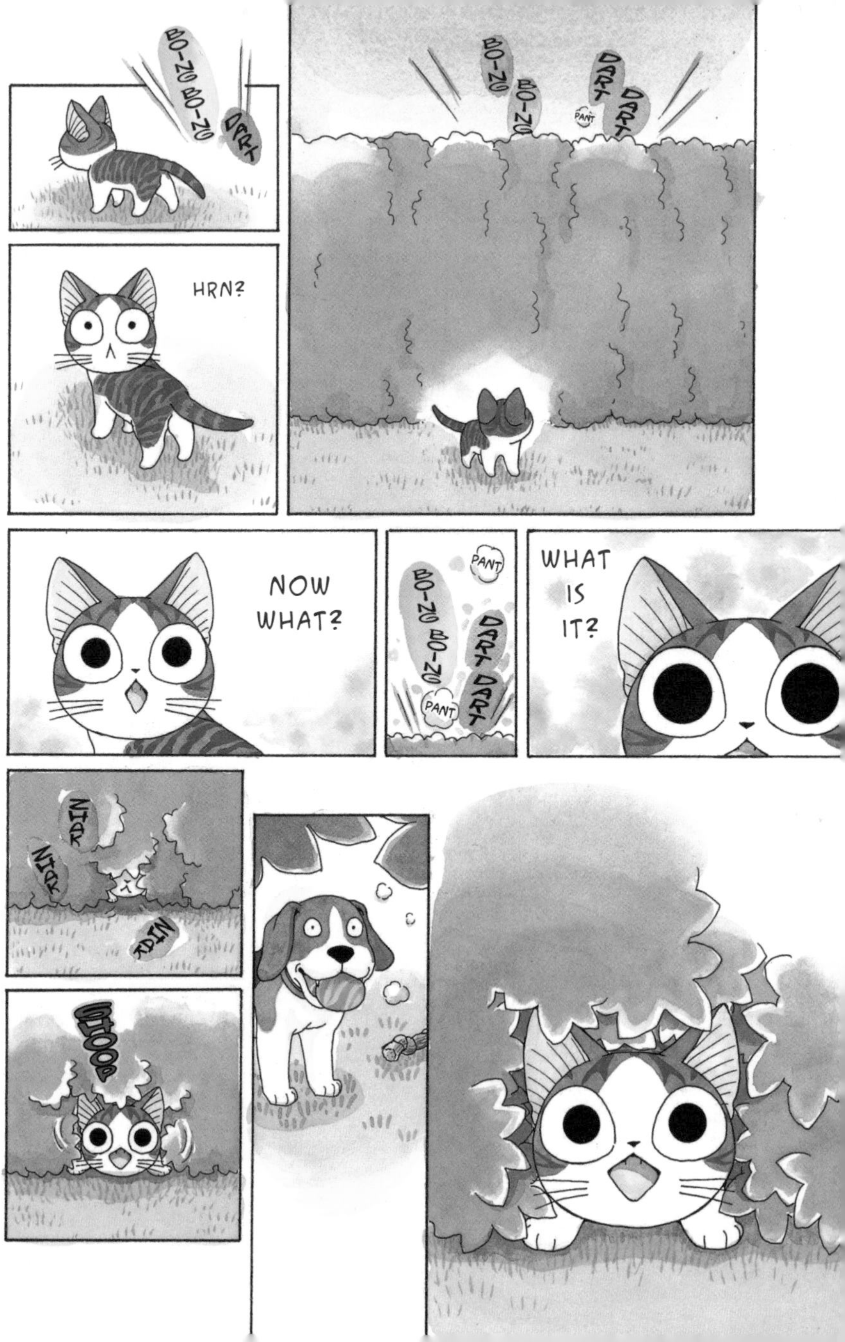

BOING BOING
DART
HRN?
BOING BOING
PANT
DART DART
NOW WHAT?
PANT
BOING BOING
PANT
DART DART
WHAT IS IT?
SHOOP

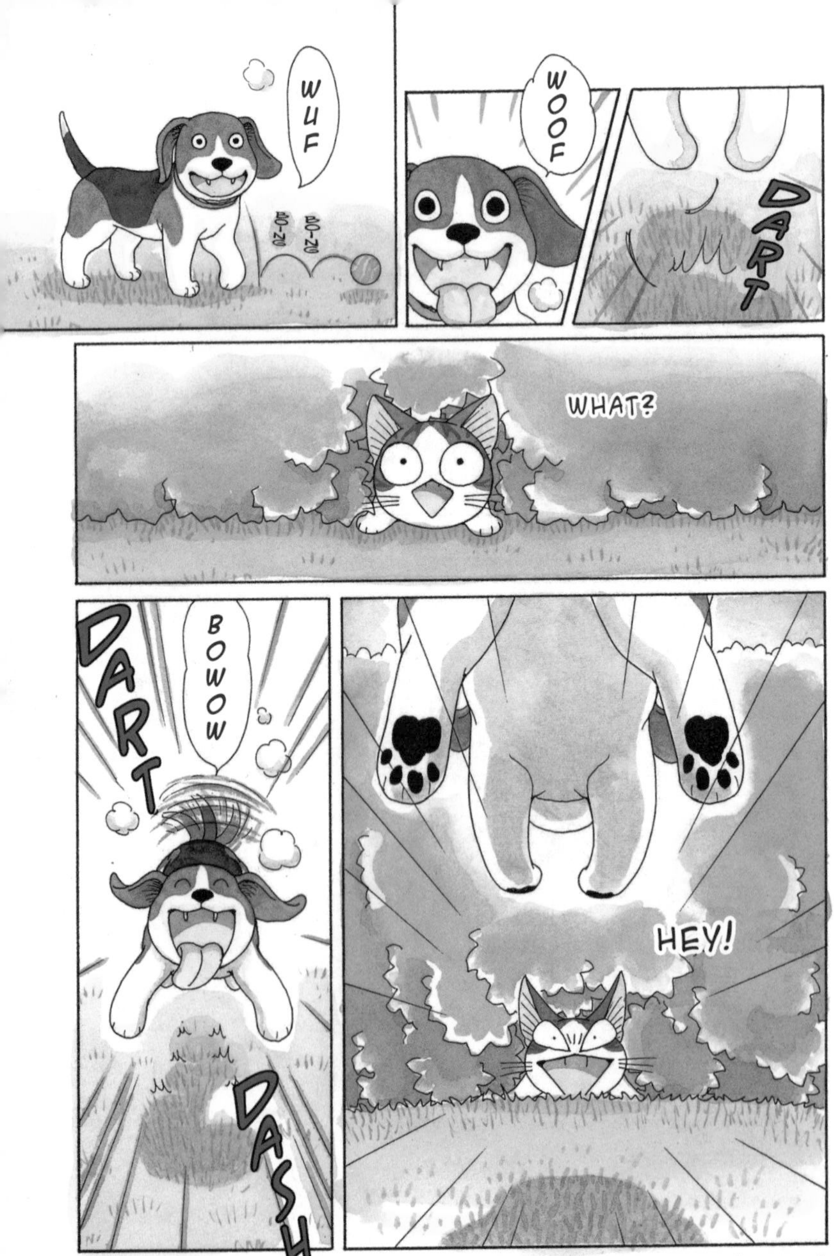
WUF
BOING BOING
WOOF
DART
WHAT?
DART
BOWOW
DASH
HEY!

the end

homemade 70: a cat figures out

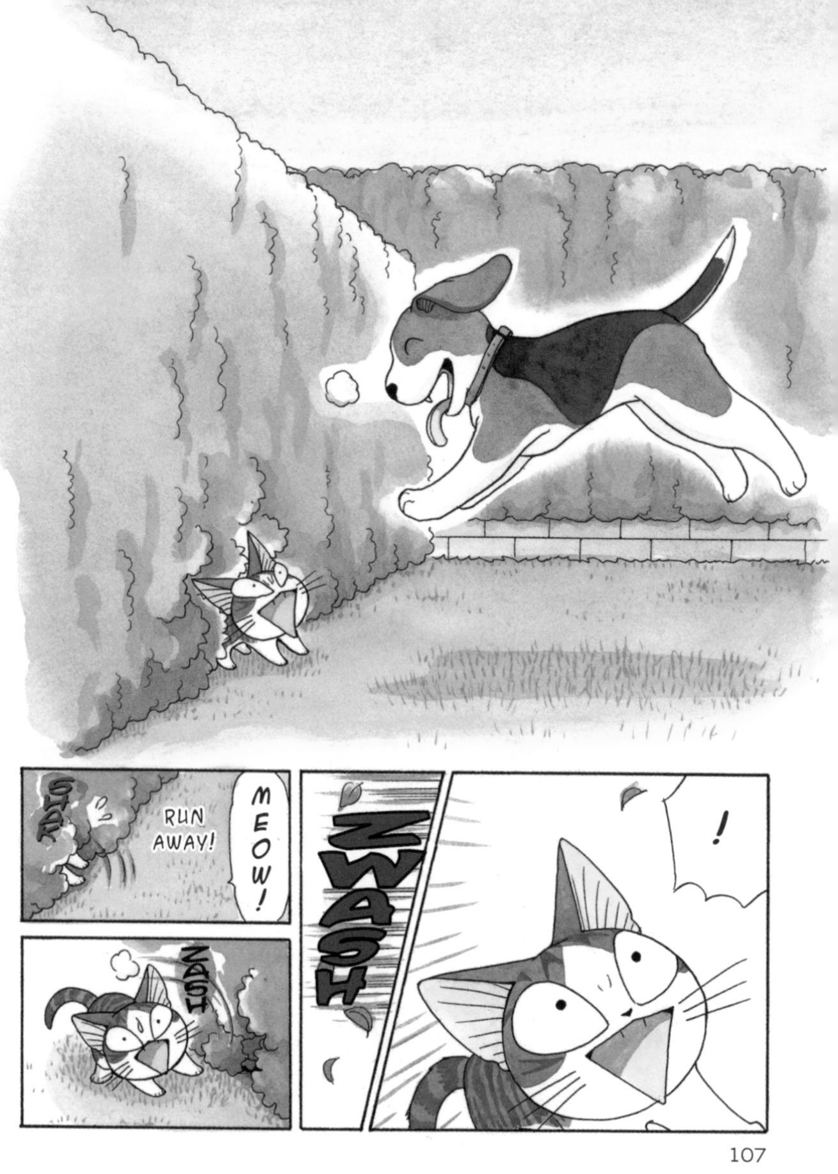
RUN AWAY!
MEOW!
ZWASH
ZWASH
!

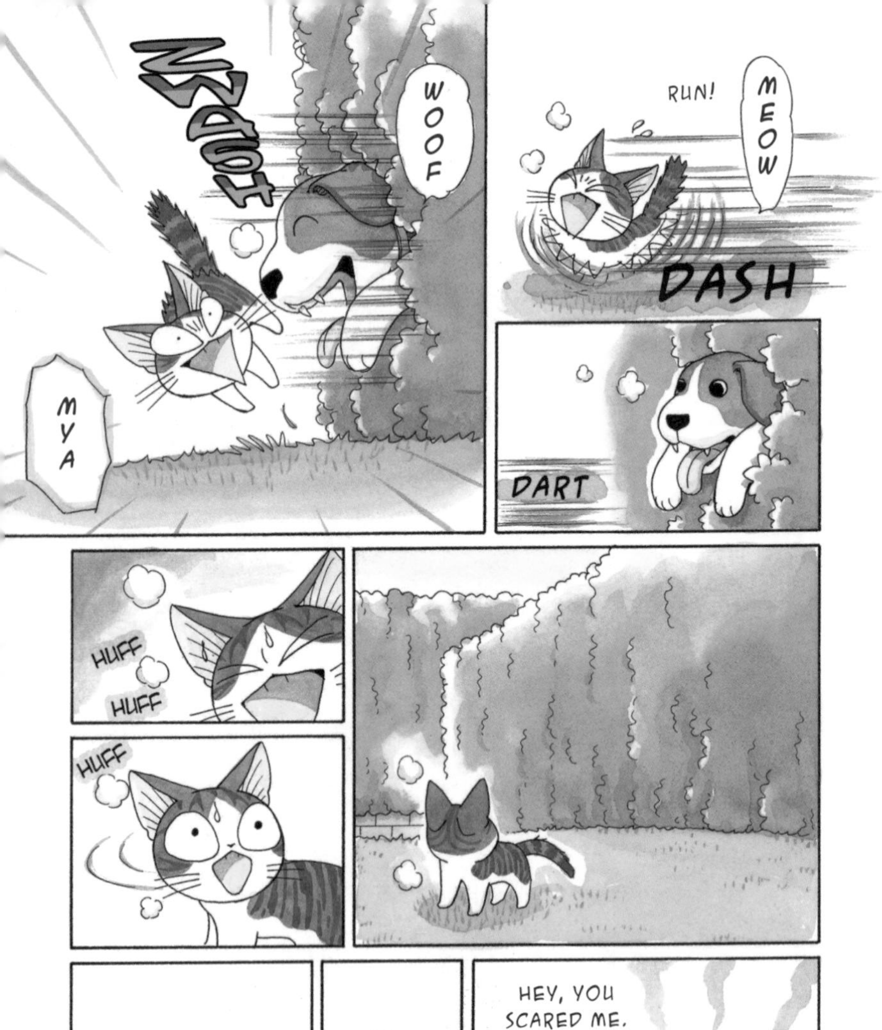
HOOSH
WOOF
MYA
RUN!
MEOW
DASH
DART
HUFF
HUFF
HUFF
HA
HEY, YOU SCARED ME.

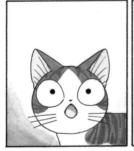

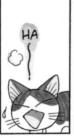

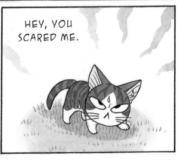

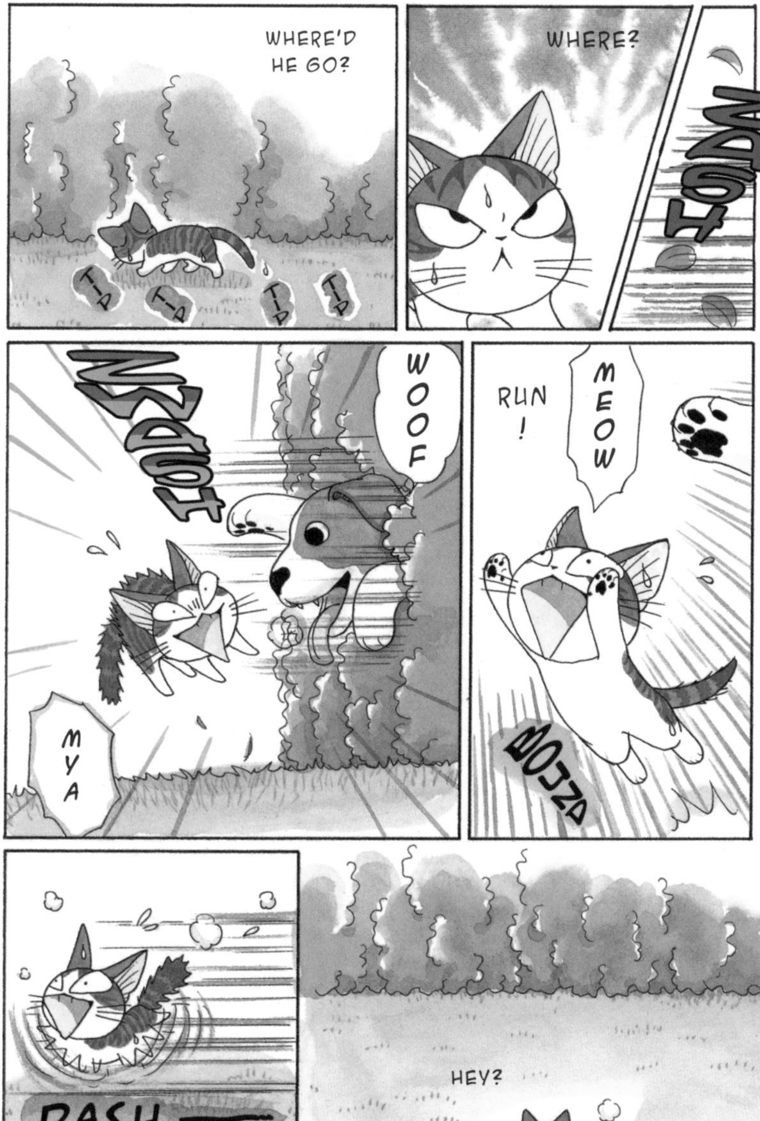
WHERE'D HE GO?
WHERE?
WHOOSH
WOOF
MYA
RUN!
MEOW
DASH
HEY?

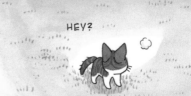

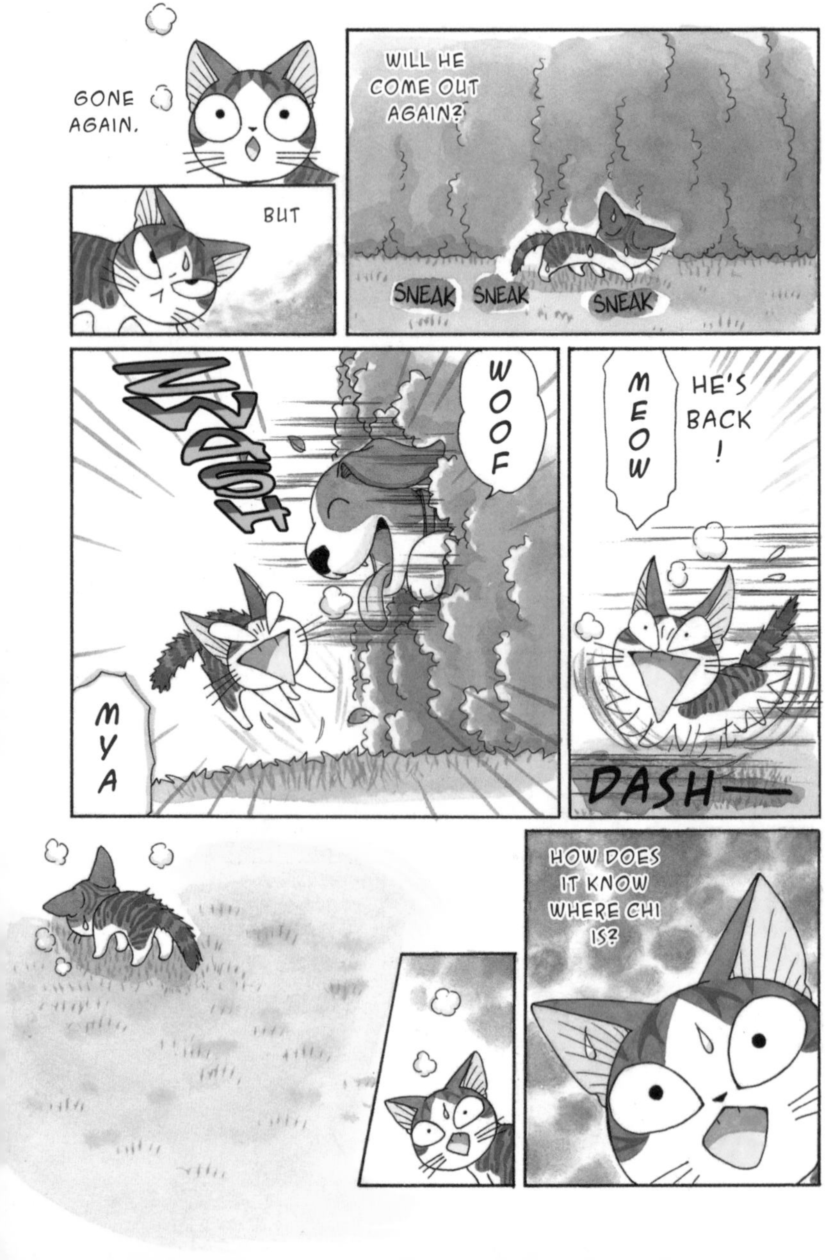

GONE AGAIN.
BUT
WILL HE COME OUT AGAIN?
SNEAK
SNEAK
SNEAK
MYA
WOOF
MEOW
HE'S BACK!
DASH—
HOW DOES IT KNOW WHERE CHI IS?

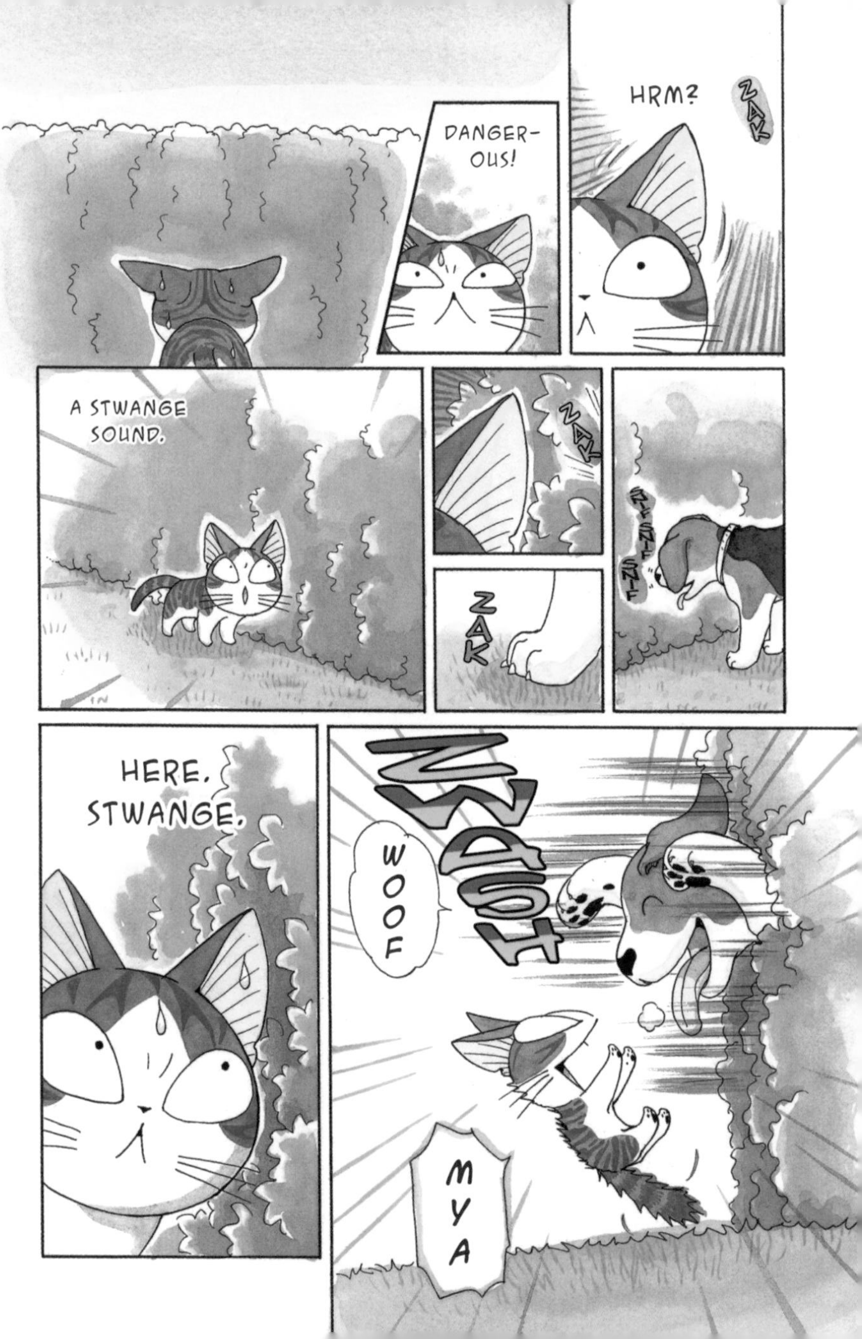
DANGER-
OUS!
HRM?
ZAK
A STWANGE
SOUND.
ZAK
ZAK
SNIF SNIF
SNIF
HERE.
STWANGE.
WOOF
FOOSH
MYA

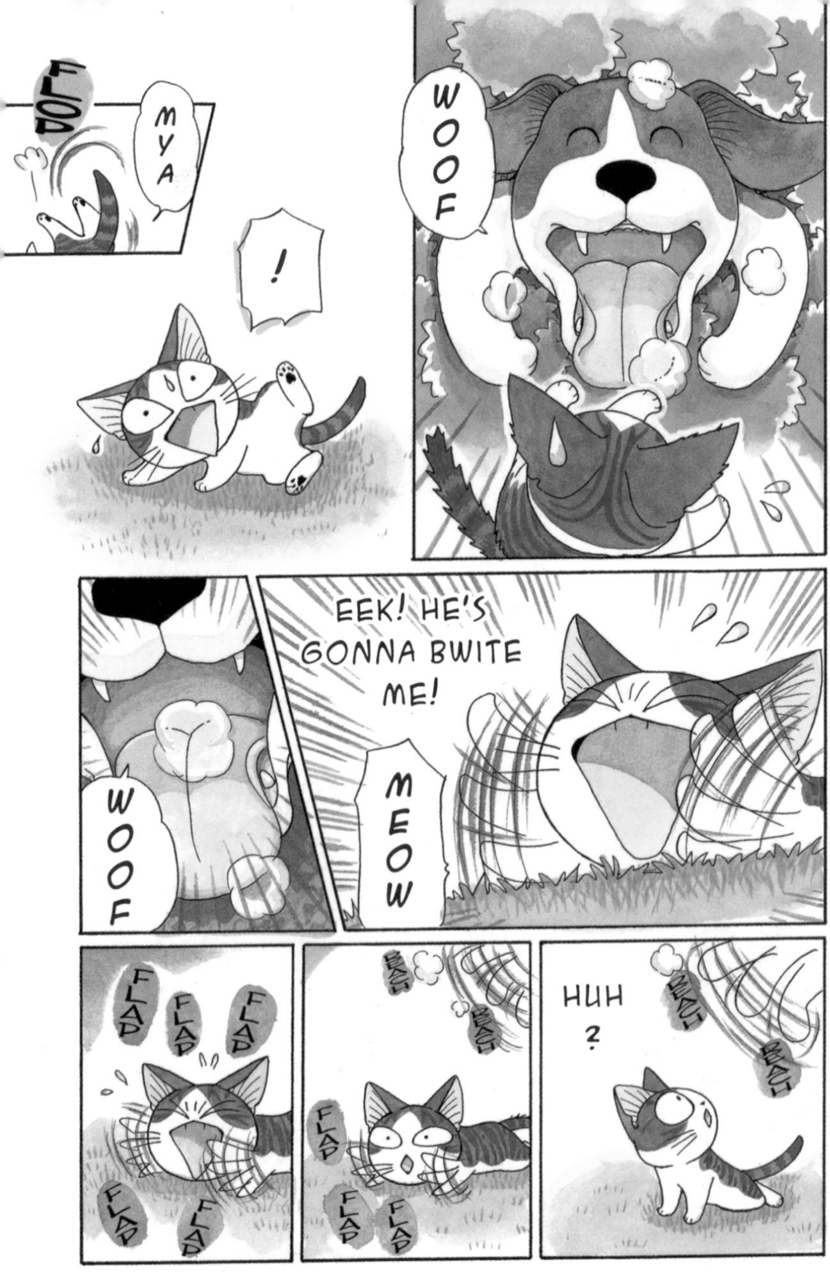
FLOP
MYA
!
WOOF
WOOF
EEK! HE'S GONNA BWITE ME!
MEOW
FLAP
FLAP
FLAP
FLAP
FLAP
FLAP
FLAP
FLAP
HUH?

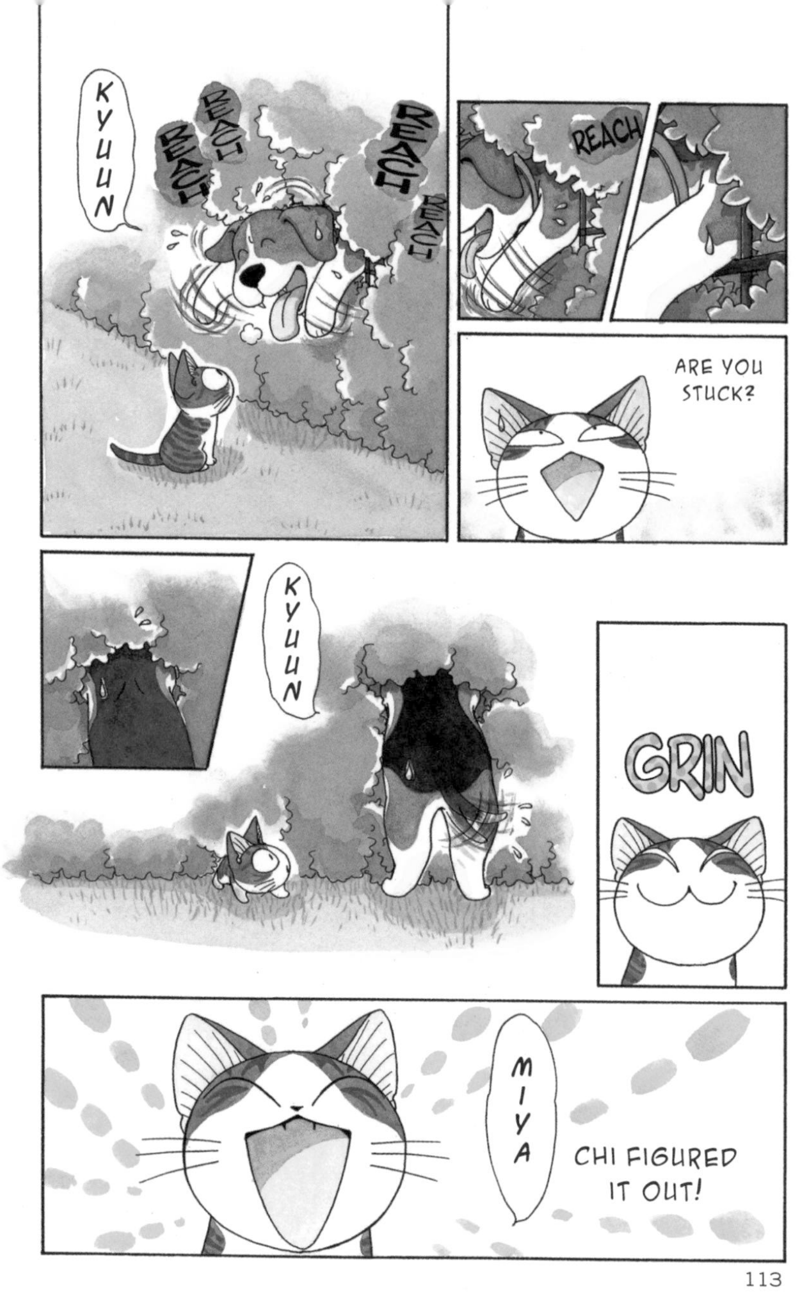
KYUUN
REACH
REACH
REACH
REACH
REACH
ARE YOU STUCK?
KYUUN
GRIN
MIYA
CHI FIGURED IT OUT!

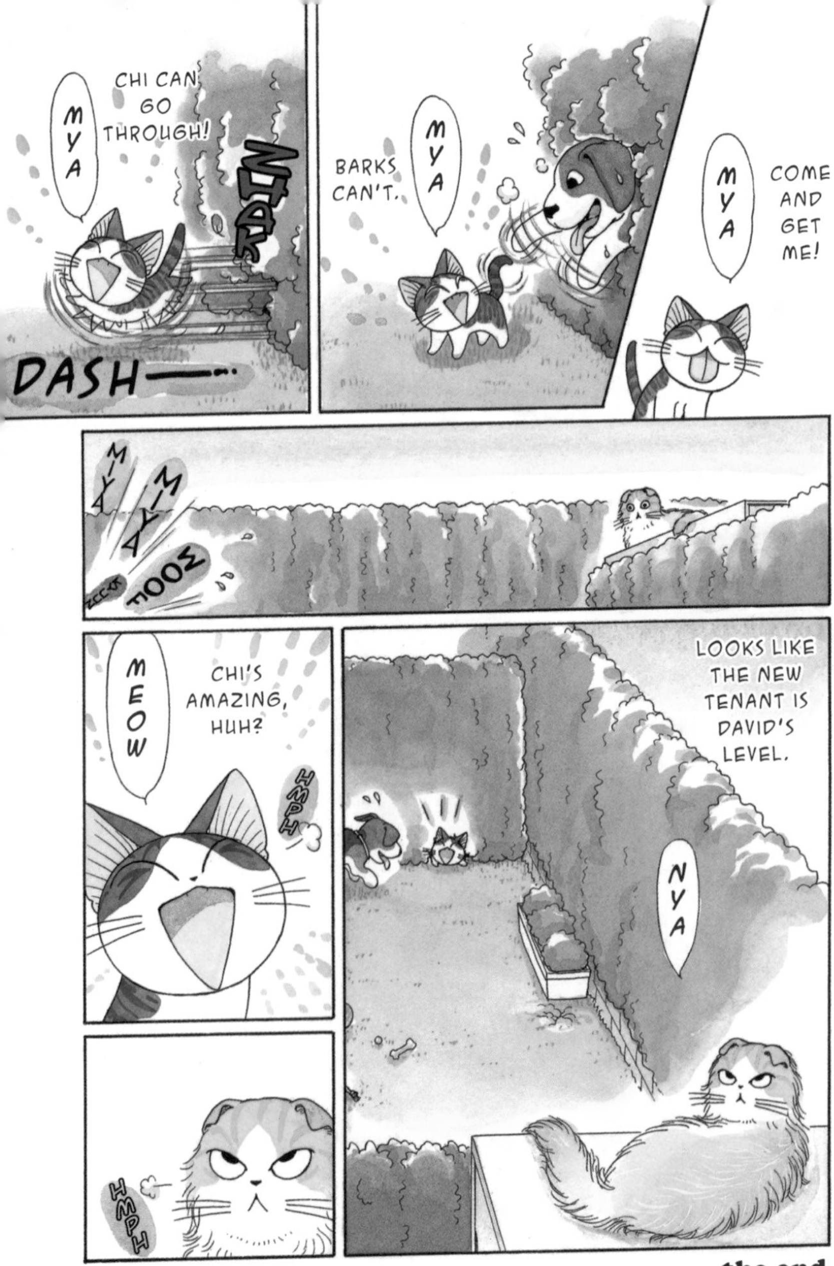
MYA
CHI CAN GO THROUGH!
THWAK
DASH—
BARKS CAN'T.
MYA
MYA
COME AND GET ME!
MIYA
MIYA
WOOF
MEOW
CHI'S AMAZING, HUH?
HMPH
LOOKS LIKE THE NEW TENANT IS DAVID'S LEVEL.
NYA
HMPH

the end

homemade 71: a cat hides out

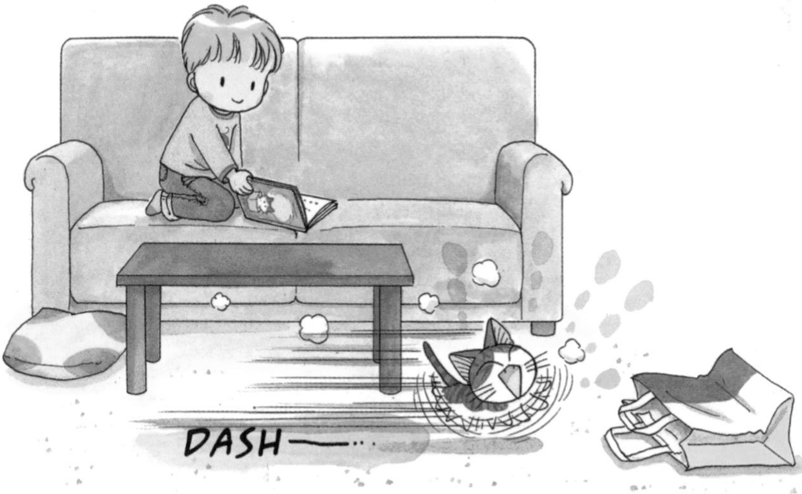
DASH—...

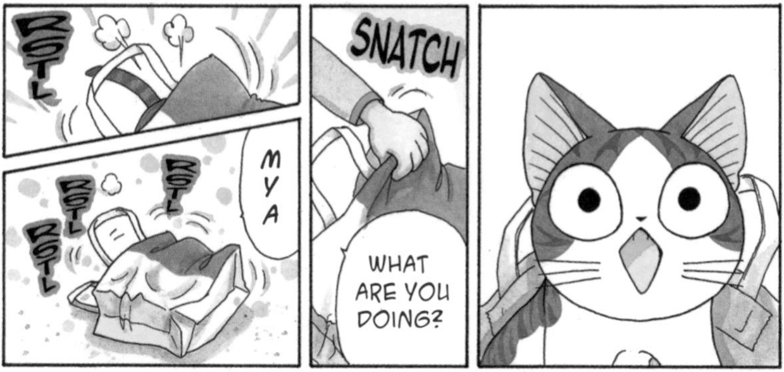
RSTL
RSTL
RSTL
RSTL
MYA
SNATCH
WHAT ARE YOU DOING?

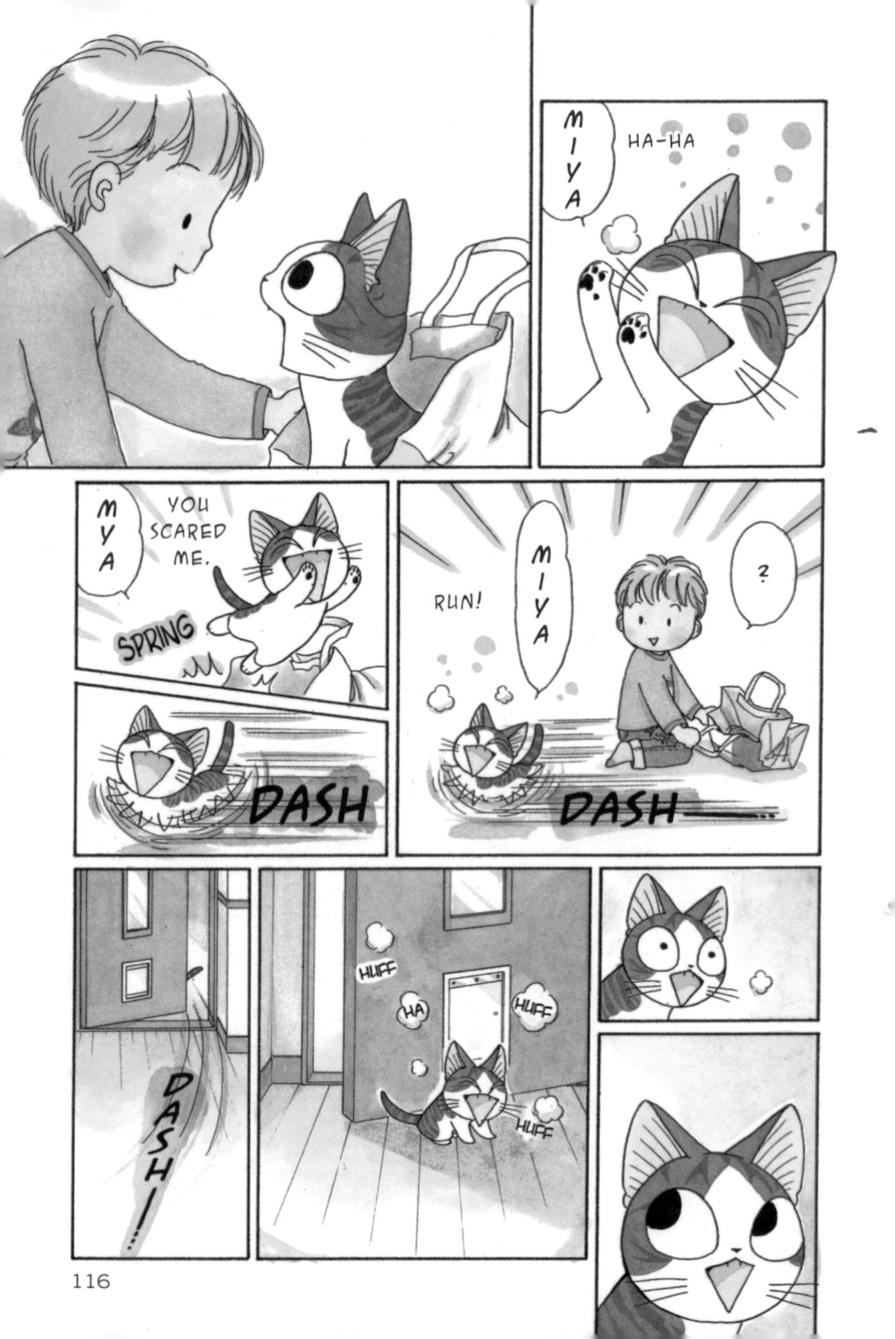
MIYA
HA-HA
MYA
YOU SCARED ME.
SPRING
RUN!
MIYA
?
DASH
DASH
DASH!
HUFF
HA
HUFF
HUFF

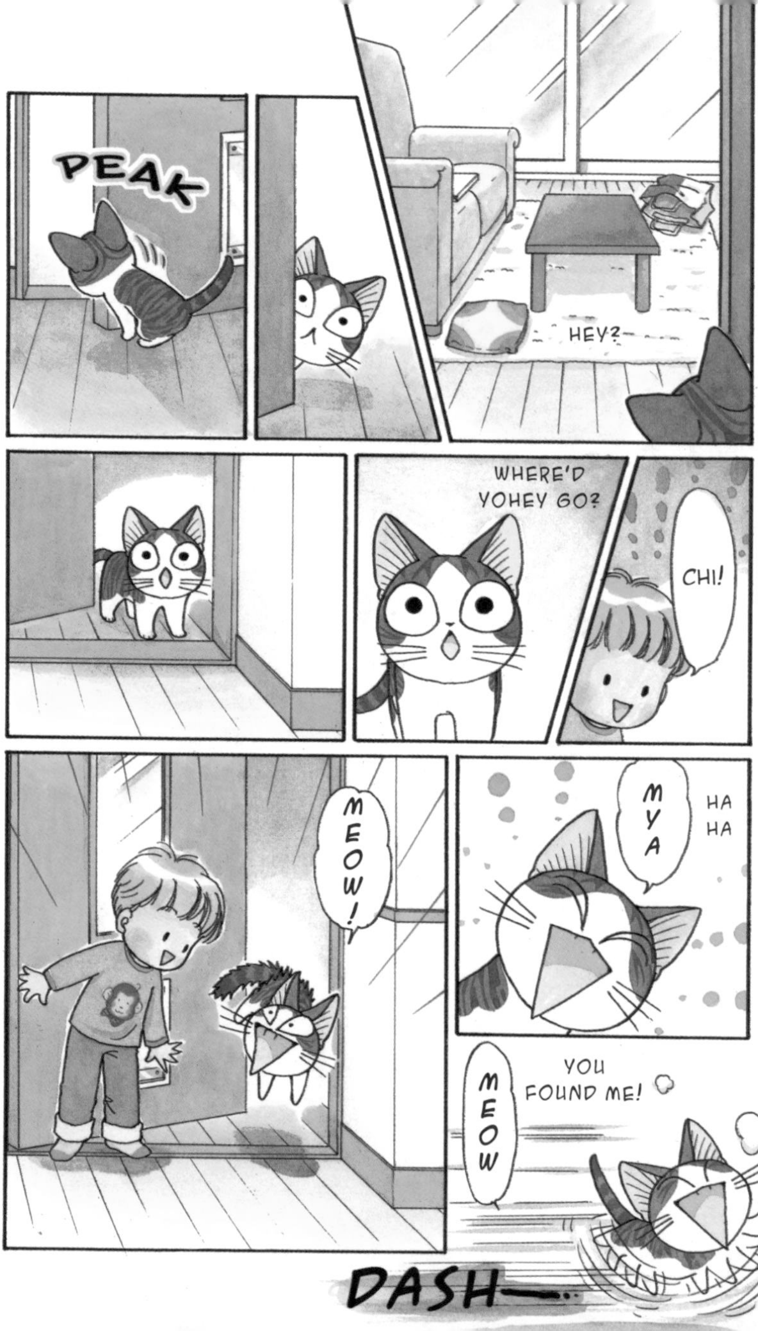
PEAK
HEY?
WHERE'D YOHEY GO?
CHI!
MEOW!
MYA
HA HA
YOU FOUND ME!
MEOW
DASH

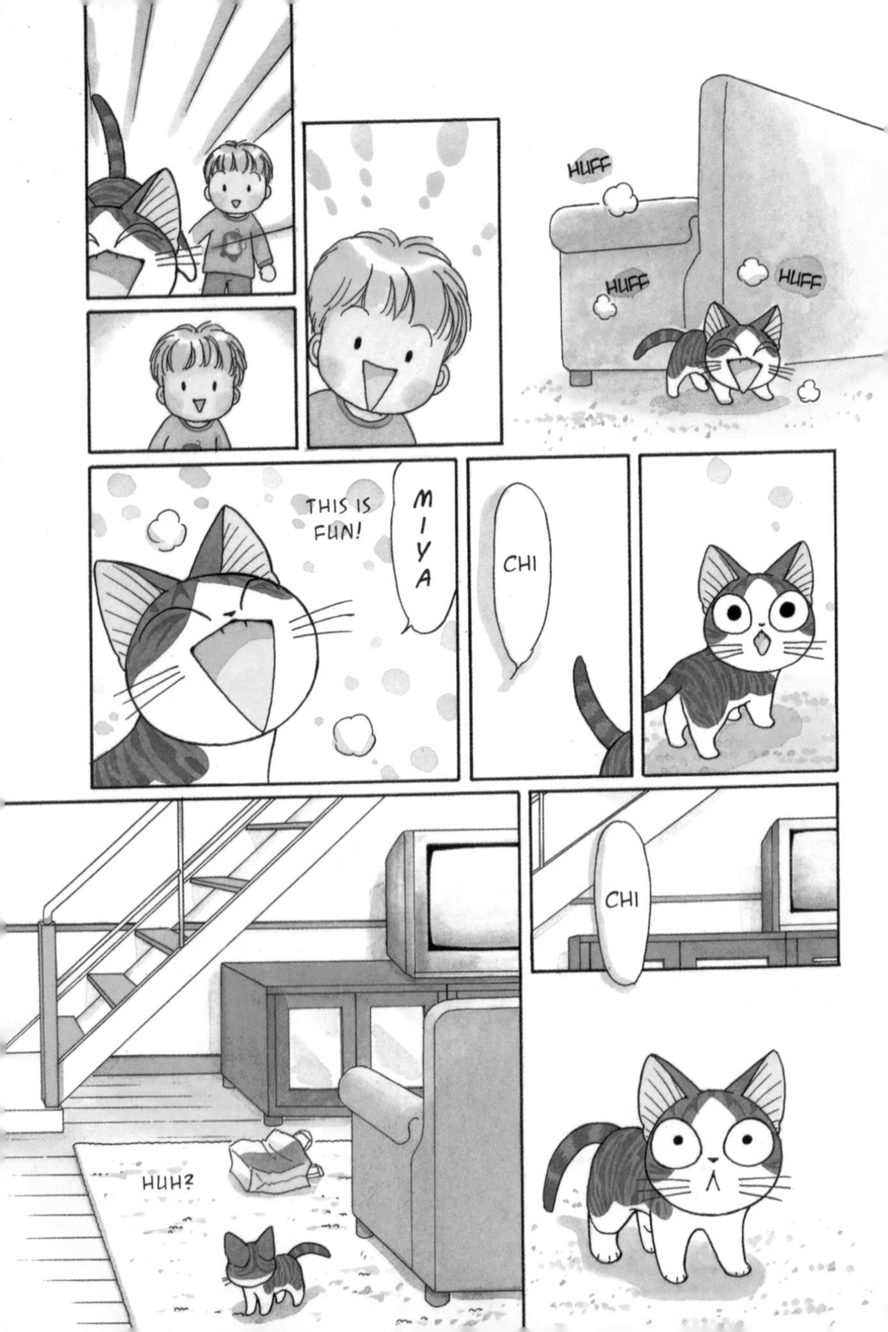
HUFF
HUFF
HUFF
THIS IS FUN!
MIYA
CHI
HUH?
CHI

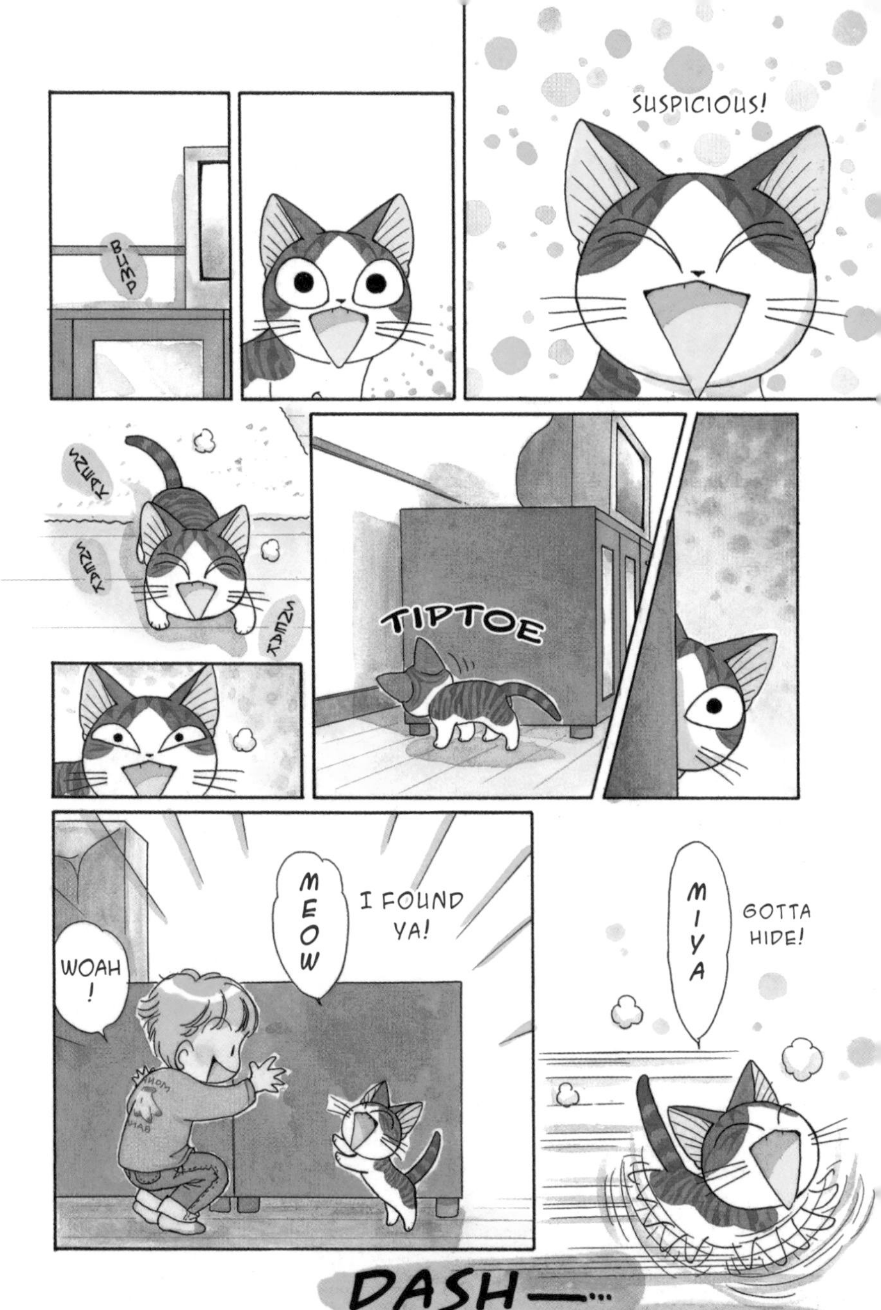
BUMP
SUSPICIOUS!
SNEAK
SNEAK
SNEAK
TIPTOE
WOAH!
MEOW
I FOUND YA!
MIYA
GOTTA HIDE!
DASH—...

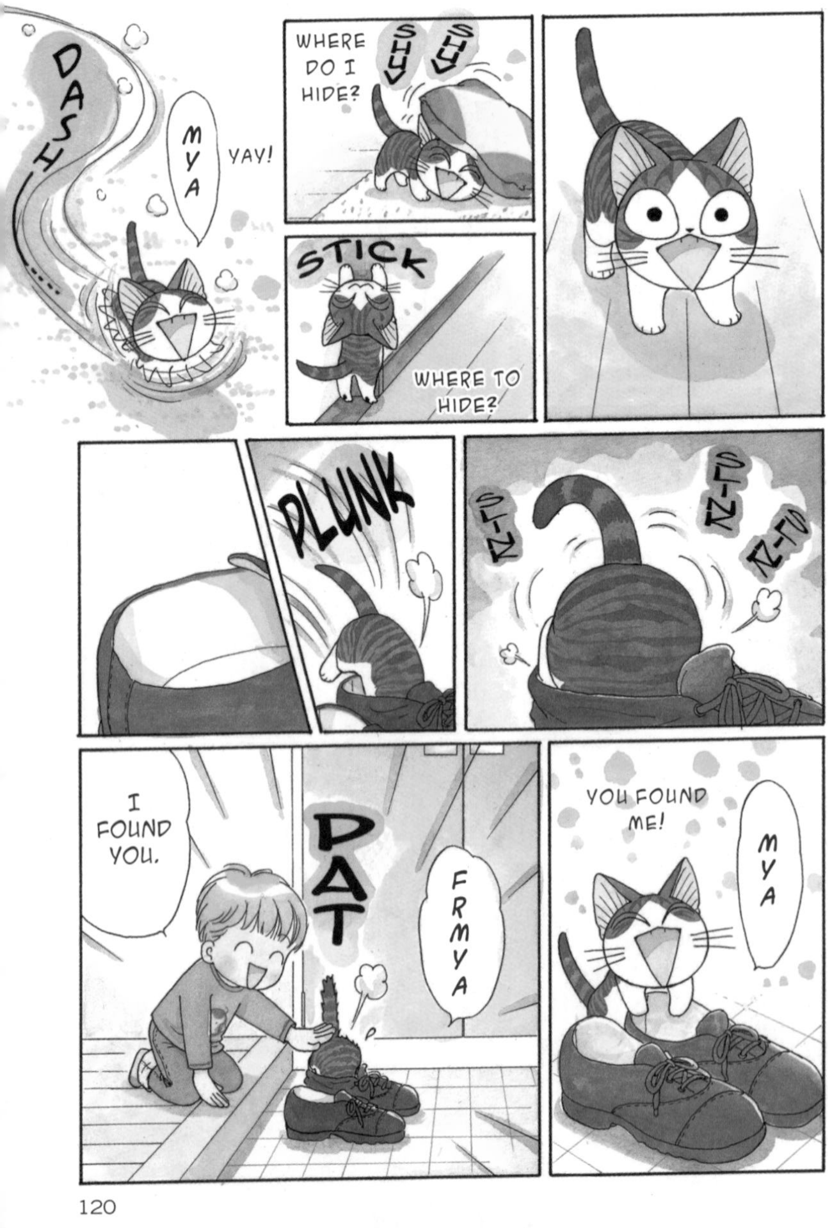
DASH
MYA
YAY!
WHERE DO I HIDE?
SHUV
SHUV
STICK
WHERE TO HIDE?
PLUNK
SINK
SINK
SINK
I FOUND YOU.
PAT
FRMYA
YOU FOUND ME!
MYA

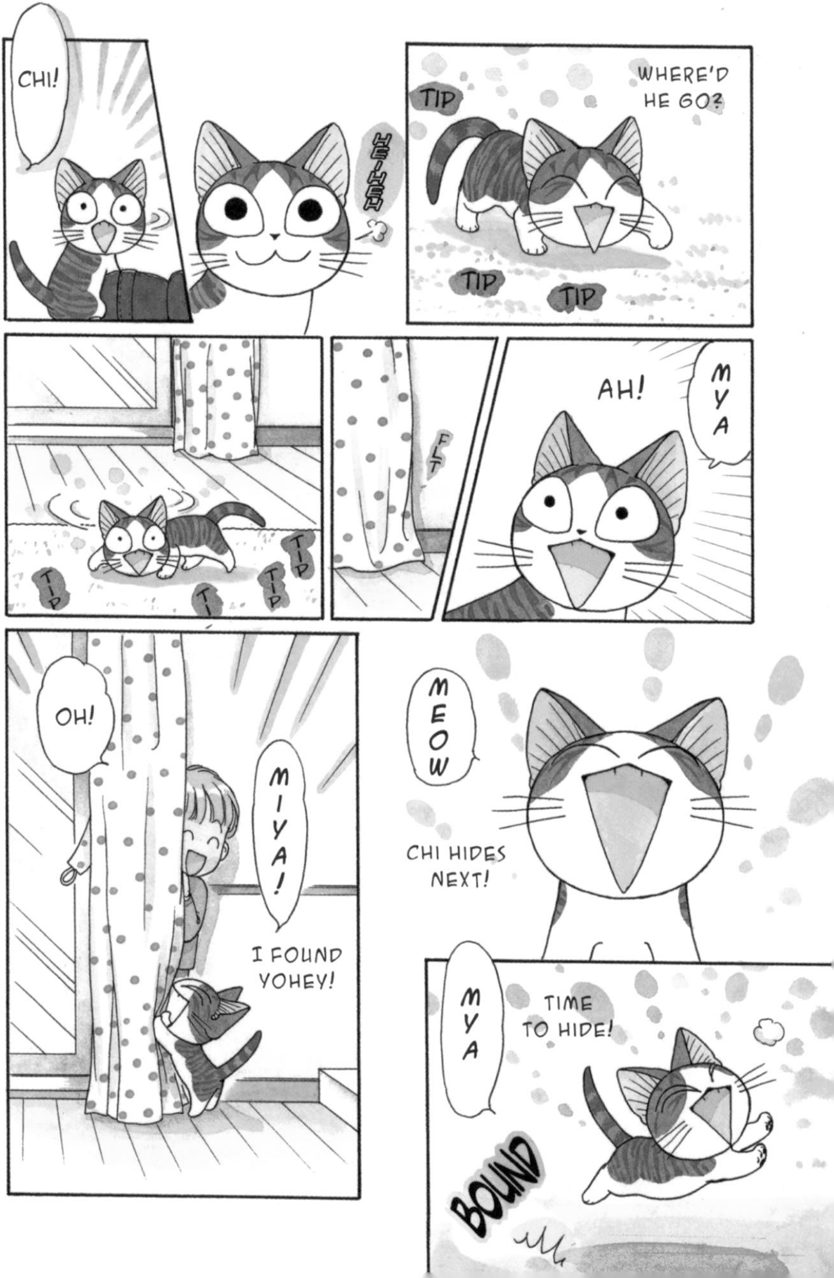
CHI!
HE-HEH
WHERE'D HE GO?
TIP
TIP
TIP
TIP
TIP
TIP
FLT
AH!
MYA
OH!
MIYA!
I FOUND YOHEY!
MEOW
CHI HIDES NEXT!
MYA
TIME TO HIDE!
BOUND

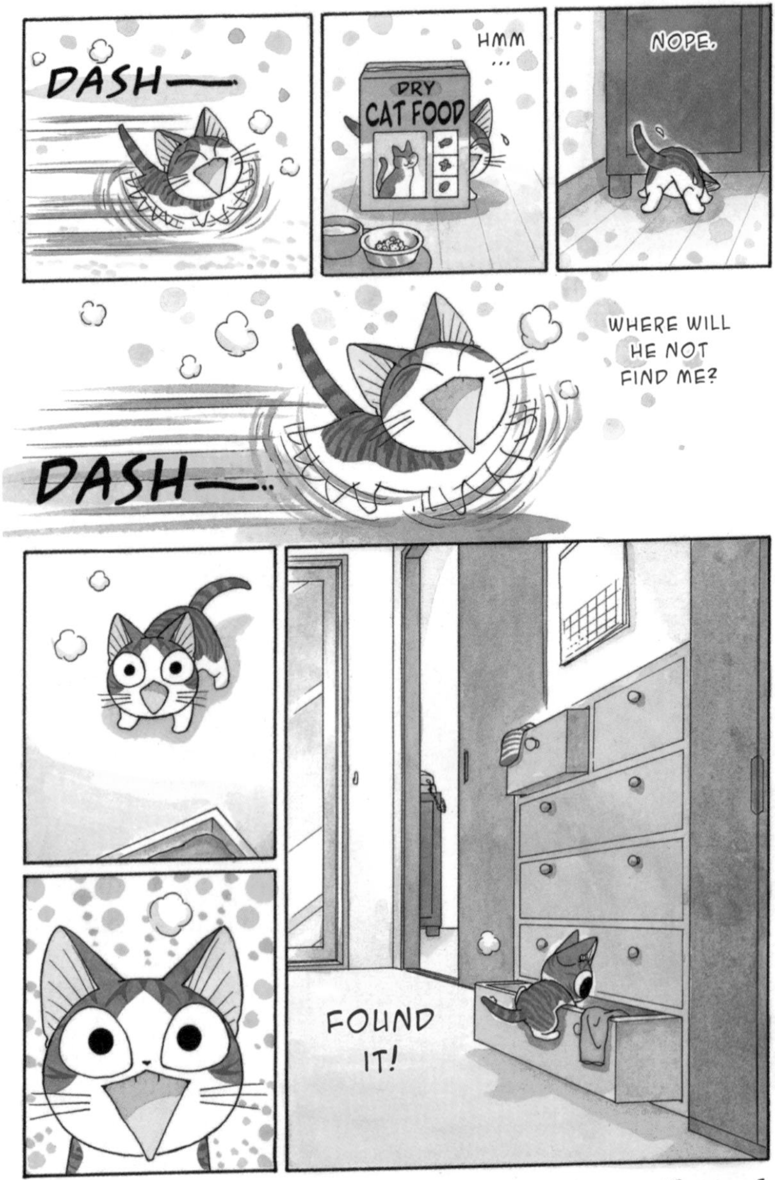
DASH—
DRY CAT FOOD
HMM …
NOPE.
WHERE WILL HE NOT FIND ME?
DASH—..
FOUND IT!

the end

homemade 72: a cat hides out some more

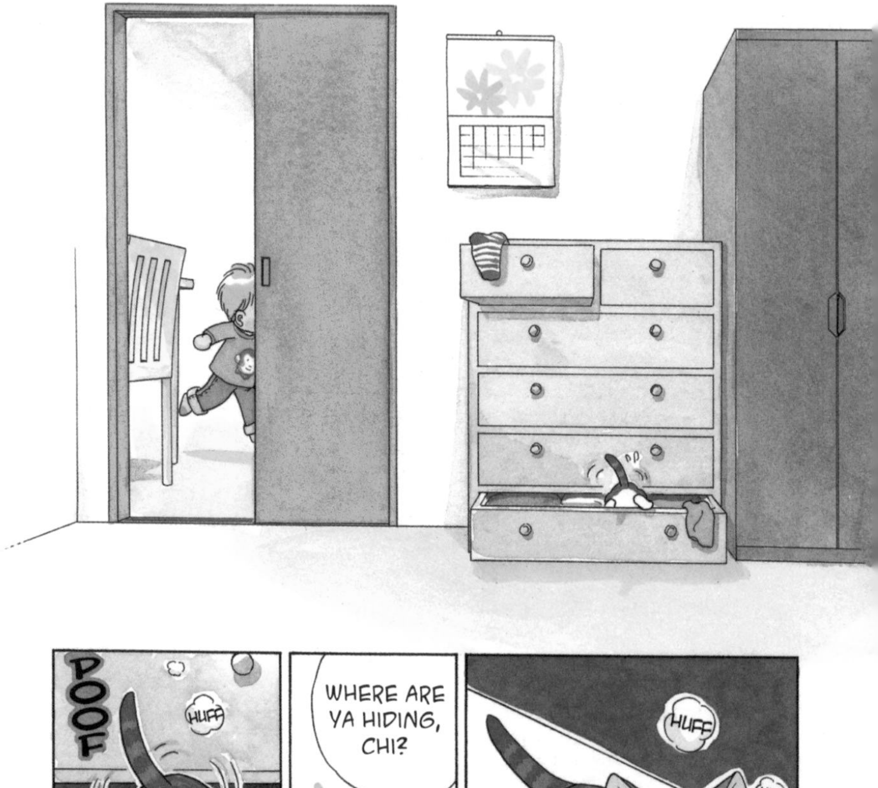

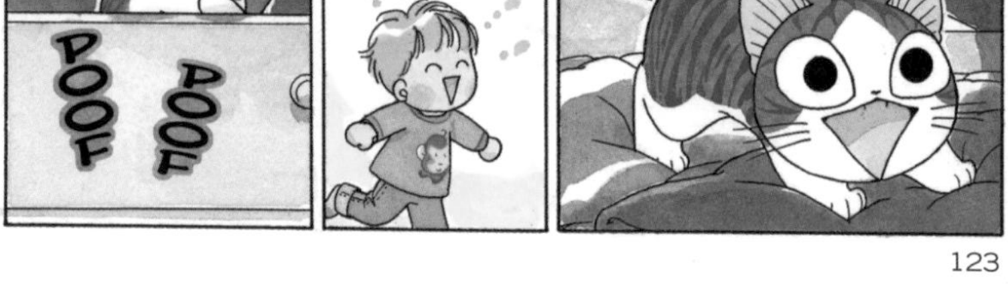
POOF
HUFF
POOF
POOF
WHERE ARE YA HIDING, CHI?
HUFF
HUFF

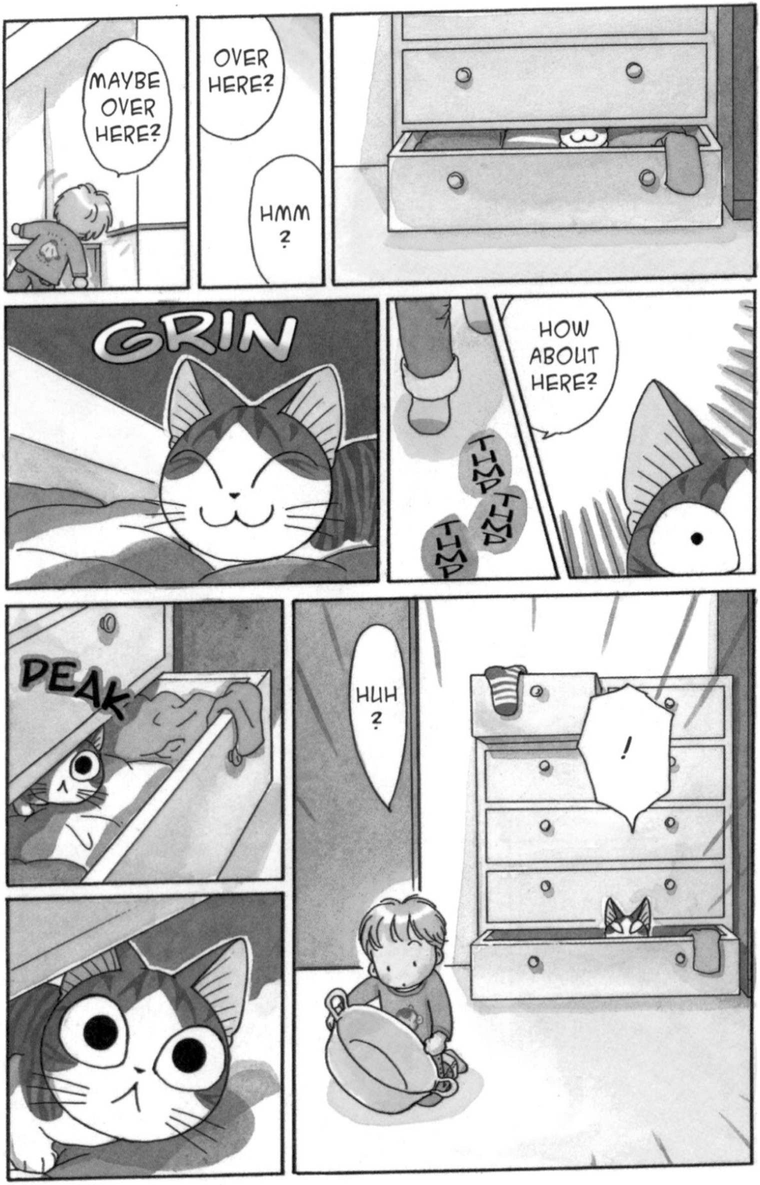
MAYBE OVER HERE?
OVER HERE?
HMM ?
GRIN
HOW ABOUT HERE?
THMP THMP THMP
PEAK
HUH ?
!

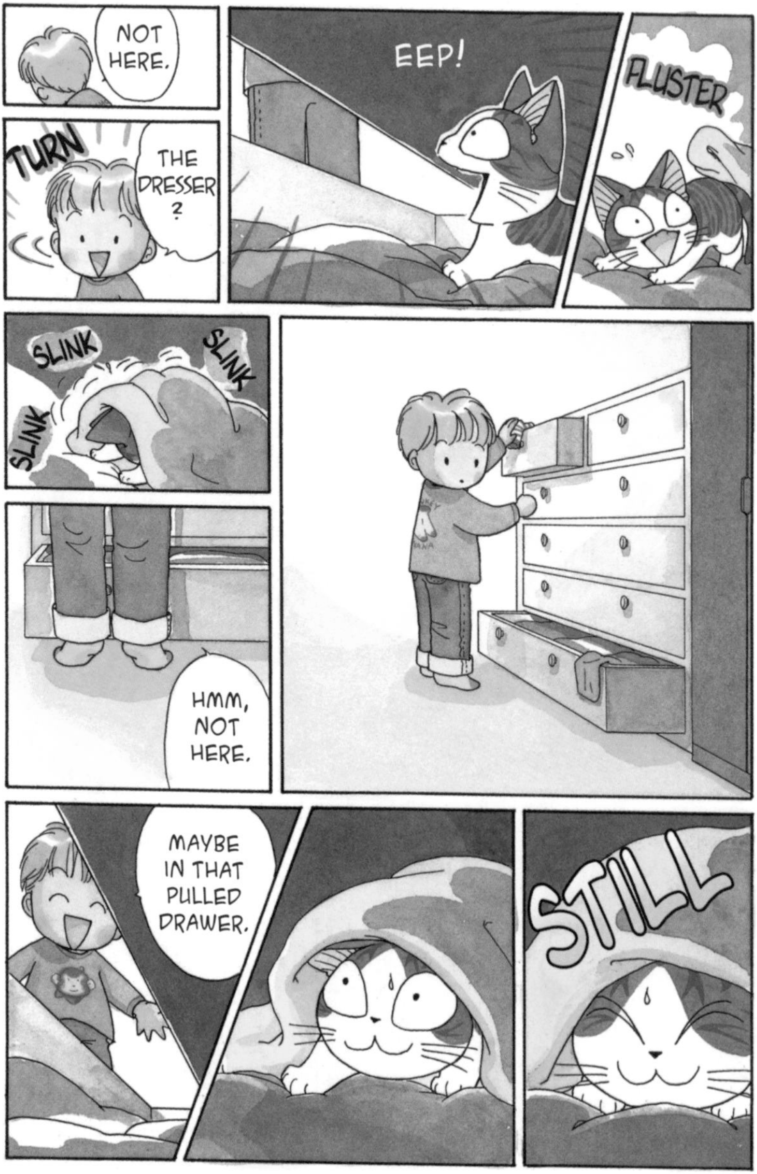
NOT HERE.
EEP!
FLUSTER
TURN
THE DRESSER?
SLINK
SLINK
SLINK
HMM, NOT HERE.
MAYBE IN THAT PULLED DRAWER.
STILL

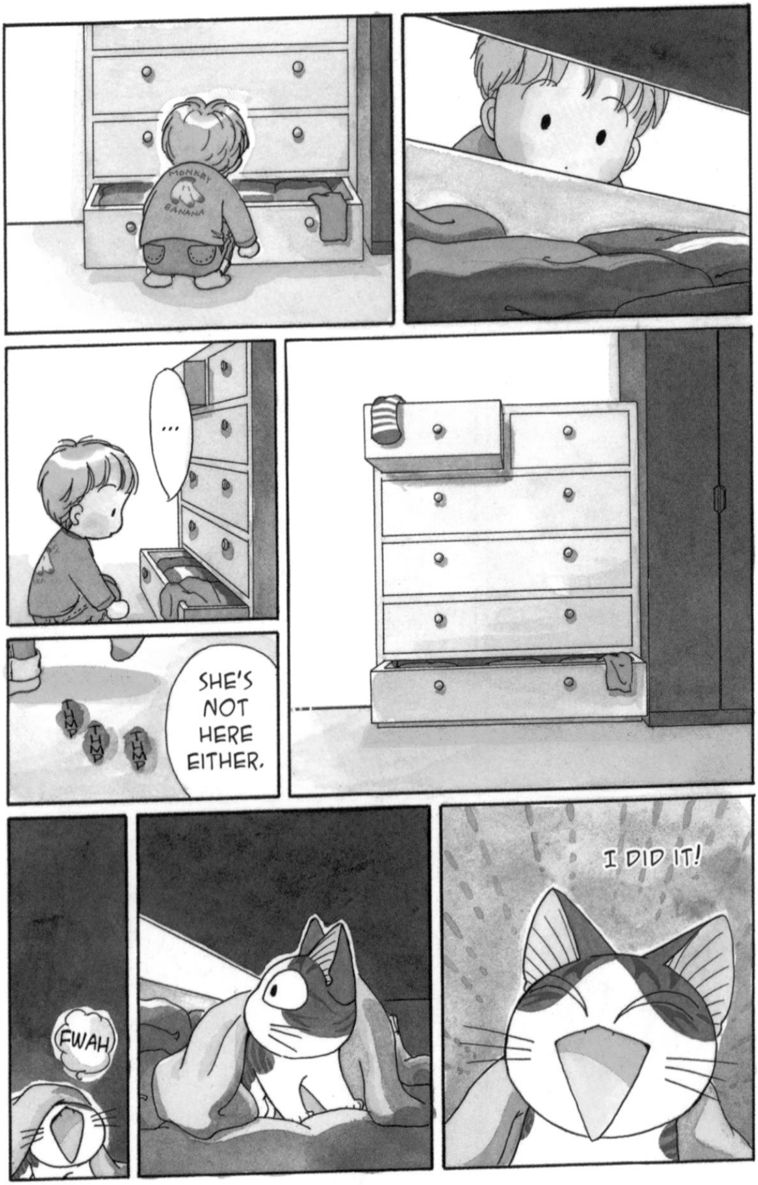
MONKEY
BANANA
...
THMP
THMP
THMP
SHE'S NOT HERE EITHER.
FWAH
I DID IT!

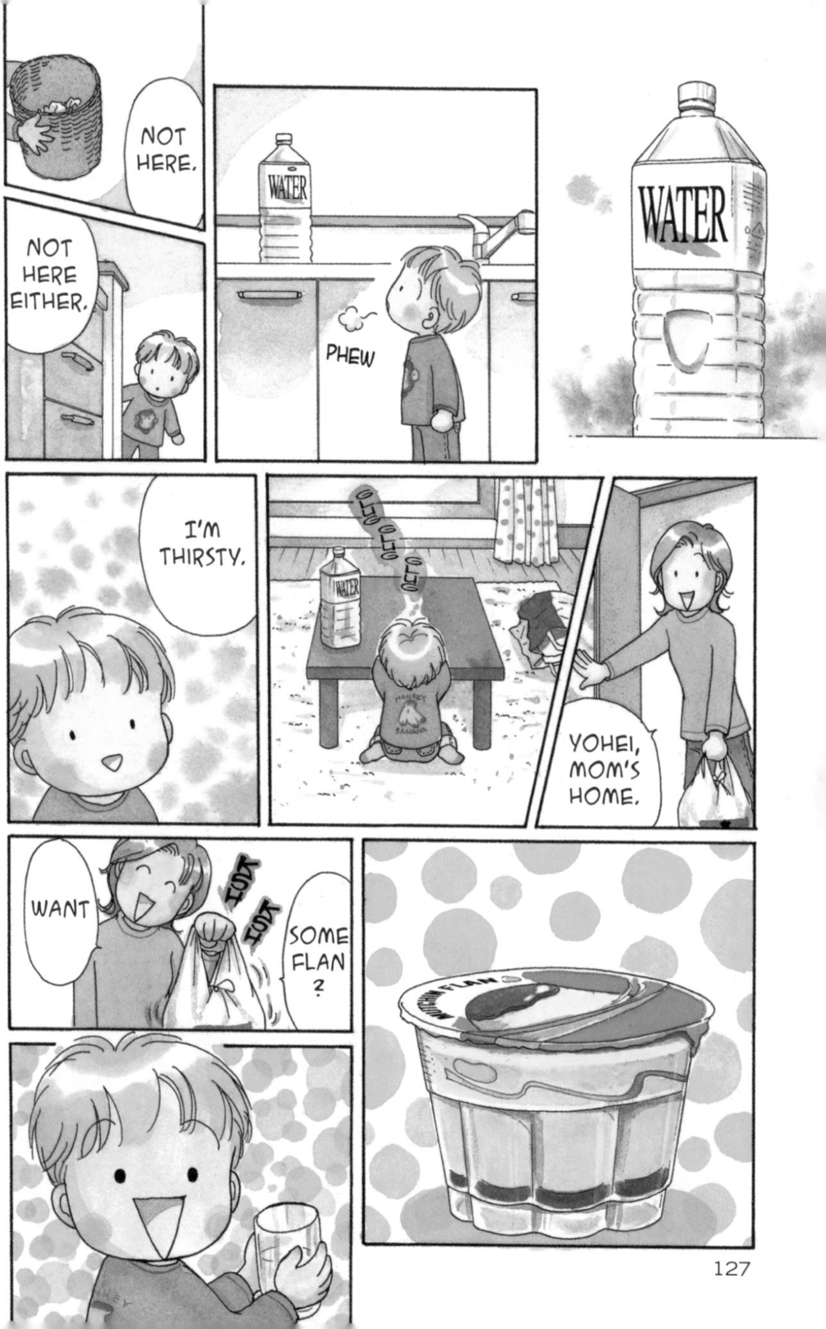
NOT HERE.
NOT HERE EITHER.
WATER
PHEW
WATER
I'M THIRSTY.
GLUG GLUG GLUG
WATER
YOHEI, MOM'S HOME.
WANT
SOME FLAN ?

IF I STAY HERE, I'LL WIN!

GRIN

DEFINITELY!

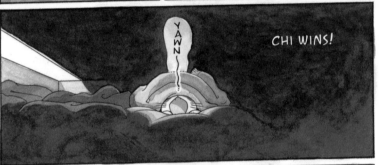
YAWN

CHI WINS!

HUP

HEY, NUDG SHUP

FALL-ING OUT.

LEFT OPEN. NUDG

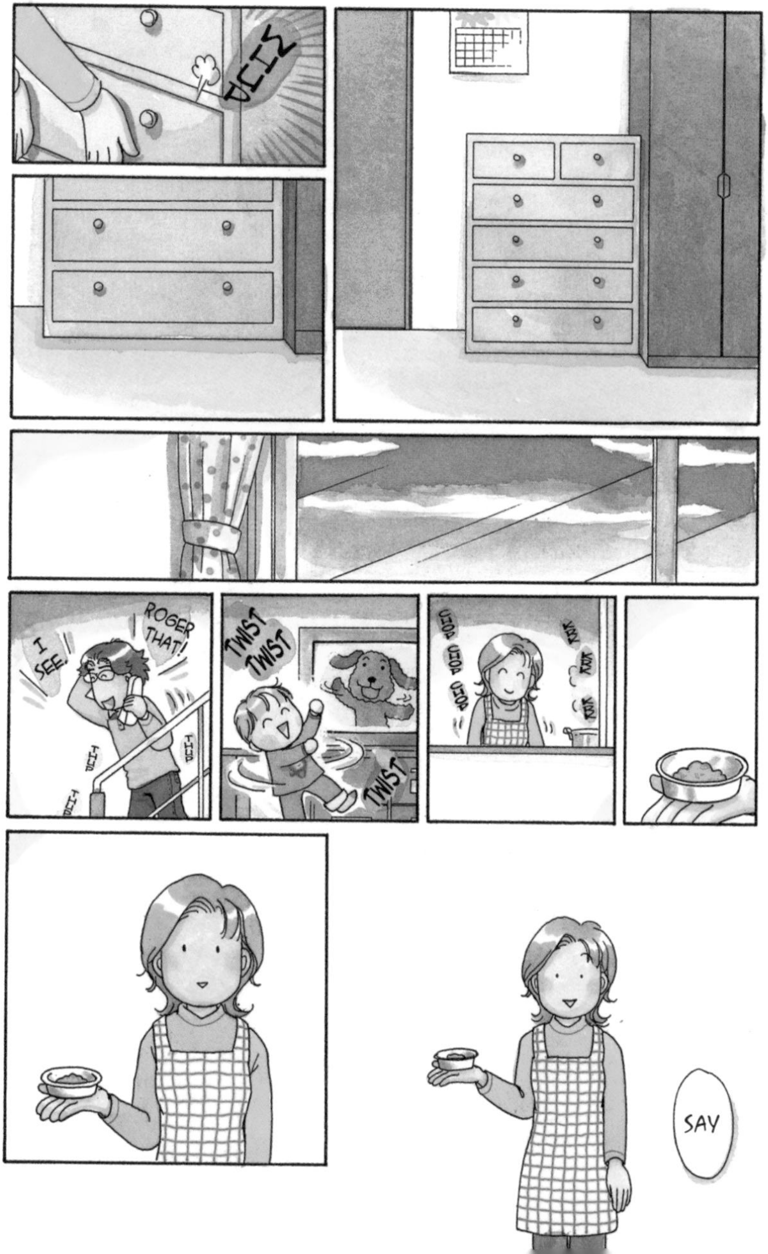
SLID
I SEE.
ROGER THAT!
THUD
THUD
THUD
TWIST TWIST
TWIST
CHOP CHOP CHOP
SAY

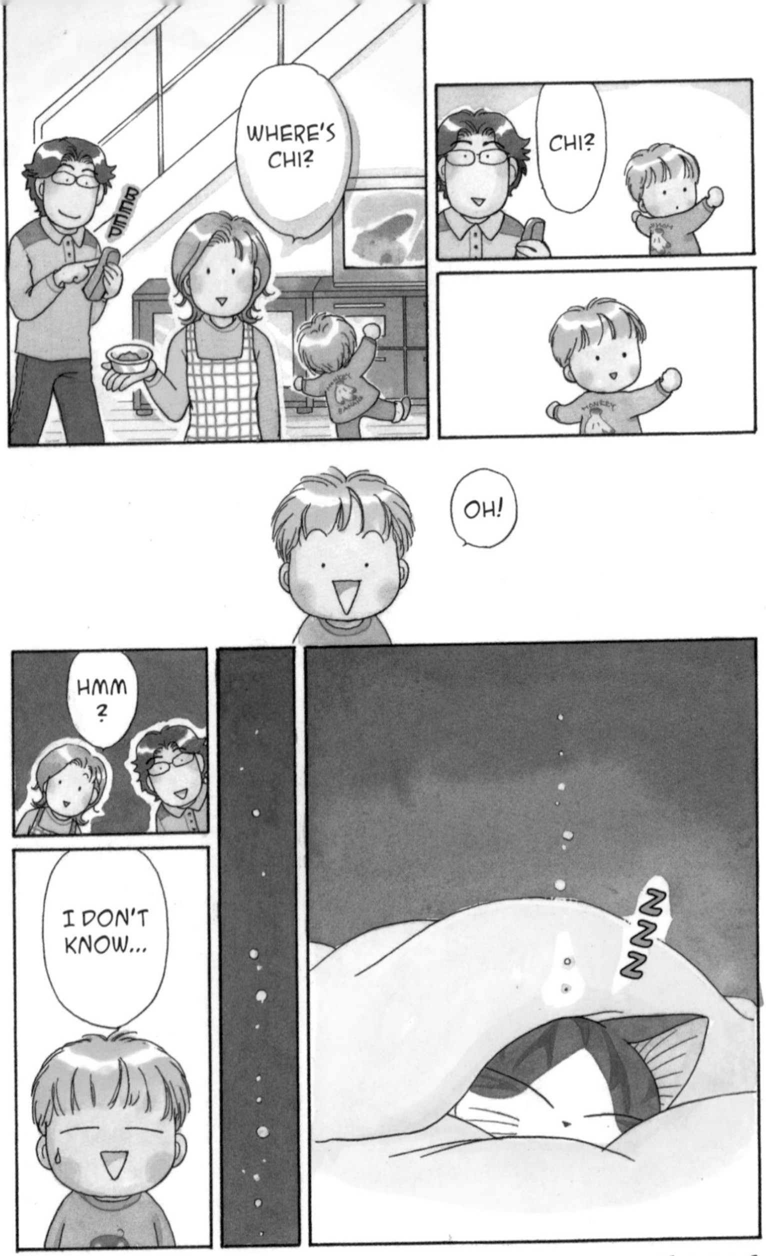
BEEP
WHERE'S CHI?
CHI?
OH!
HMM ?
I DON'T KNOW...
ZZZ

the end

homemade 73: a cat is sought

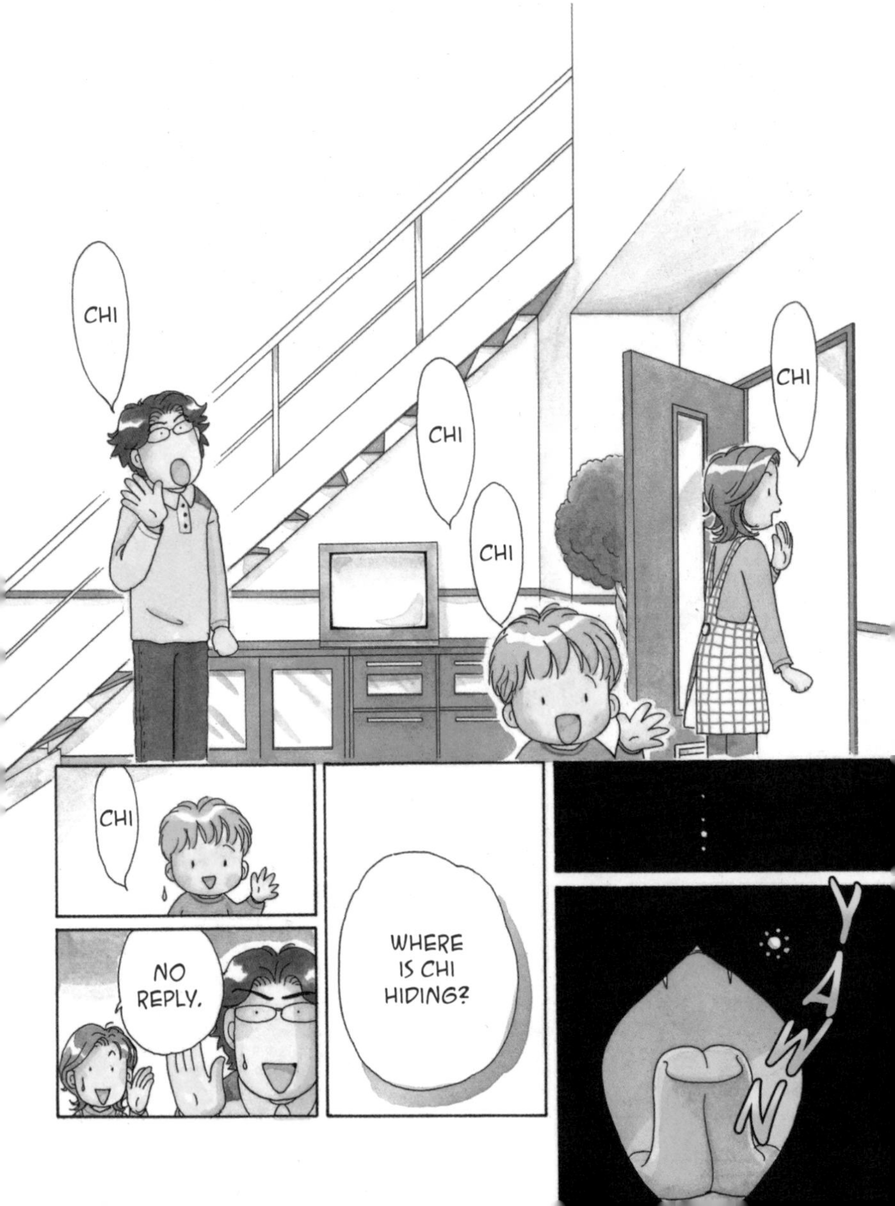
CHI
CHI
CHI
CHI
CHI
NO REPLY.
WHERE IS CHI HIDING?
...
YAWN

WHERE AM I?

AND WHAT WAS CHI DOING?

HUH

UM...

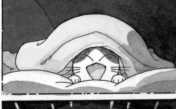

CALM DOWN AND THINK.

WHERE DOES CHI LIKE TO HIDE?

RIGHT!

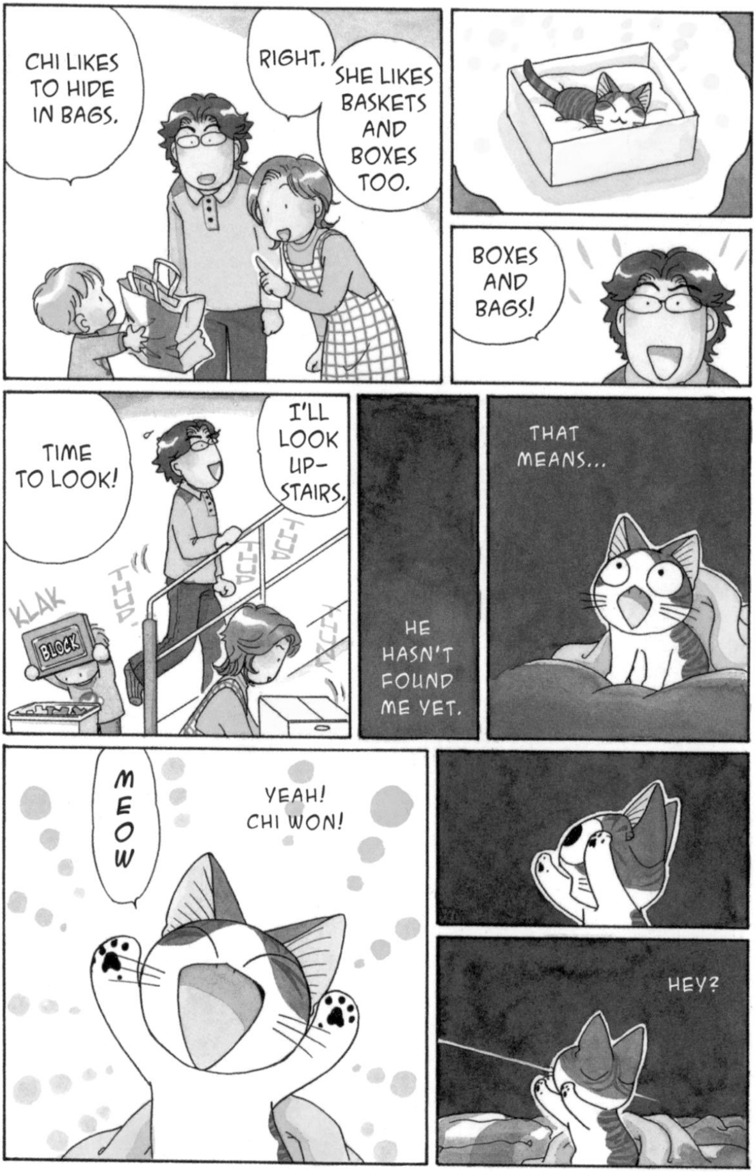
CHI LIKES TO HIDE IN BAGS.
RIGHT.
SHE LIKES BASKETS AND BOXES TOO.
BOXES AND BAGS!
TIME TO LOOK!
I'LL LOOK UP-STAIRS.
THUD
THUD
THUD
KLAK
BLOCK
THUD
HE HASN'T FOUND ME YET.
THAT MEANS...
MEOW
YEAH! CHI WON!
HEY?

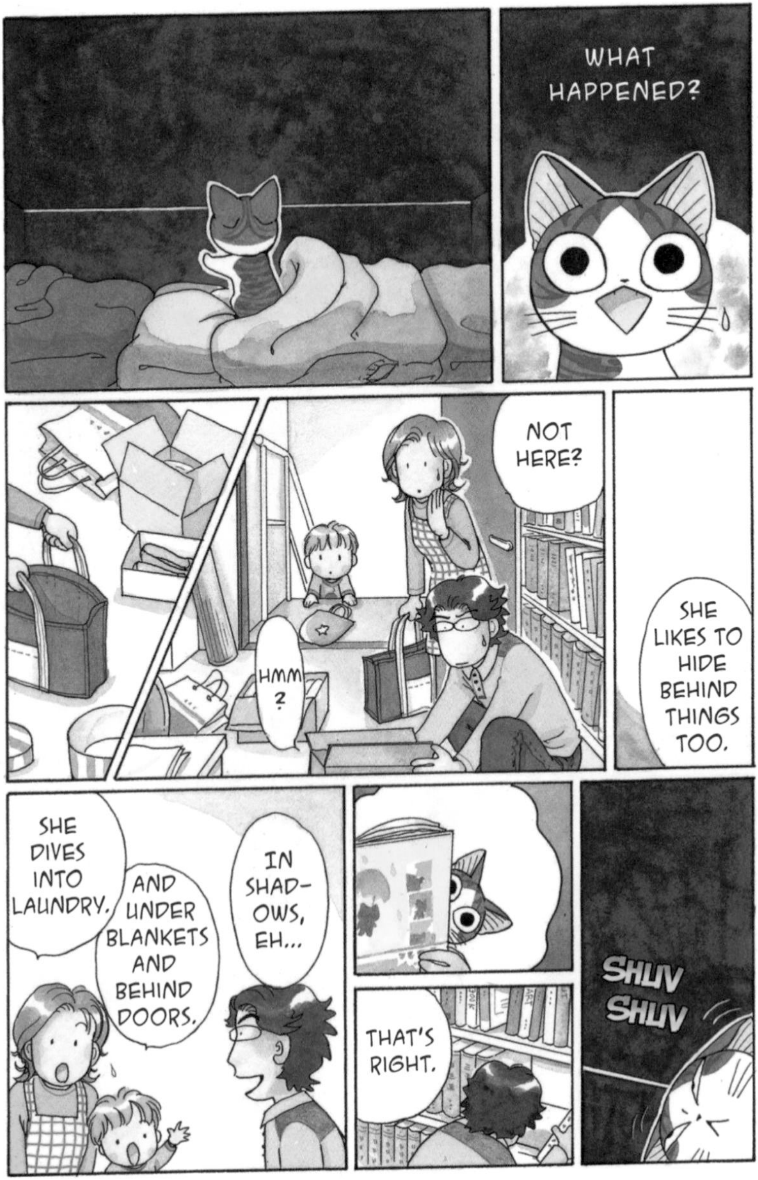
WHAT HAPPENED?
NOT HERE?
HMM ?
SHE LIKES TO HIDE BEHIND THINGS TOO.
SHE DIVES INTO LAUNDRY.
AND UNDER BLANKETS AND BEHIND DOORS.
IN SHAD-OWS, EH...
THAT'S RIGHT.
SHUV SHUV

CHI CANNOT GET OUT.

SKFF SKFF SKFF

THOUGH I WON AT HIDE-N-SEEK!

I DON'T FEEL LIKE I WON.

RUMM

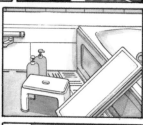

SHE'S GONE.

WHERE ELSE COULD SHE BE?

SOAP

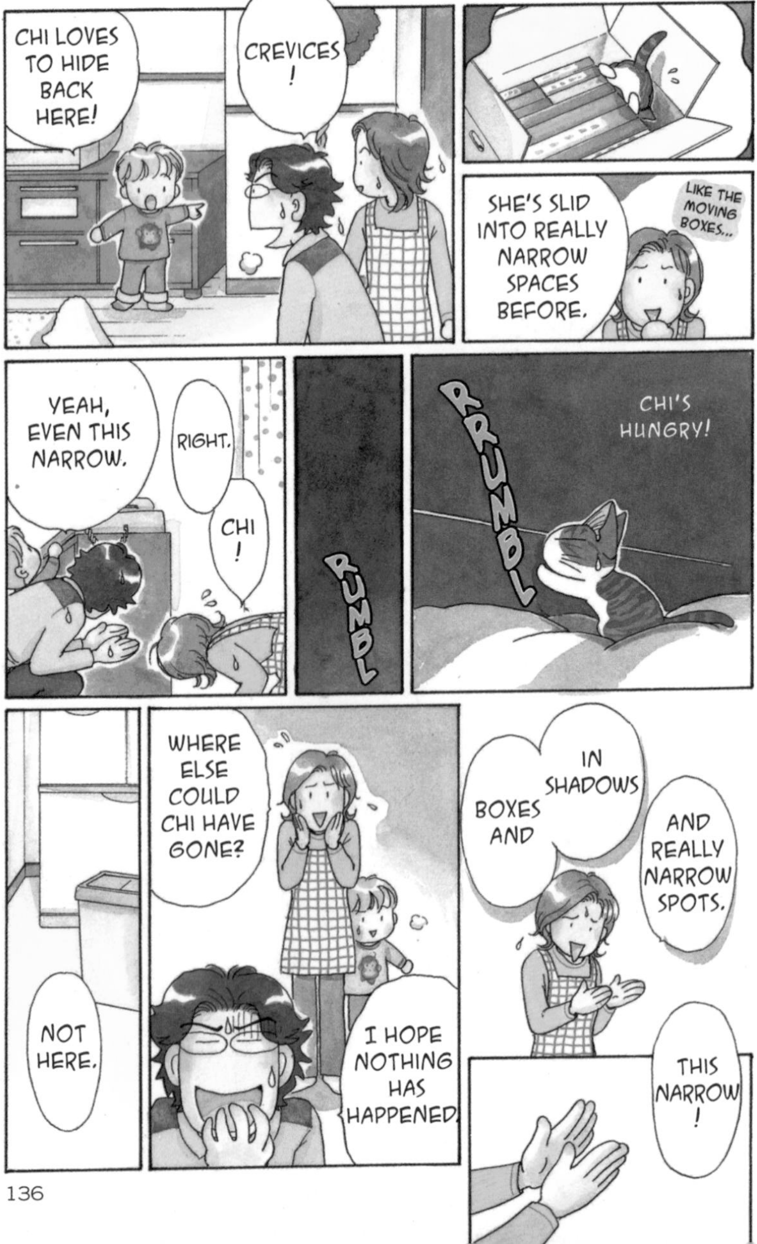
CHI LOVES TO HIDE BACK HERE!
CREVICES!
SHE'S SLID INTO REALLY NARROW SPACES BEFORE.
LIKE THE MOVING BOXES...
YEAH, EVEN THIS NARROW.
RIGHT.
CHI!
RUMBL
RRUMBL
CHI'S HUNGRY!
NOT HERE.
WHERE ELSE COULD CHI HAVE GONE?
I HOPE NOTHING HAS HAPPENED.
BOXES AND
IN SHADOWS
AND REALLY NARROW SPOTS.
THIS NARROW!

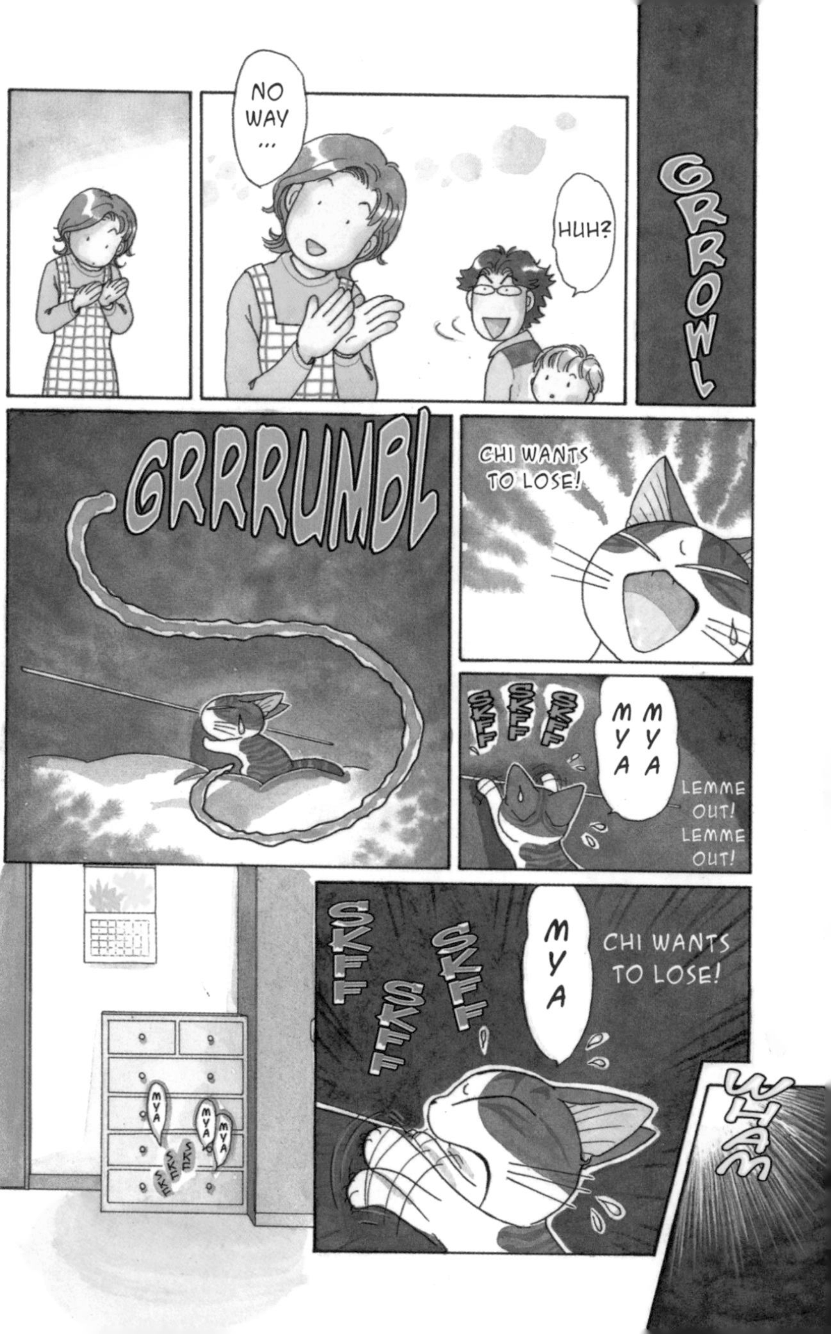
NO WAY ...
HUH?
GRROWL
GRRRUMBL
CHI WANTS TO LOSE!
SKFF SKFF SKFF
MYA MYA
LEMME OUT! LEMME OUT!
MYA MYA MYA
SKF SKF SKF
SKFF SKFF SKFF
MYA
CHI WANTS TO LOSE!
WHAM

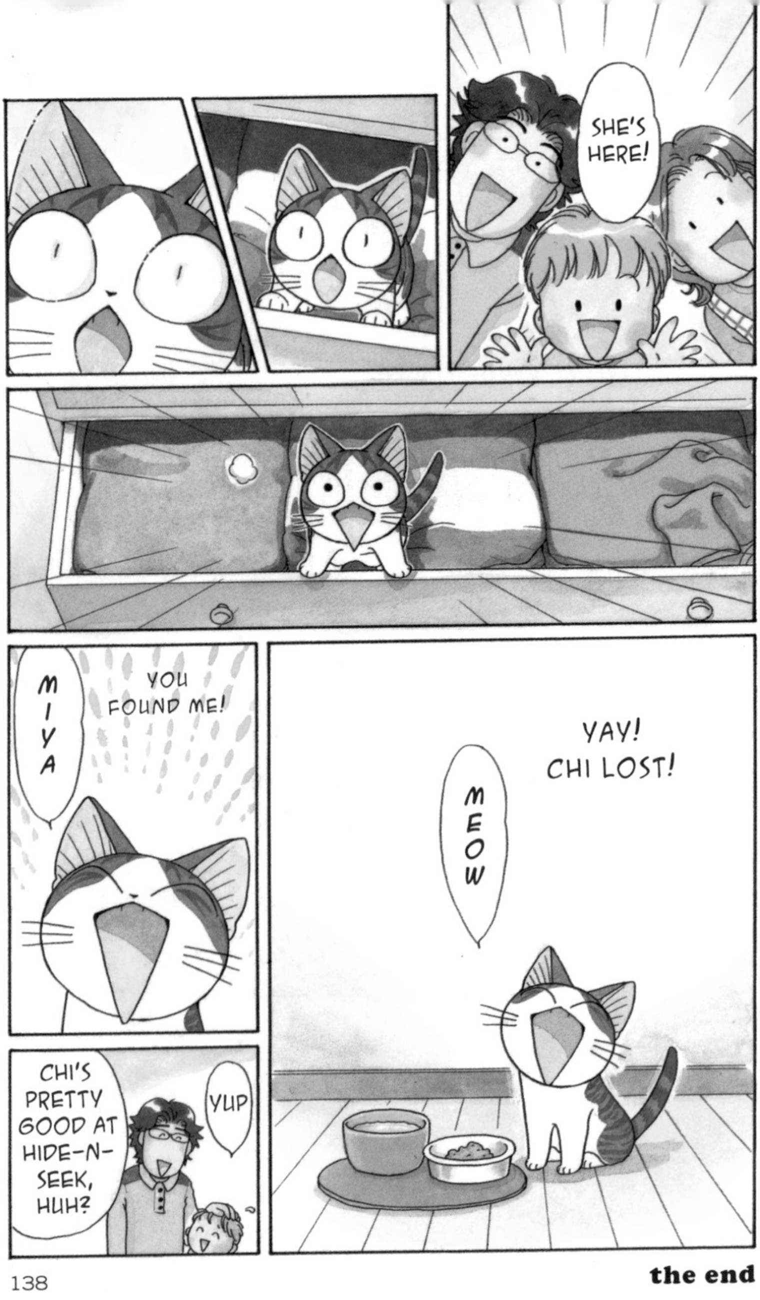
SHE'S HERE!
MIYA
YOU FOUND ME!
CHI'S PRETTY GOOD AT HIDE-N-SEEK, HUH?
YUP
YAY! CHI LOST!
MEOW

the end

homemade 74: a cat chases

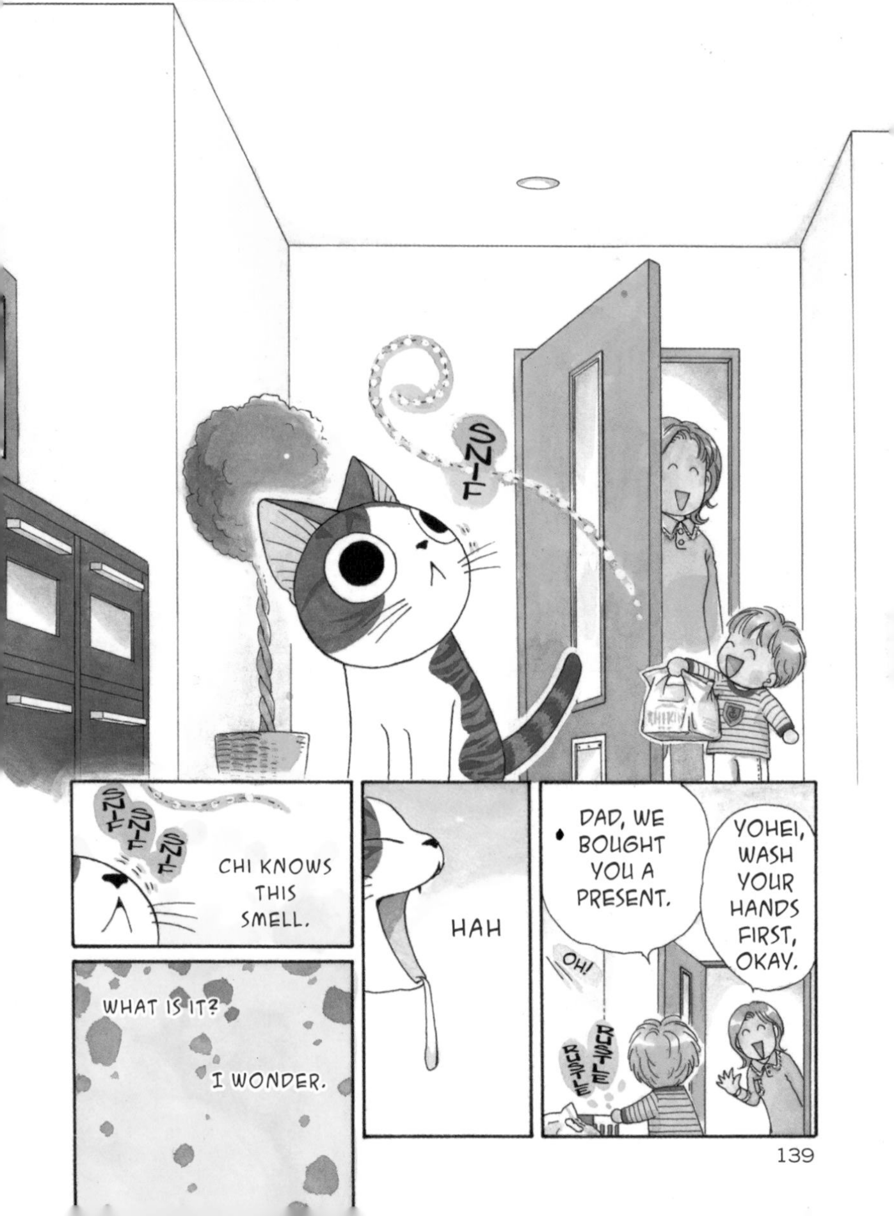
SNIFF
SNIFF SNIFF SNIFF
CHI KNOWS THIS SMELL.
WHAT IS IT?
I WONDER.
HAH
DAD, WE BOUGHT YOU A PRESENT.
YOHEI, WASH YOUR HANDS FIRST, OKAY.
OH!
RUSTLE RUSTLE

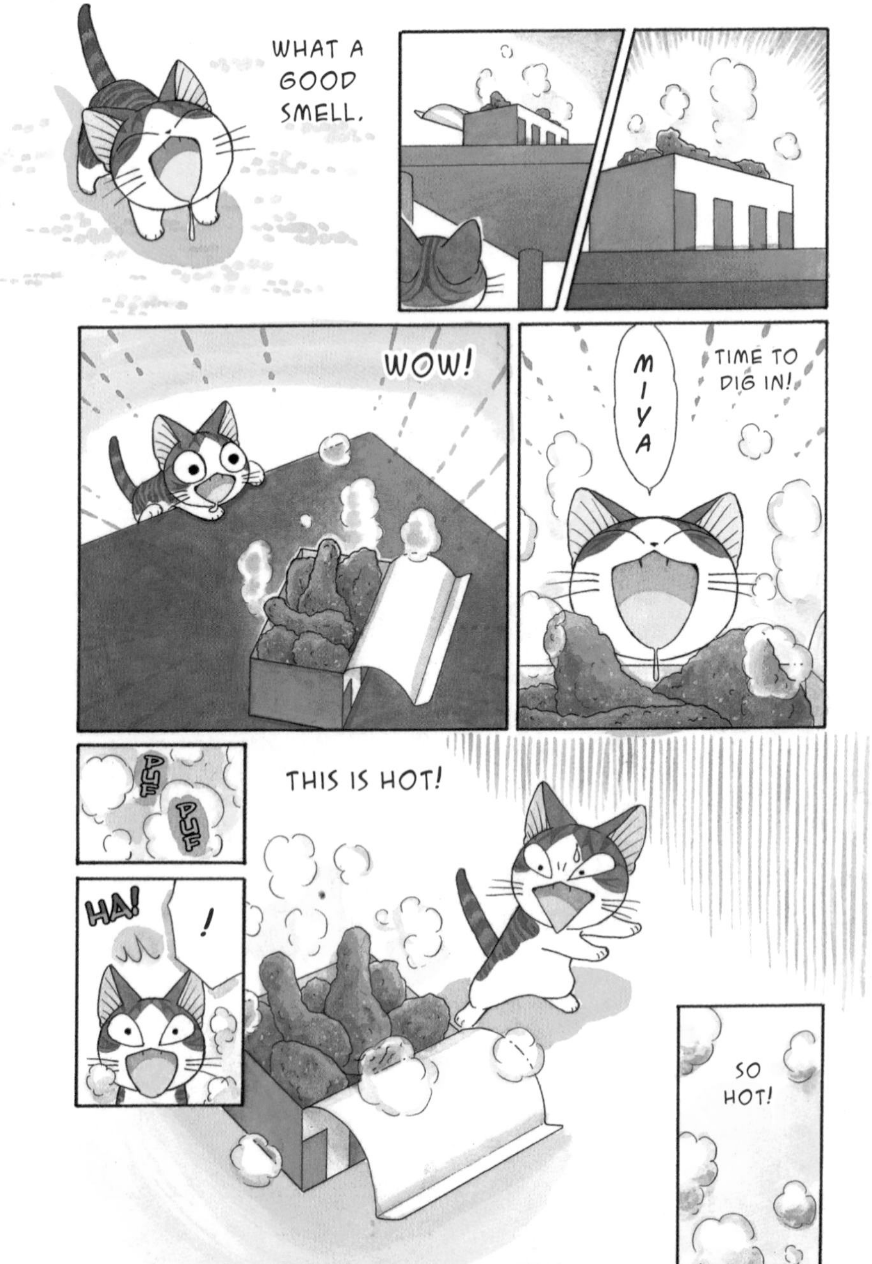
WHAT A GOOD SMELL.
WOW!
MIYA
TIME TO DIG IN!
PUF
PUF
HA!
!
THIS IS HOT!
SO HOT!

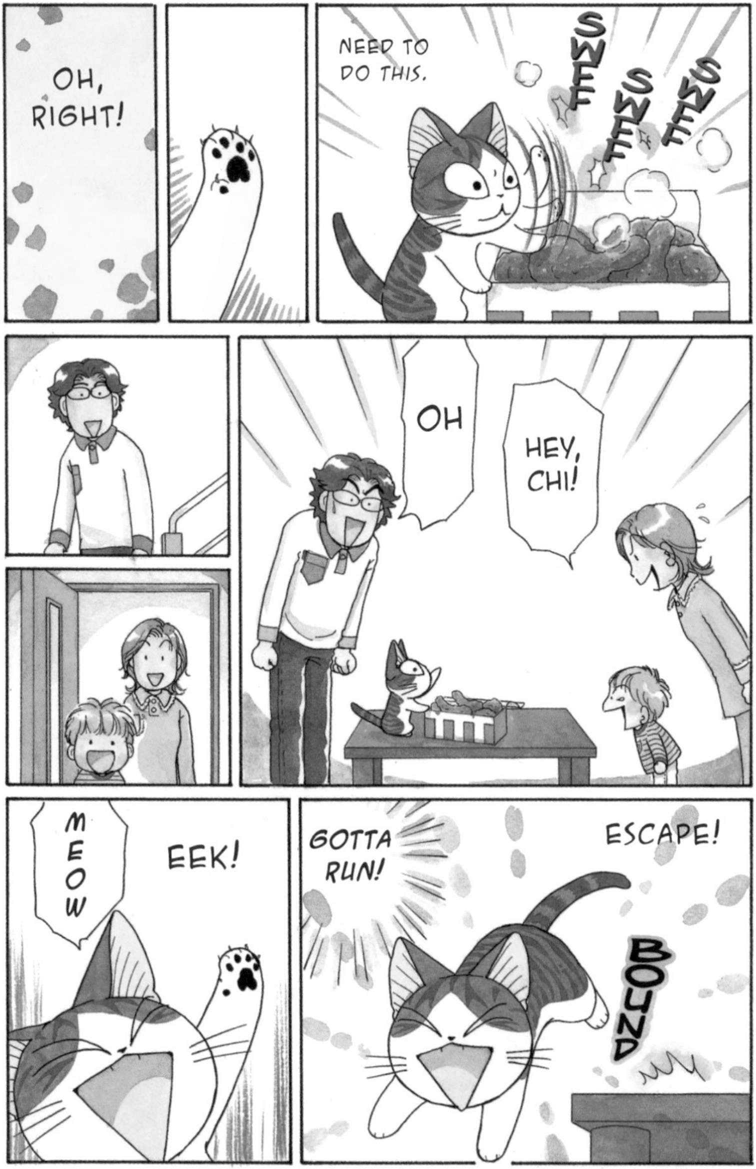
OH, RIGHT!
NEED TO DO THIS.
SWEF SWEF SWEF
OH
HEY, CHI!
MEOW
EEK!
GOTTA RUN!
ESCAPE!
BOUND

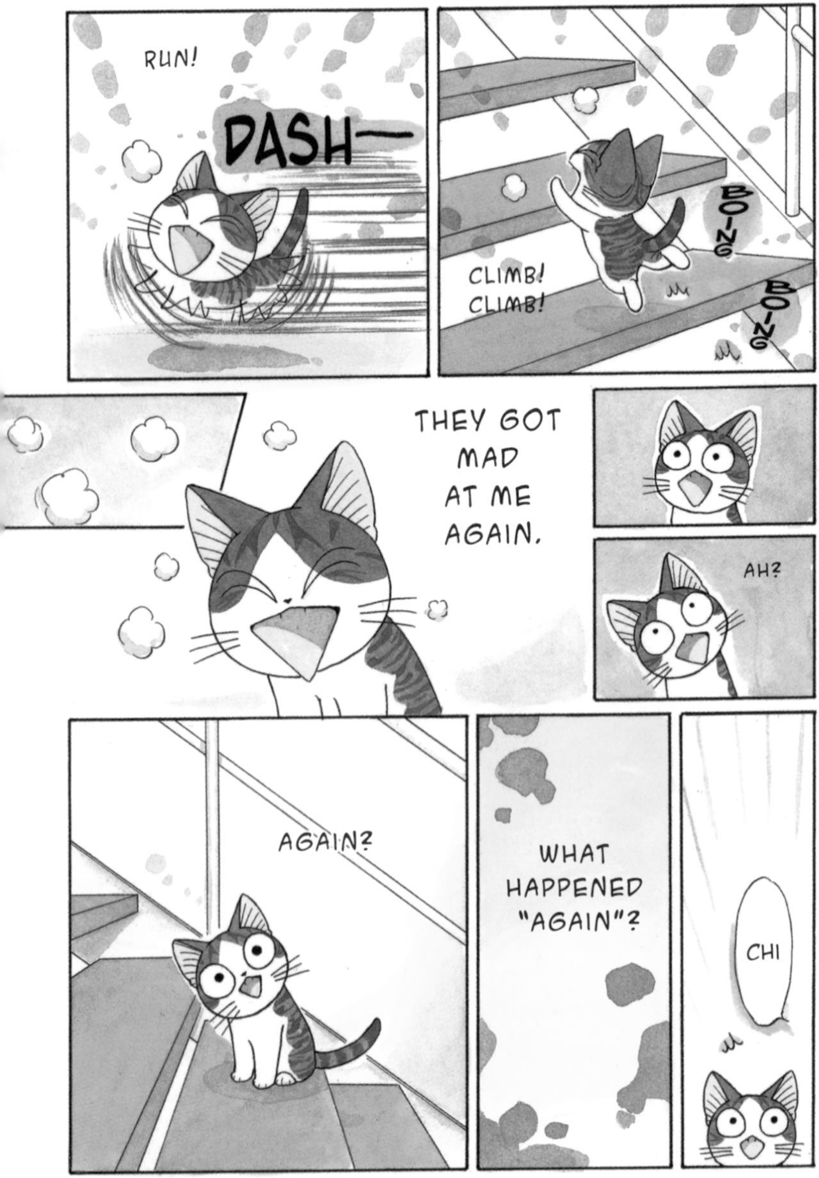
RUN!
DASH—
CLIMB!
CLIMB!
BOING
BOING
THEY GOT MAD AT ME AGAIN.
AH?
AGAIN?
WHAT HAPPENED "AGAIN"?
CHI

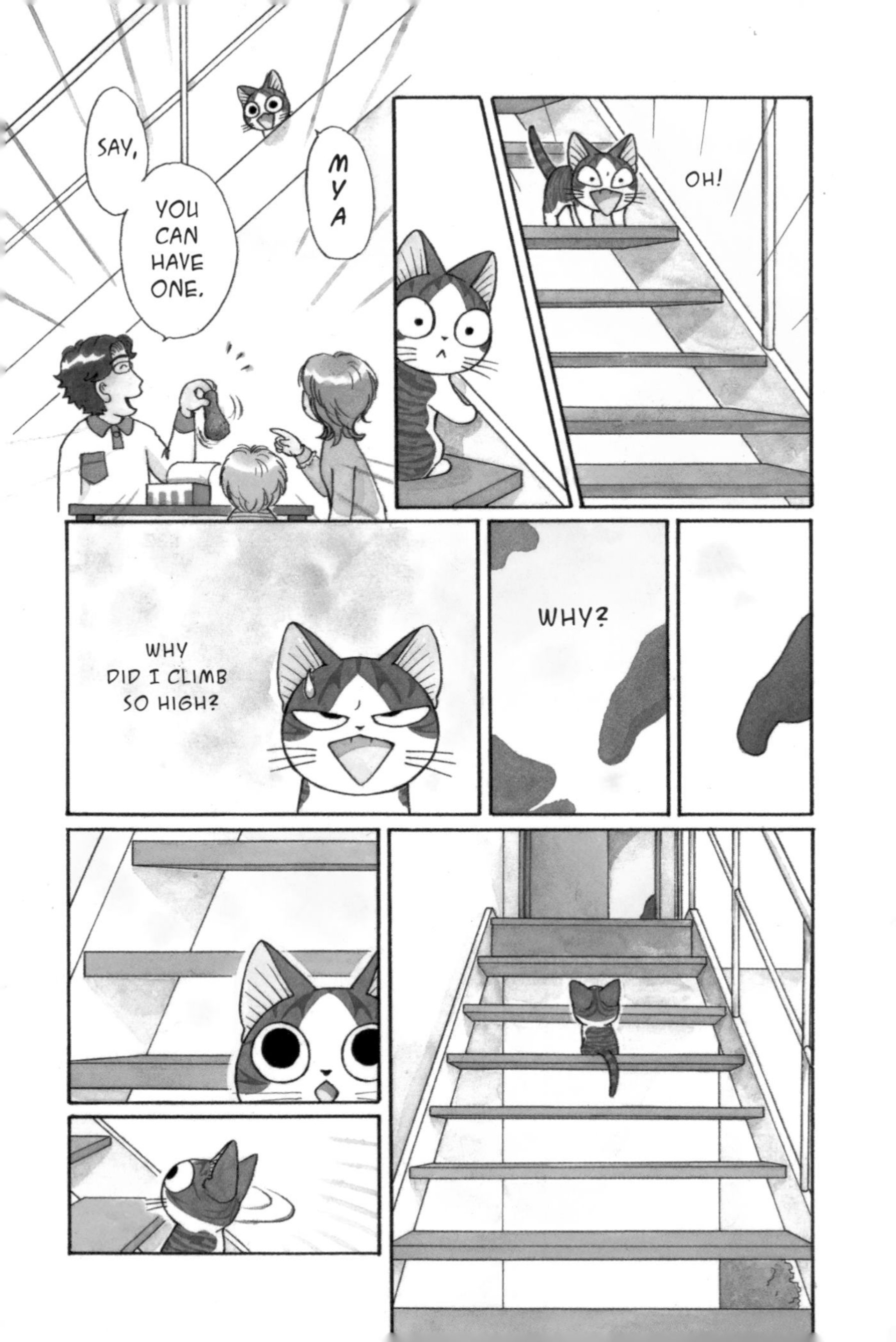
SAY,
YOU CAN HAVE ONE.
MYA
OH!
WHY DID I CLIMB SO HIGH?
WHY?

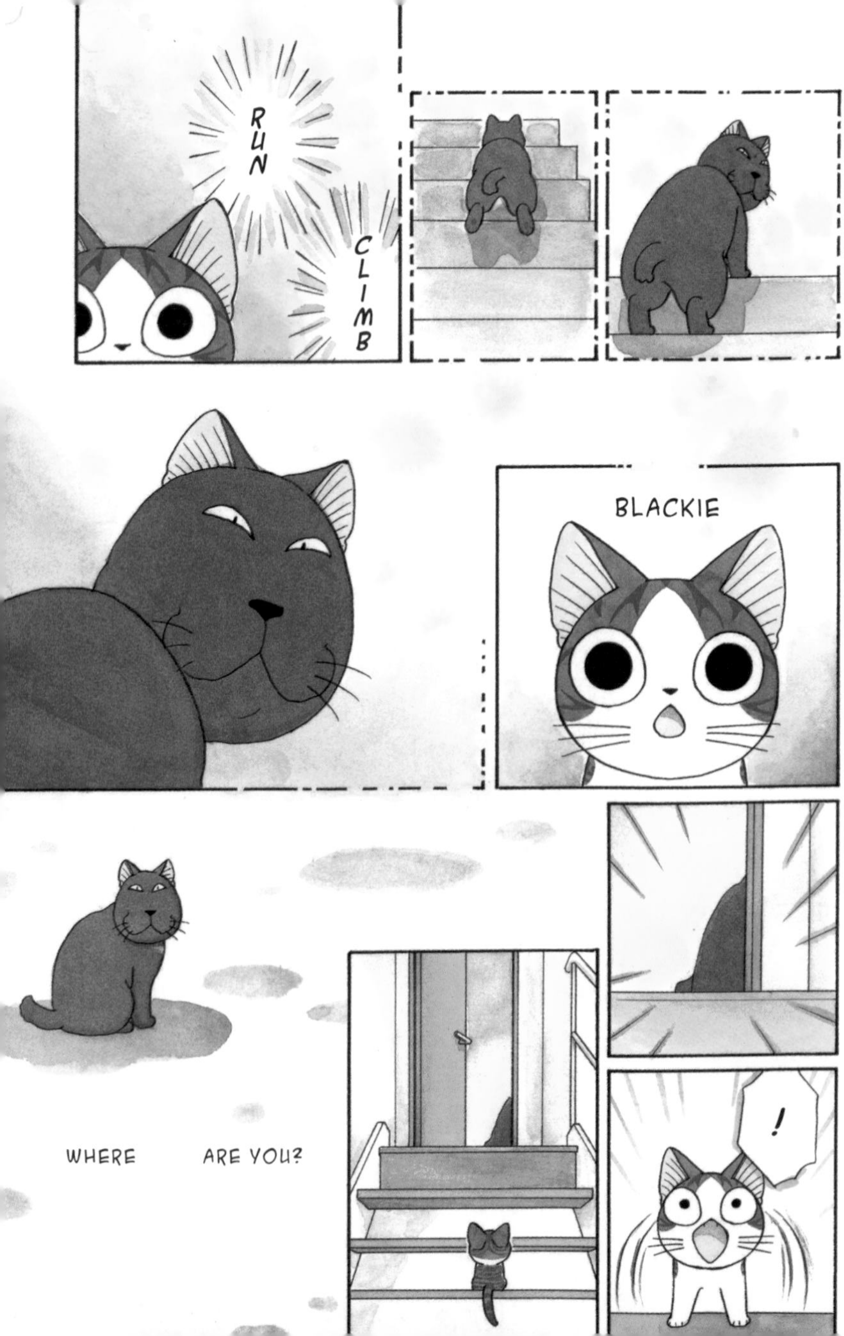
RUN
CLIMB
BLACKIE
WHERE
ARE YOU?
!

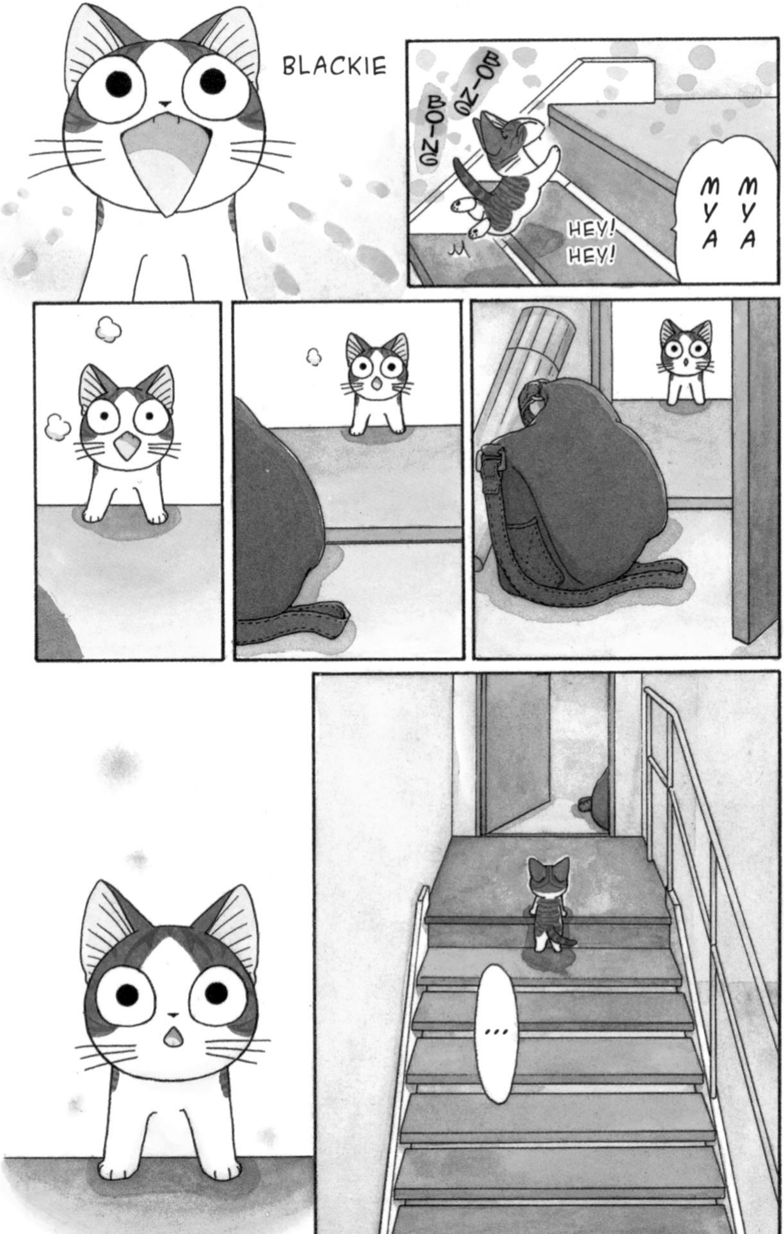
BLACKIE
BOING BOING
HEY! HEY!
MYA MYA
...

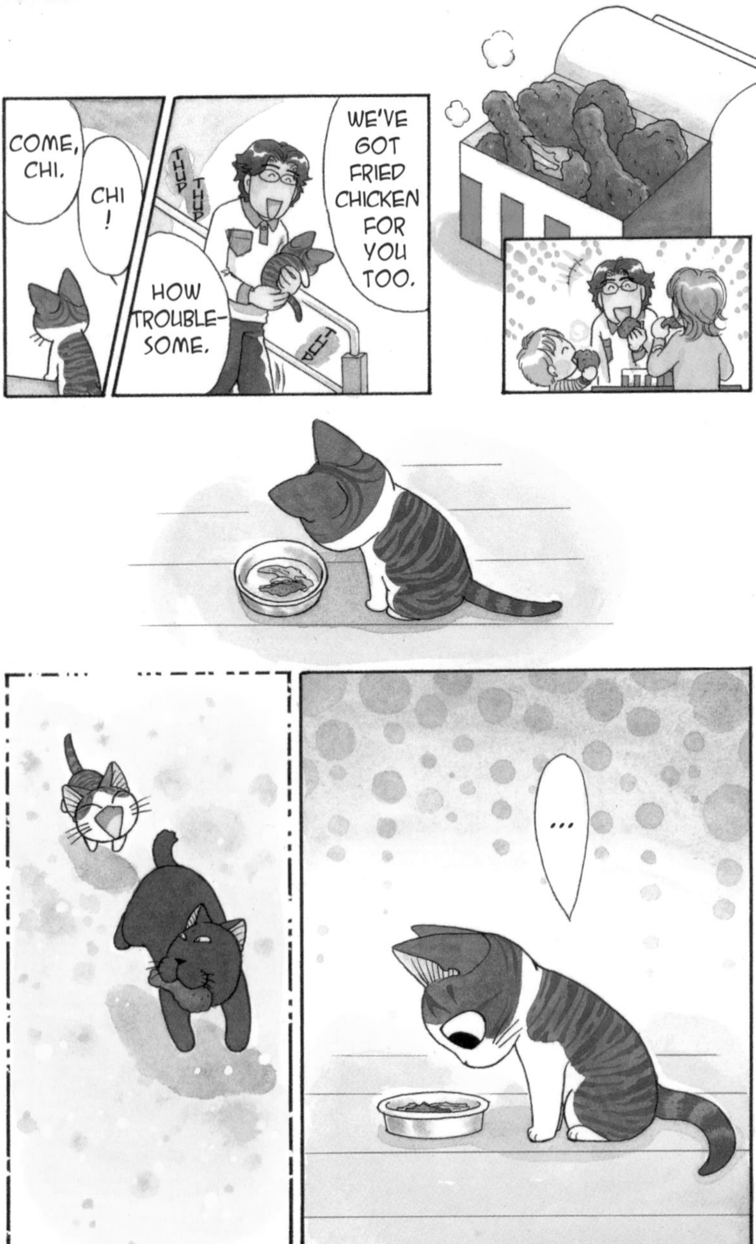
COME, CHI.
CHI!
THUP THUP
WE'VE GOT FRIED CHICKEN FOR YOU TOO.
HOW TROUBLE-SOME.
...

the end

Special Collaboration Manga

TWO FUNNY FELINES CHI & KURO

Risa Ito
creator of "Oy, Pi-tan"

×

Konami Kanata
creator of "Chi's Sweet Home"

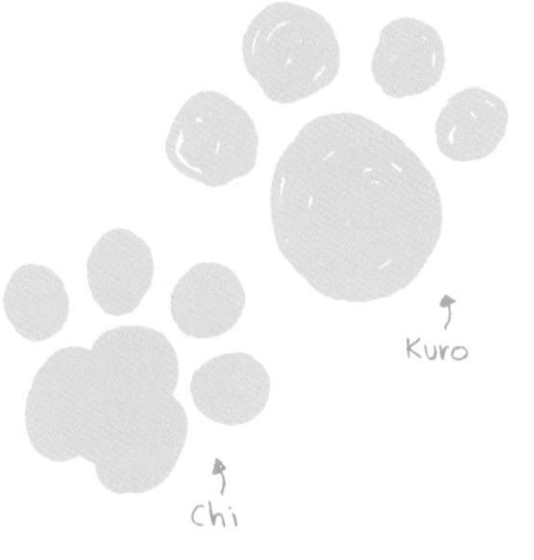
Kuro
Chi

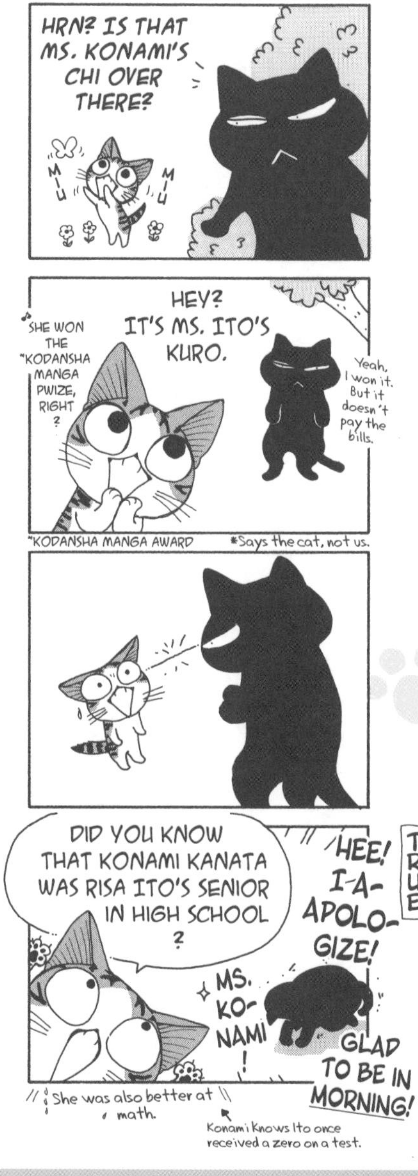
HRN? IS THAT MS. KONAMI'S CHI OVER THERE?
MIU
MIU
HEY? IT'S MS. ITO'S KURO.
SHE WON THE *KODANSHA MANGA PWIZE, RIGHT?
Yeah, I won it. But it doesn't pay the bills.
*KODANSHA MANGA AWARD
*Says the cat, not us.
DID YOU KNOW THAT KONAMI KANATA WAS RISA ITO'S SENIOR IN HIGH SCHOOL?
TRUE
HEE! I-A-APOLO-GIZE!
MS. KO-NAMI!
GLAD TO BE IN MORNING!
She was also better at math.
Konami Knows Ito once received a zero on a test.

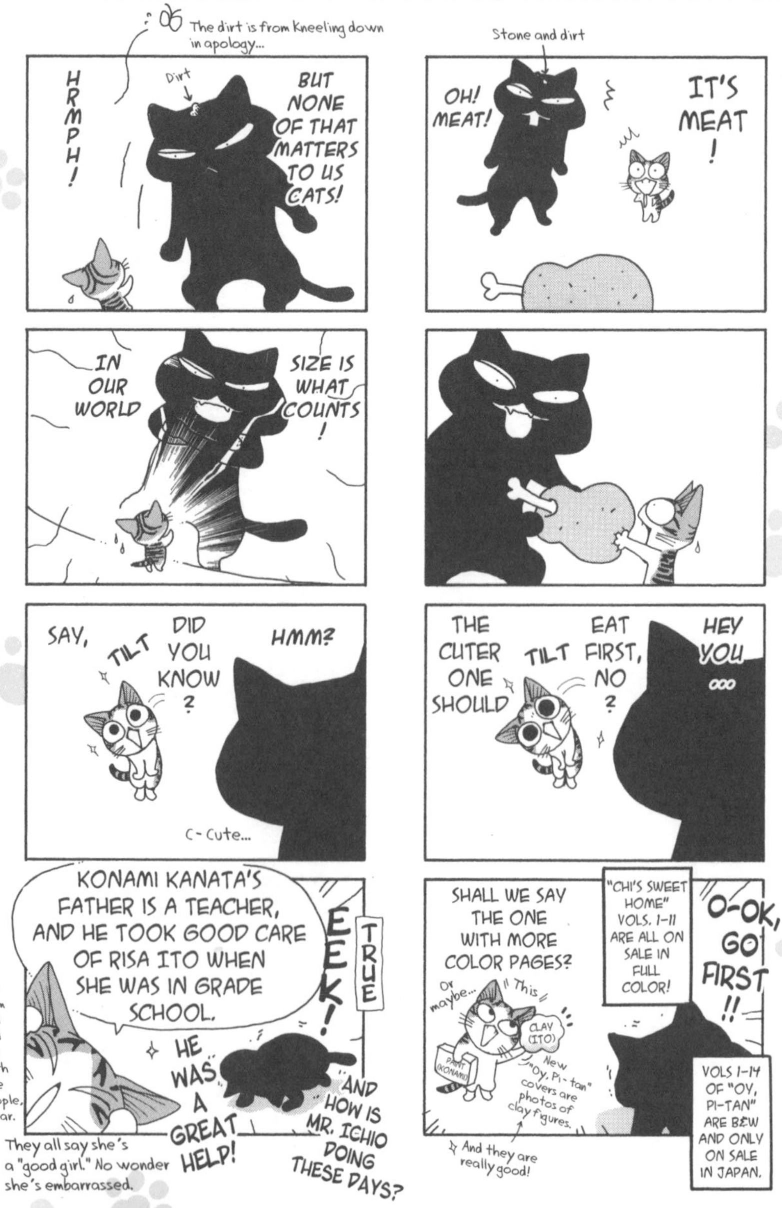
The dirt is from kneeling down in apology...
Dirt
HRMPH!
BUT NONE OF THAT MATTERS TO US CATS!
Stone and dirt
OH! MEAT!
IT'S MEAT!
IN OUR WORLD
SIZE IS WHAT COUNTS!
SAY,
TILT
DID YOU KNOW?
HMM?
C-Cute...
THE CUTER ONE SHOULD
TILT
EAT FIRST, NO?
HEY YOU...
KONAMI KANATA'S FATHER IS A TEACHER, AND HE TOOK GOOD CARE OF RISA ITO WHEN SHE WAS IN GRADE SCHOOL.
EEK!
TRUE
Her mom and dad are both nice people, I hear.
HE WAS A GREAT HELP!
AND HOW IS MR. ICHIO DOING THESE DAYS?
They all say she's a "good girl." No wonder she's embarrassed.
SHALL WE SAY THE ONE WITH MORE COLOR PAGES?
"CHI'S SWEET HOME" VOLS. 1-11 ARE ALL ON SALE IN FULL COLOR!
Or maybe...
This
CLAY (ITO)
PAINT (KONAMI)
New "Oy, Pi-tan" covers are photos of clay figures.
And they are really good!
O-OK, GO FIRST!!
VOLS 1-14 OF "OY, PI-TAN" ARE BEW AND ONLY ON SALE IN JAPAN.

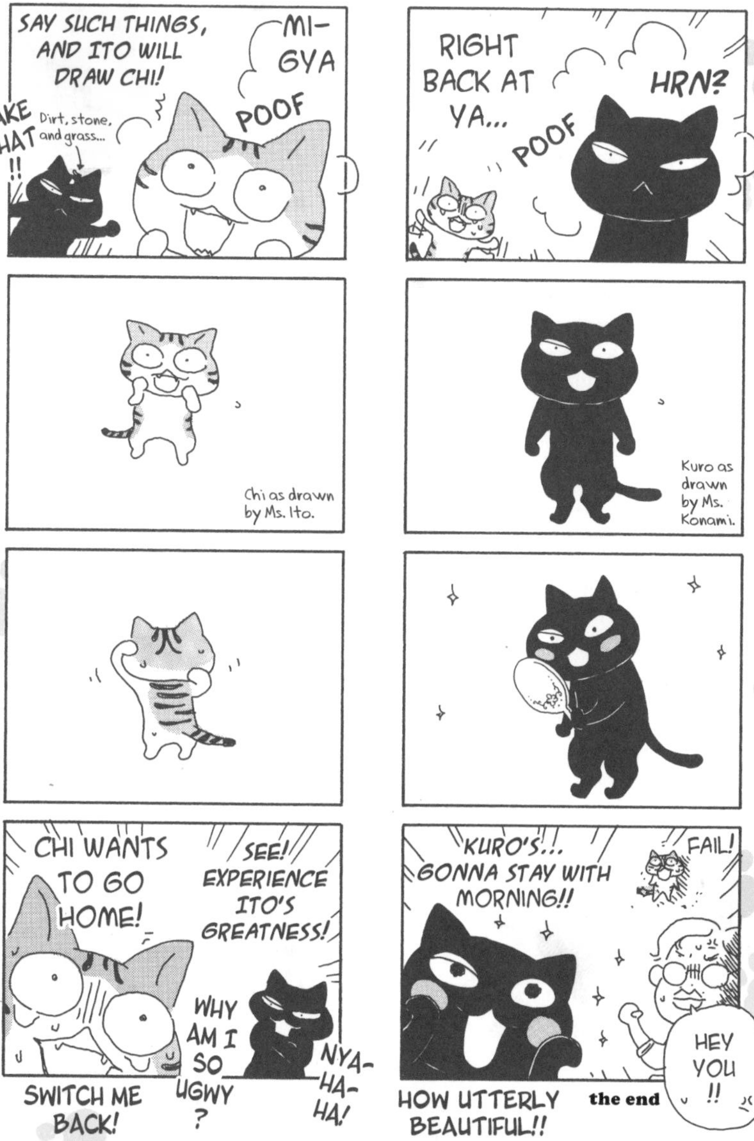
SAY SUCH THINGS, AND ITO WILL DRAW CHI!
MI-GYA
POOF
TAKE THAT !!
Dirt, stone, and grass...
RIGHT BACK AT YA...
HRN?
POOF
Chi as drawn by Ms. Ito.
Kuro as drawn by Ms. Konami.
CHI WANTS TO GO HOME!
SEE! EXPERIENCE ITO'S GREATNESS!
WHY AM I SO UGWY ?
NYA-HA-HA!
SWITCH ME BACK!
KURO'S... GONNA STAY WITH MORNING!!
FAIL!
HEY YOU !!
HOW UTTERLY BEAUTIFUL!!
the end

TWIN SPI

Space has never seemed so close and yet so far!

"It's easy to see why the series was a smash hit in its native land…
Each page contains more genuine emotion than an entire space fleet's
worth of similarly themed stories."
—*Publishers Weekly*

Now Available Digitally!
16 Volumes, $4.99 each

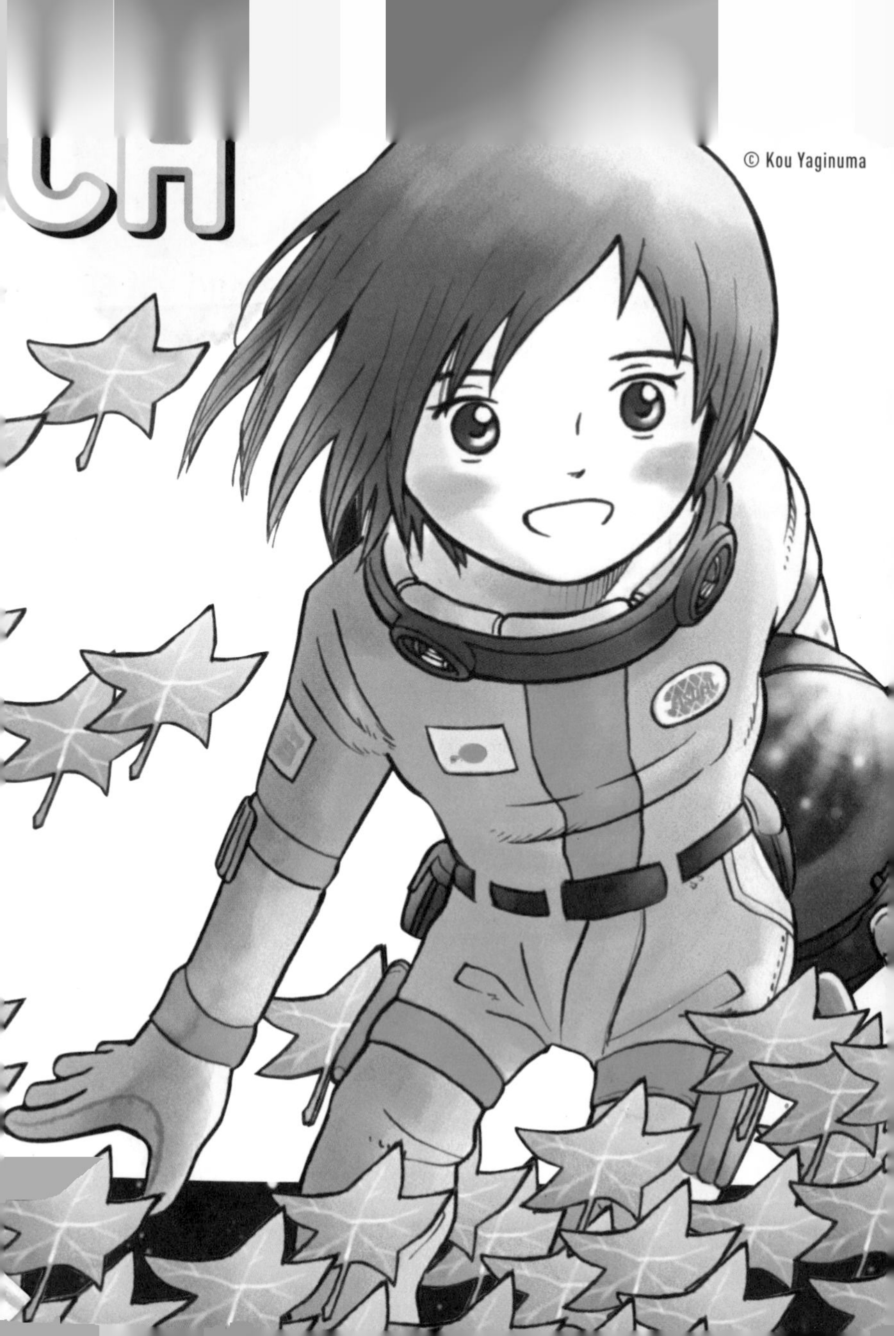
© Kou Yaginuma

Chi's Sweet Home, volume 4

Translation - Ed Chavez
Production - Hiroko Mizuno
Glen Isip
Tomoe Tsutsumi

First published in Japan in 2007 by Kodansha, Ltd., Tokyo
Publication for this English edition arranged through Kodansha, Ltd., Tokyo
English language version produced by Vertical, Inc.

Translation provided by Vertical, Inc., 2010
Published by Vertical, Inc., New York

Originally published in Japanese as *Chiizu Suiito Houmu* by Kodansha, Ltd., 2006-2007
Chiizu Suiito Houmu first serialized in *Morning*, Kodansha, Ltd., 2004-

Oy, Pi-tan illustrated by Risa Ito, 2007

ISBN: 978-1-934287-96-5

Manufactured in the United States of America

First Edition

Fourth Printing

Vertical, Inc.
451 Park Avenue South, 7th Floor
New York, NY 10016
www.vertical-inc.com

Special thanks to: Risa Ito & K. Kitamoto